The State of Black America 2009

Message to the President

Foreword by Martin Luther King, III

AN OFFICIAL PUBLICATION OF THE  National Urban League   www.nul.org

Library of Congress Control Number: 77-647469
ISBN- 0-914758-02-0
EAN: 9780914758020

The State of Black America® 2009

Message to the President

Editor-in-Chief
Stephanie J. Jones

Editorial Director
Lisa Bland Malone

Managing Editors
Larry Williamson
Rose Jefferson-Frazier

Associate Editors
Dr. Valerie R. Wilson
Gail L. Thomas
Mark McArdle

Bakri Design
President and Creative Director
Pooja Bakri

Charts
Cari Colclough

Cover Illustration
Jakob Lunden

CONTENTS

APPENDICES

The American Narrative

By Martin Luther King, III

Since the dawn of slavery, African Americans have been constructing a peoples' narrative, "a coherent arrangement of facts and myths
explaining the group's past and present and embodying their hopes
for the future." *The State of Black America 2009: Message to the
President* is an important chapter in the narrative of African
Americans today.

As in the past, *The State of Black America 2009* tells of both the
triumphs and tragedies of the African-American experience as it
sets the plot for the rest of the story. Perhaps most striking in this
now-unfolding chapter is a new character: a black man who is now
the most powerful person in the world.

Since Barack Obama's election, I have been asked more than a
few times if the first African-American president is the realization or
fulfillment of my father's dream. In other words, is this the end of
the story?

The answer is simple: President Obama represents an important
step toward realizing the dream of Dr. King. However, his election is
not the fulfillment of the Dream. This is because President Obama is
not the only character in this narrative, nor is he the story's only writer.

The American narrative cannot realize its greatest promise
unless the narratives of all its peoples are part of that promise. In
other words, realizing the American Dream must be a complete possibility for every American, not just for the self-interested individual or
the privileged few. It is not reserved for a majority's tyranny or restrict-
ed to a minority's autocracy. "We are tied together in the single

garment of destiny, caught in an inescapable network of mutuality. And whatever affects one directly affects all indirectly," my father said. "For some strange reason I can never be what I ought to be until you are what you ought to be. And you can never be what you ought to be until I am what I ought to be."

My father saw that this nation could not realize its fullest potential unless each and every American has "the untrammeled opportunity to fulfill his or her total individual capacity without regard to race, creed, color" or any other qualifier. This opportunity is, in essence, my father's dream.

But, as this volume describes, too many African Americans are hindered from realizing their fullest potential because of an inadequate education, too many remain on the margins of our economy because of a lack of employment opportunities or access to capital to run their own businesses, and too many find themselves relegated to a mutually-reinforcing cycle of generational poverty. So long as the education, healthcare, employment and other disparities documented in *The Equality Index* persist among various racial and ethnic groups, as long as the opportunities for adequate and affordable housing, wealth creation, and full civil rights are beyond their reach, the American Dream can never be their reality.

Each essay contained within this edition of *The State of Black America* represents a view of those facts and myths that shape the narrative. They will clearly demonstrate that we have not yet realized the full potential of the American dream. But they also offer solutions that can lead us in the right direction.

I hope that *The State of Black America 2009: Message to the President* will find its way to the desks of decision makers from the White House to both Houses of Congress to every state house and to local governments throughout the nation. I also hope that it will lead to a national dialogue that spawns an agenda with support from the private sector and its civic counterpart. With this hope we can hasten the realization of my father's dream so that the narratives of all Americans can be one.

FROM THE PRESIDENT'S DESK

By Marc H. Morial
President and CEO

The State of Black America 2009: Message to the President comes in the midst of one of the worst economic crises our nation has ever faced. It also comes on the heels of the Inauguration of the first African-American President of the United States of America.

Last November, the American people voted for hope over fear and, in a watershed moment, elected Barack Hussein Obama as the next President of the United States, renewing the nation's founding promise of freedom, equality and opportunity for all. Barack Obama's election shattered perhaps the most impenetrable of the glass ceilings that have kept so many generations of minorities and women from dreaming big dreams and reaching their full potential. Never again will any young boy or girl of color in America be shackled with the awful certainty of "not in my lifetime" and it was certainly one of the moments when I was most proud to be an American.

However, despite this lofty achievement, as then-Senator Obama wrote in his Foreword to *The State of Black America 2007: Portrait of the Black Male,* there are still two stories to tell about Black America. One story, of accomplishment, prosperity and increased political power, fills us with pride and hope. However, the other story is very different: Fewer than 50 percent of African Americans graduate from high school in many major American cities. Our prisons are disproportionately populated by African-American males. The economic crisis is hitting our communities especially hard, leaving huge numbers of African Americans without homes, jobs or life savings. We see an unemployment rate that's double that of whites, and wide academic achievement gaps.

In this shifting economic sea, the overall 2009 Equality Index is down 0.4% from 71.5% in 2008 to 71.1% in 2009, the social justice index decreased 2% from 62.1% to 60.4%, and the economic index decreased from 57.6% to 57.4% and was the lowest index value. Much of the information available was from 2006 and 2007 (as not all the data is available on an annual basis); therefore, 2008 does not accurately reflect the real effect of the current recession, and many unemployment statistics don't reflect those not fully employed, working part time with little or no benefits.

Taken together, these facts underscore the reality that the election of the first black president does not mean we can now all close up shop and go home. Instead, it is more important than ever that the National Urban League and other organizations and individuals committed to positive change must work even harder to lift up our communities and move this country forward.

In this edition of *The State of Black America,* leading experts analyze these conditions and outline innovative steps that President Obama and the Congress need to move this country and our urban communities forward toward full economic and social equity.

But, as important as such analysis and recommendations are, this year's report goes even further. We also offer the voices of ordinary people whose voices are rarely heard in national political discussions but who are the most deeply impacted by the policies and programs these discussions generate. These men and women offer a very personal and poignant perspective of how public policies affect real people and what our president and government can and should do to help them help themselves.

Their experiences and reflections demonstrate the fallacy of the notion that the federal government is unnecessary or that it cannot function effectively. While we do believe in a robust private sector, we also know that strong and effective federal government is just as essential. The aftermath of Hurricane Katrina and the current banking scandals provide ample evidence of the catastrophic ramifications of a government's failure to safeguard its citizens in time of disaster and financial crisis. We can and must expect government services that fully meet the needs of its citizens. And African Americans and other disadvantaged people also can never forget the pivotal role that government must play in protecting the civil rights of all persons.

During his remarks to the Urban League Movement at our 2008 Annual Conference in Orlando, Florida last August, then-Senator Obama reminded us that the presidential election was not so much about him as it was about us. He stressed that change comes from the bottom up, not the other way around. It is up to all of us—as citizens and advocates—to take an even more active role in governance at all levels and to make our voices heard from City Hall to the State House to the halls of Congress to the White House.

We welcome this new vision the Obama administration brings to Washington and to America. But this vision can only become a reality if *we* make it so.

The State of Black America 2009: Message to the President, is an essential part of the National Urban League's effort to bring about this vision by working with the new Administration to tackle the nation's deepening domestic challenges. I hope that it encourages and inspires each of you to join us in working to help President Obama fulfill the promise he made to us last summer "to build a nation worthy of our children's future."

Introduction to the 2009 Equality Index

by Valerie Rawlston Wilson, Ph.D.
National Urban League Policy Institute

On January 20, 2009, nearly 1.5 million people crowded the national mall as millions more across the world tuned in to witness Barack Obama, the first African-American president of the United States of America, take the oath of office. Inauguration Day 2009 echoed the day just 40 years earlier when Dr. Martin Luther King, Jr. delivered his famous "I Have a Dream" speech from the steps of the Lincoln Memorial at the opposite end of the mall.

As the Obama Administration ushers in a new era of hope, change, and to some extent, unity for this nation, many are asking whether racial barriers have now been erased in America. Are discrimination, division and inequality antiquated relics of the past? For a quick answer to that question, one has but to review some of the sobering statistics presented in the 2009 Equality Index. Ironically, even as an African-American man holds the highest office in the country, African Americans remain twice as likely as whites to be unemployed, three times more likely to live in poverty and more than six times as likely to be incarcerated. These statistics represent persistent inequalities that have existed in American society for years and while some might argue that the prospect of closing these gaps seems bleak in light of the current recession, I would suggest that even this cloud has potential for a silver lining. History has shown that unless policies are targeted to address the underlying causes of inequality, an economic downturn only amplifies the existing gaps between black and white America; however, rebuilding an economy that creates jobs as well as provides viable opportunities for disadvantaged populations to tap into and benefit from the resulting economic growth, could have huge implications for the future of inequality in America.

Interpreting the Equality Index

The Equality Index can be interpreted as the relative status of blacks and whites in American society, measured according to five areas—economics, health, education, social justice and civic engagement. For any given measure, the index represents the ratio of blacks to whites.[1] To use median household income as an example, an index of 61% = $31,969/$52,423, where $31,969 is the median household income for blacks and $52,423 is the median household income for whites. Equality would be indicated by an index of 100%. Therefore, an Equality Index less than 100% suggests that blacks are doing worse relative to whites, and an Equality Index greater than 100% suggests that blacks are doing better than whites.

The overall Equality Index is a weighted average of indices calculated for each of the five sub-categories—economics, health, education, social justice and civic engagement. In turn, the indices for each of the five sub-categories are themselves weighted averages of indices calculated from individual variables (like the example of median household income used above) available from nationally representative data sources. The appropriate data sources and data years are indicated in the accompanying tables at the end of this chapter.

What's New in the 2009 Equality Index?

The 2009 Equality Index stands at 71.1% compared to a revised 2008 index of 71.5%. Revisions to the previous year's index are done for greater comparability across years and reflect data points that have been corrected, removed from the current year's index or re-weighted so that less emphasis is placed on older data. Relative to 2008, the change in this year's overall index was marginal, indicating a general continuation of the status quo. Economics remains the area with the greatest degree of inequality (from 57.6% in 2008 to 57.4% in 2009), followed by social justice (from 62.1% to 60.4%), health (from 73.3% to 74.4%), education (from 78.6% to 78.5%) and civic engagement (from 100.3% to 96.3%). A comparison of the revised 2008 and 2009 Equality Index is shown in Figure 1.

Figure 1

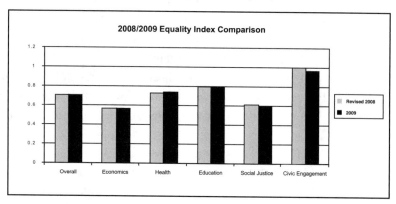

The two areas with the greatest decline were civic engagement (-4 percentage points) and social justice (-1.7 percentage points). Although civic engagement saw the biggest decline in this year, it was still the highest of the five sub-indices. The score declined largely because the most recent voter turnout data was from 2006, which corresponds with the congressional election when turnout is traditionally lower. The 2008 Index included voter turnout data from the 2004 presidential election. Therefore, when the 2008 presidential data is released this score should improve. There were also small declines in volunteering and union representation. Most of the decline in the social justice index was in the area of victimization. Specifically, there was a 31-percentage point decline between 2005 and 2007 (data years reported by CDC) in the index of the percentage of high school students carrying weapons on school property. This is almost a total reversal of the 40-percentage points increase reported in last year's index.

Health was the only sub-index that increased (1.1 percentage points). This was largely due to a narrowing of the gap for those without health insurance, particularly among those eligible for coverage by public insurance programs. Nonetheless, according to the most recent data (2007), nearly 1 out of 5 African Americans (19.5%) still do not have health insurance.

Economic Inequality and the Jobless Recovery

Foremost on everyone's mind this year is the economy. While the 2009 economics sub-index does not fully capture the current state of the economy—it includes both pre- and post-recession statistics—it is useful, however, to examine changes in some key economic indicators that occurred during the course of the economic recovery that ended December 2007 relative to the previous economic expansion of the 1990s.

The economic expansion that took place between November 2001 and December 2007 (73 months long)[2] has been referred to as a jobless recovery. During this time, the economy added only 6.2 million private sector jobs, compared to twice as many (12.5 million) during the first 73 months of the previous expansion and 21.5 million for the entire duration of the expansion which lasted from March 1991 through March 2001.[3] In fact, during the 2001-2007 expansion, it took 30 months to recover the jobs lost during the preceding recession. By contrast, this milestone was reached only 18 months into the 1991-2001 recovery.

As a major stimulus of economic growth, the rate at which the economy produces jobs has a major impact on important household economic characteristics like income, poverty, unemployment and home ownership. Figures 2 – 5 show the percent change in these four areas for blacks and whites during three periods of time: (1) from the trough to the peak of the 1991 – 2001 expansion, (2) the first six years of the 1991 expansion (same length of time as the 2001 expansion) and (3) from the trough to the peak of the 2001 – 2007 expansion.[4] Table 1 contains the actual numbers corresponding to each of these periods of time for blacks and whites.

Figures 2 – 5 show that the percent change in each of the selected indicators—median household income, poverty, unemployment and homeownership—was significantly lower during the 2001–2007 expansion than during the 1991–2001 expansion.[5] In fact, there was actually a decline in real median household income (-1.7% for blacks; -3.9% for whites) and an increase in the rate of poverty (7.9% for blacks; 5.1% for whites) during the 2001–2007 economic recovery.

Figure 2

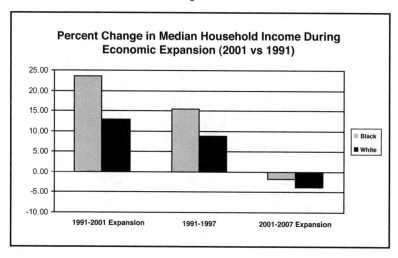

Figure 3

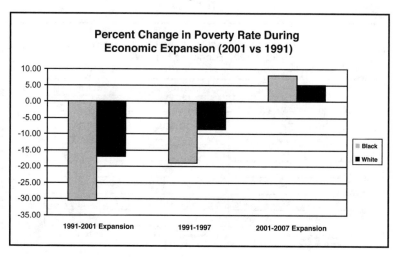

Figure 4

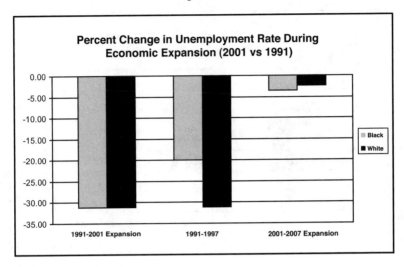

Figure 5

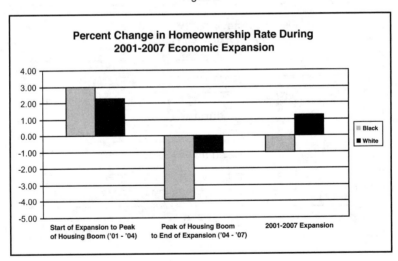

By contrast, during the first six years of the 1991–2001 recovery, real median income for African-American households grew by 15.6 percent while the real median income of white households grew by 8.9 percent; poverty rates declined by 19 percent and 8.5 percent, respectively. For the duration of the 1990s expansion, real median household income grew by 23.6 percent for African Americans and by 13 percent for whites, while poverty rates declined by 30.6 percent and 17 percent, respectively. Although unemployment declined for both groups during each of the most recent expansions, the six year decline for African Americans during the 1991 – 2001 expansion was nearly six times greater than the decline during the 2001–2007 expansion. For whites, the magnitude of the difference was thirteen times.

In terms of home ownership, 1991 data was not available by race, so the point of reference for the comparison was the peak of the housing boom in 2004—halfway through the expansion. Interestingly, despite the higher growth in home ownership among African Americans (2.9 percent) relative to whites (2.3 percent) that occurred between 2001 and 2004 (start of expansion to peak of housing boom), between 2004 and 2007 (peak of the housing boom to peak of expansion) growth in home ownership dropped precipitously; -3.9 percent for African Americans and -1.0 percent for whites. In the end, between 2001 and 2007 (duration of the expansion), whites still saw a net gain in the rate of homeownership (1.2 percent) while African Americans experienced a net loss (-1.0 percent).

Table 1

Selected Economic Statistics by Race for Recent Economic Expansions								
Year	Median Household		Poverty Rate		Unemployment Rate		Home Ownership Rate	
	Black	White	Black	White	Black	White	Black	White
Start of 1990s Expansion (1991)	$27,922	$47,988	32.7	9.4	12.5	6.1		
Six Years into 1990s Expansion (1997)	$32,266	$52,266	26.5	8.6	10	4.2		
End of 1990s Expansion/Start of 2001 Expansion (2001)	$34,514	$54,230	22.7	7.8	8.6	4.2	47.7	74.3
Peak of Housing Boom (2004)							49.1	76
End of 2001 Expansion (2007)	$33,916	$52,115	24.5	8.2	8.3	4.1	47.2	75.2

Five Years of the Equality Index

This year marks the sixth year the National Urban League has published the Equality Index, providing an opportunity to reflect upon observed five-year trends in some key statistics over this period of time. Because there have been a number of revisions to the overall index since its inception, comparing specific variables over time, rather than the overall index or sub-indices, will prove to be a more consistent and accurate way of measuring changes. Table 2

Table 2

Five Year Comparison of Selected Equality Index Variables	2005 Equality Index			2009 Equality Index			
	Black	White	Index	Black	White	Index	Data Years
Economics							
Median Household Income (2007 dollars)	33,421	53,862	61%	33,916	52,115	65.0%	2003, 2007
Poverty Rate	24.1%	10.2%	42%	24.5%	8.2%	33.0%	2003, 2007
Unemployment Rate	10.8%	4.7%	43%	10.1%	5.2%	51.0%	2004, 2008
Home Ownership Rate	48.1%	75.4%	64%	47.2%	75.2%	63.0%	2003, 2007
Health							
People Without Health Insurance, % of population	19.7%	10.1%	51%	19.5%	10.4%	53%	2002, 2007
Uninsured Children, %	13.9%	7.8%	56%	12.2%	7.3%	60.0%	2002, 2007
Education							
Educational Attainment: At Least High School (25 yrs. and over), % of population	80.1%	85.1%	94%	82.3%	90.6%	91%	2003, 2007
Educational Attainment: At Least Bachelor's (25 yrs. and over), % of population	17.3%	27.6%	63%	18.5%	31.8%	58%	2003, 2007
Preprimary School Enrollment	67.7%	65.0%	104%	66.7%	68.3%	98%	2002, 2006
College Enrollment (Graduate or undergraduate): ages 14 and over, % of population	8.2%	7.0%	119%	6.6%	6.1%	108%	2002, 2006
Social Justice							
Incarceration rate: prisoners per 100,000	3,950	503	13%	2,142	332	16%	2003, 2007
Prisoners as a % of Arrests	24.6%	7.8%	32%	23.5%	8.3%	35%	2001, 2007

displays selected variables from the 2005 Equality Index and the current 2009 Index suggesting that progress has been mixed.

The indices for two of the four economic variables included in Table 1—the poverty rate and the homeownership rate—declined between 2003 and 2007 (data years) as whites did better in these areas while African Americans did worse. On the other hand, the improvement seen in the indices of the other two variables—median household income and unemployment rate—resulted from the opposite effect. Real median household income decreased by $1,747 for whites, but increased by $495 for African Americans. Similarly, the unemployment rate increased by 0.2 percentage point for whites and decreased almost one percentage point for African Americans. However, despite these positive changes for African Americans, they remained twice as likely to be unemployed and had a median household income of less than two-thirds that of white Americans.

In the area of education, attainment and enrollment data suggest that although achievement in these areas is similar for blacks and whites, over the four-year period observed, there has been a growing, rather than a diminishing, gap. For example, although educational attainment improved for both groups between 2003 and 2007, it has done so more quickly for whites than for African Americans. On the other hand, preprimary school enrollment and college enrollment were areas of divergence. African-American enrollment declined at both the preprimary (-1.3 percentage points) and college (-1.4 percentage points) level while white enrollment increased at the preprimary level (-3.3 percentage points) and decreased slightly (-0.9 percentage point) at the college level.

In the area of health, between 2002 and 2007 (data years) there were some improvements in the health insurance gap overall (2 percentage points) and for children (3 percentage points) with the most ground being made among uninsured African-American children who went from almost 14 percent to 12 percent. Under the heading of social justice, the incarceration rate declined for both whites and African Americans between 2003 and 2007, resulting in a 3 percentage-point increase in the incarceration rate index. A decline in prisoners as a percentage of arrests for African Americans (-1.7 percentage points) also contributed to a 3 percentage-point increase in the index for this variable.

Conclusion

Reflecting again upon the inauguration of President Obama, one can't help but acknowledge the profound symbolism of the moment. For, although the steps of the U.S. Capital are only 1.9 miles from the Lincoln Memorial, the journey from where Dr. King stood to where President Obama now stands took 40 years to travel. The question therefore is not whether racism is dead, but how long will it take to travel the many other distances distorted by its legacy? The clock is ticking.

NOTES

[1] For negative outcomes like death rates or incarceration rates, the ratio is white-to-black so that the interpretation of the index (less than 100% suggests that blacks are doing worse relative to whites, and greater than 100% suggests that blacks are doing better than whites) is preserved.

[2] These are the dates identified by the Business Cycle Dating Committee of the National Bureau of Economic Research.

[3] All job growth numbers are the author's calculations based on Bureau of Labor Statistics data.

[4] The Census Bureau's March 2007 Current Population Survey is the source for the median income (http://www.census.gov/hhes/www/income/histinc/h17.html) and poverty (http://www.census.gov/hhes/www/poverty/histpov/perindex.html , Table 2) statistics in the *Equality Index*. Therefore, although November 2001 is the official start of the 2001-2007 expansion, changes in median income and poverty will be measured from March 2001 to March 2007. This will be compared to the six-year changes from March 1991 – March 1997, corresponding to the March 1991- March 2001 expansion. The home ownership statistics in the *Equality Index* are 2007 annual averages based on the Census Bureau's monthly Current Population Survey (http://www.census.gov/hhes/www/housing/hvs/annual07/ann07t20.html). The unemployment rates in the *Equality Index* are the 2008 annual averages (not seasonally adjusted) reported by the Bureau of Labor Statistics (www.bls.gov)

NATIONAL URBAN LEAGUE
EQUALITY INDEX™
2009

Global Insight, Inc.
Ana Orozco and Robert Tomarelli

The Equality Index of Black America

Updated Series ■ New Series (Index = 0.71)

	Source	Year	Black	White	Index	DIFF ('09-'08)
ECONOMICS (30%)						
Median Income (0.25)						
Median Household Income (Real), Dollars	Census	2007	33,916	52,115	65%	0.02
Median Male Earnings, Dollars	ACS	2007	35,652	50,139	71%	(0.01)
Median Female Earnings, Dollars	ACS	2007	31,035	36,398	85%	(0.01)
Poverty (0.15)						
Population Living Below Poverty Line, %	Census	2007	24.5	8.2	33%	(0.00)
Population Living Below 50% of Poverty Line, %	Census	2007	11.2	3.4	30%	(0.02)
Population Living Below 125% of Poverty Line, %	Census	2007	30.7	11.4	37%	0.00
Population Living Below Poverty Line (Under 18), %	Census	2007	34.5	10.1	29%	(0.01)
Population Living Below Poverty Line (18-64), %	Census	2007	19.8	7.7	39%	(0.00)
Population Living Below Poverty Line (65 and Older), %	Census	2007	23.2	7.4	32%	0.01
Employment Issues (0.20)						
Unemployment Rate, %	BLS	2008	10.1	5.2	51%	0.02
Unemployment Rate-Male, %	BLS	2008	11.4	5.5	48%	0.02
Unemployment Rate-Female, %	BLS	2008	8.9	4.9	55%	0.02
Unemployment Rate-Persons 16-19, %	BLS	2008	31.2	16.8	54%	0.07
Percent Not in Workforce-Ages 16 to 19, %	BLS	2008	70.6	56.9	81%	0.01
Percent Not in Workforce-Ages 16 and Older, %	BLS	2008	36.3	33.7	93%	0.00
Labor Force Participantion Rate, %	BLS	2008	63.7	66.3	96%	0.00
LFPR 16 to 19, %	BLS	2008	29.4	43.1	68%	(0.00)
LFPR 20 to 24, %	BLS	2008	68.0	76.3	89%	(0.00)
LFPR over 25-Less than High School Grad, %	BLS	2008	39.8	47.7	83%	0.02
LFPR over 25-High School Graduate, No College, %	BLS	2008	65.7	62.0	106%	0.01
LFPR over 25-Some College, No Degree, %	BLS	2008	73.8	68.6	108%	(0.00)
LFPR over 25-Associate's Degree, %	BLS	2008	78.4	76.1	103%	0.01

The Equality Index of Black America

Updated Series ■ New Series (Index = 0.71)

	Source	Year	Black	White	Index	DIFF ('09-'08)
LFPR Over 25-Some College or Associate Degree, %	BLS	2008	75.2	71.2	106%	0.00
LFPR Over 25-College Graduate, %	BLS	2008	81.5	77.5	105%	(0.02)
Employment to Pop. Ratio, %	BLS	2008	57.3	62.8	91%	(0.01)
Housing & Wealth (0.34)						
Home Ownership, %	Census	2007	47.2	75.2	63%	(0.00)
Mortgage Application Denial Rate (Total), %	HMDA	2007	32.6	14.6	45%	(0.04)
Mortgage Application Denial Rate (Male), %	HMDA	2007	35.0	17.7	50%	(0.05)
Mortgage Application DenialRate (Female), %	HMDA	2007	32.6	16.7	51%	(0.04)
Mortgage Application Denial Rate (Joint), %	HMDA	2007	26.9	11.0	41%	(0.04)
Home Improvement Loans Denials (Total), %	HMDA	2007	55.6	33.3	60%	(0.00)
Home Improvement Loans Denials (Male), %	HMDA	2007	56.8	37.9	67%	(0.01)
Home Improvement Loans Denials (Female), %	HMDA	2007	57.1	37.7	66%	(0.00)
Home Improvement Loans Denials (Joint), %	HMDA	2007	51.5	28.2	55%	(0.01)
Percent of High-Priced Loans (More than 3% above Treasury)	HMDA	2007	34.0	10.5	31%	(0.02)
Median Home Value, Dollars	Census	2000	80,600	123,400	65%	
Median Wealth, 2005 Dollars	PSID	2005	10,000	109,100	9%	0.01
Median Equity in Home, Dollars	Census	2002	40,000	79,200	51%	(0.04)
Percent Investing in 401k, %	EBRI	2005	27.0	36.8	73%	0.05
Percent Investing in IRA, %	EBRI	2005	9.9	27.7	36%	(0.02)
U.S. Firms by Race (% Compared to Employment Share)	Census	2002	0.51	0.95	54%	
Digital Divide (0.05)						
Households with Computer at Home, %	Census	2003	44.6	66.6	67%	
Households with the Internet, %	Census/NTIA	2007	46.3	68.9	67%	0.07
Adult Users with Broadband Access, %	Pew Inter.	2008	43.0	57.0	75%	(0.08)
Transportation (0.01)						
Car Ownership, %	Census	2002	67.1	88.4	76%	(0.03)

The Equality Index of Black America

Legend: Updated Series | New Series | (Index = 0.71)

	Source	Year	Black	White	Index	DIFF ('09-'08)
Means of Transportation to Work: Drive Alone, %	ACS	2007	71.3	79.6	90%	0.01
Means of Transportation to Work: Public Transportation, %	ACS	2007	11.6	2.9	25%	0.01
Economic Weighted Index					**57.4%**	(0.002)
HEALTH INDEX (25%)						
Death Rates & Life Expectancy (0.45)						
Life Expectancy at Birth	CDC	2005	73.2	78.3	93%	0.00
Male	CDC	2005	69.5	75.7	92%	0.00
Female	CDC	2005	76.5	80.8	95%	0.00
Life Expectancy at 65 (Additional Expected Years)	CDC	2005	17.2	18.8	91%	0.00
Male at 65	CDC	2005	15.2	17.2	88%	0.00
Female at 65	CDC	2005	18.7	20.0	94%	0.00
Death Rates						
Age-Adjusted Death Rates (per 100,000)–all causes	CDC	2005	1,034.5	796.6	77%	0.01
Age-Adjusted Death Rates (per 100,000)–Male	CDC	2005	1,275.3	945.4	74%	0.01
Age-Adjusted Death Rates (per 100,000)–Female	CDC	2005	860.5	677.7	79%	0.01
Age-Adjusted Death Rates (per 100,000)–Heart Disease	CDC	2005	275.6	210.7	76%	0.01
Ischemic Heart Disease	CDC	2005	173.7	145.2	84%	0.01
Age-Adjusted Death Rates (per 100,000)–Stroke (Cerebrovascular)	CDC	2005	66.3	45.0	68%	(0.00)
Age-Adjusted Death Rates (per 100,000)–Cancer	CDC	2005	226.8	187.0	82%	0.01
Trachea, Bronchus, and Lung	CDC	2005	59.6	55.5	93%	0.01
Colon, Rectum, and Anus	CDC	2005	25.2	17.2	68%	(0.03)
Prostate (Male)	CDC	2005	54.1	22.8	42%	0.00
Breast (Female)	CDC	2005	33.4	24.0	72%	(0.03)
Age-Adjusted Death Rates (per 100,000)–Chronic Lower Respiratory	CDC	2005	31.1	47.2	152%	(0.04)
Age-Adjusted Death Rates (per 100,000)–Influenza and Pneumonia	CDC	2005	22.1	20.3	92%	0.05
Age-Adjusted Death Rates (per 100,000)–Chronic Liver Disease and Cirrhosis	CDC	2005	7.8	8.7	112%	0.03

Updated Series | **New Series** | **(Index = 0.71)**

The Equality Index of Black America

	Source	Year	Black	White	Index	DIFF ('09-'08)
Age-Adjusted Death Rates (per 100,000)–Diabetes	CDC	2005	47.7	21.5	45%	0.01
Age-Adjusted Death Rates (per 100,000)–HIV	CDC	2005	19.8	1.8	9%	0.00
Unintentional Injuries	CDC	2005	39.5	41.0	104%	(0.03)
Motor Vehicle-Related Injuries	CDC	2005	14.5	15.5	107%	0.01
Age-Adjusted Death Rates (per 100,000)–Suicide	CDC	2005	5.4	12.9	239%	0.04
Age-Adjusted Death Rates (per 100,000)–Suicide Males	CDC	2005	9.4	21.2	226%	0.11
Age-Adjusted Death Rates (per 100,000)–Suicide Males Ages 15-24	CDC	2005	11.5	18.4	160%	0.04
Age-Adjusted Death Rates (per 100,000)–Suicide Females	CDC	2005	1.9	5.3	279%	(0.21)
Age-Adjusted Death Rates (per 100,000)–Suicide Females Ages 15-24	CDC	2005	1.7	3.9	229%	0.48
Age-Adjusted Death Rates (per 100,000)–Homicide	CDC	2005	21.8	2.7	12%	(0.01)
Age-Adjusted Death Rates (per 100,000)–Homicide Male	CDC	2005	38.5	3.5	9%	(0.01)
Age-Adjusted Death Rates (per 100,000)–Homicide Males Ages 15-24	CDC	2005	84.1	4.7	6%	(0.00)
Age-Adjusted Death Rates (per 100,000)–Homicide Female	CDC	2005	6.2	1.8	29%	0.01
Age-Adjusted Death Rates (per 100,000)–Homicide Females Ages 15-24	CDC	2005	8.8	2.0	23%	(0.03)
Age-Adjusted Death Rates (per 100,000) by Age Cohort: >1 Male	CDC	2005	1,437.2	625.7	44%	(0.01)
Age-Adjusted Death Rates (per 100,000) by Age Cohort: 1-4 Male	CDC	2005	46.7	29.9	64%	0.04
Age-Adjusted Death Rates (per 100,000) by Age Cohort: 5-14 Male	CDC	2005	27.0	17.4	64%	(0.04)
Age-Adjusted Death Rates (per 100,000) by Age Cohort: 15-24 Male	CDC	2005	172.1	105.8	61%	(0.02)
Age-Adjusted Death Rates (per 100,000) by Age Cohort: 25-34 Male	CDC	2005	254.3	134.1	53%	0.01
Age-Adjusted Death Rates (per 100,000) by Age Cohort: 35-44 Male	CDC	2005	395.5	236.1	60%	0.00
Age-Adjusted Death Rates (per 100,000) by Age Cohort: 45-54 Male	CDC	2005	948.6	517.2	55%	0.01
Age-Adjusted Death Rates (per 100,000) by Age Cohort: 55-64 Male	CDC	2005	1,954.3	1,079.6	55%	0.00
Age-Adjusted Death Rates (per 100,000) by Age Cohort: 65-74 Male	CDC	2005	3,747.3	2,584.5	69%	0.00
Age-Adjusted Death Rates (per 100,000) by Age Cohort: 75-84 Male	CDC	2005	7667.1	6,420.4	84%	(0.00)
Age-Adjusted Death Rates (per 100,000) by Age Cohort: 85+ Male	CDC	2005	13,809.8	15,401.3	112%	0.04
Age-Adjusted Death Rates (per 100,000) by Age Cohort: >1 Female	CDC	2005	1,179.7	496.5	42%	(0.01)

The Equality Index of Black America

Updated Series | New Series | (Index = 0.71)

	Source	Year	Black	White	Index	DIFF ('09-'08)
Age-Adjusted Death Rates (per 100,000) by age cohort: 1-4 Female	CDC	2005	36.7	22.2	60%	0.01
Age-Adjusted Death Rates (per 100,000) by Age Cohort: 5-14 Female	CDC	2005	19.4	12.9	66%	0.05
Age-Adjusted Death Rates (per 100,000) by Age Cohort: 15-24 Female	CDC	2005	51.2	42.2	82%	(0.00)
Age-Adjusted Death Rates (per 100,000) by Age Cohort: 25-34 Female	CDC	2005	109.8	62.1	57%	0.03
Age-Adjusted Death Rates (per 100,000) by Age Cohort: 35-44 Female	CDC	2005	250.0	137.0	55%	0.02
Age-Adjusted Death Rates (per 100,000) by Age Cohort: 45-54 Female	CDC	2005	568.4	298.7	53%	0.01
Age-Adjusted Death Rates (per 100,000) by Age Cohort: 55-64 Female	CDC	2005	1,103.6	677.2	61%	0.01
Age-Adjusted Death Rates (per 100,000) by Age Cohort: 65-74 Female	CDC	2005	2,341.5	1,729.6	74%	0.00
Age-Adjusted Death Rates (per 100,000) by Age Cohort: 75-84 Female	CDC	2005	5,236.7	4,579.7	87%	0.01
Age-Adjusted Death Rates (per 100,000) by Age Cohort: 85+ Female	CDC	2005	12,789.9	13,683.1	107%	0.01
Physical Condition (0.10)						
Overweight and Obese: 18+ years (% of Population)	CDC	2007	35.5	36.7	103%	(0.01)
Overweight-Men 20 Years and Over (% of Population)	CDC	2003-2006	36.0	39.4	109%	(0.03)
Overweight-Women 20 Years and Over (% of Population)	CDC	2003-2006	26.4	26.3	100%	0.05
Obese (% of population)	CDC	2007	36.7	25.6	70%	0.04
Obese-Men 20 Years and Over (% of Population)	CDC	2003-2006	35.3	32.2	91%	(0.07)
Obese-Women 20 Years and Over (% of Population)	CDC	2003-2006	53.0	31.7	60%	(0.00)
Diabetes: Physician Diagnosed in Ages 20+ (% of Population)	CDC	2001-2004	11.6	6.1	53%	
AIDS Cases per 100,000 Males Ages 13+	CDC	2006	82.9	11.2	14%	0.01
AIDS Cases per 100,000 Females Ages 13+	CDC	2006	40.4	1.9	5%	0.00
Substance Abuse (0.10)						
Binge Alcohol (5 drinks in 1 day, 1x a year) Ages 18+ (% of Population)	CDC	2006	23.6	34.0	144%	0.07
Use of illicit drugs in the past month ages 12 + (% of population)	CDC	2005	9.7	8.1	84%	
Tobacco: Both Cigarette & Cigar Ages 12+ (% of Population)	CDC	2005	28.4	31.2	110%	0.00
Mental Health (0.02)						
Students Who Consider Suicide: Male (%)	CDC	2005	7.0	12.4	177%	

The Equality Index of Black America

	Source	Year	Black	White	Index	DIFF ('09-'08)
					Updated Series ■ New Series (Index = 0.71)	
Students Who Carry Out Intent and Require Medical Attention: Male (%)	CDC	2005	1.4	1.5	107%	
Students that Act on Suicidal Feeling: Male (%)	CDC	2005	5.2	5.2	100%	
Students Who Consider Suicide: Female (%)	CDC	2005	17.1	21.5	126%	
Students Who Carry Out Intent and Require Medical Attention: Female (%)	CDC	2005	2.6	2.7	104%	
Students that Act on Suicidal Feeling: Female (%)	CDC	2005	9.8	9.3	95%	
Access to Care (0.075)						
Private Insurance Payment for Health Care: Under 65 Years Old (% of Distribution)	CDC	2004	39.5	59.4	66%	
People Without Health Insurance (% of population)	Census	2007	19.5	10.4	53%	0.01
People 18 to 64 Without A Usual Source of Health Insurance (% of Adults)	Census	2007	25.4	13.7	54%	(0.01)
People in Poverty Without a Usual Source of Health Insurance (% of Adults)	Census	2007	40.8	37.9	93%	0.03
Population Under 65 Covered by Medicaid (% of population)	CDC	2006	26.2	9.5	36%	0.02
Elderly Health Care (0.03)						
Population Over 65 Covered by Medicaid (% of population)	CDC	2005	23.6	6.1	26%	
Medicare Expenditures per Beneficiary (Dollars)	CDC	2004	18,111.0	13,064.0	72%	
Pregnancy Issues (0.04)						
Prenatal Care Begins in 1st Trimester	CDC	2004	76.5	88.9	86%	
Prenatal Care Begins in 3rd Trimester	CDC	2004	5.7	2.2	39%	
Percent of Births to Mothers 18 and Under	CDC	2005	6.3	2.0	32%	0.01
Percent of Live Births to Unmarried Mothers	CDC	2005	69.9	25.3	36%	0.01
Mothers With Less than 12 Years of Education (% of Live Births)	CDC	2004	23.4	11.0	47%	
Mothers Who Smoked Cigarettes During Pregnancy (%)	CDC	2004	8.4	13.8	164%	
Low Birth Weight (% of Live Births)	CDC	2004	13.7	7.2	52%	
Very Low Birth Weight (% of Live Births)	CDC	2004	3.2	1.2	38%	
Reproduction Issues (0.01)	CDC					
Abortions (Per 100 Live Births)	CDC	2004	47.2	16.1	34%	0.01
Women Using Contraception (% in Population)	CDC	2002	57.6	64.6	89%	

The Equality Index of Black America

	Source	Year	Black	White	Index	DIFF ('09-'08)
					Updated Series / New Series	(Index = 0.71)
Delivery Issues (0.075)						
All Infant Deaths: Neonatal and Post (per 1,000 Live Births)	CDC	2005	13.6	5.8	42%	0.00
Neonatal Deaths (per 1,000 Live Births)	CDC	2005	9.1	3.7	41%	(0.00)
PostNeonatal Deaths (per 1,000 Live Births)	CDC	2005	4.5	2.1	46%	0.01
Maternal Mortality (per 100,000 Live Births)	CDC	2005	31.7	9.6	30%	0.06
Children's Health (0.1)						
Babies Breastfed (%)	CDC	1999-2001	45.3	68.7	66%	
Children without a Health Care Visit in Past 12 Months (up to 6 years old) (%)	CDC	2005-2006	4.4	5.0	114%	(0.05)
Vaccinations of Children Below Poverty: Combined Vacc. Series 4:3:1:3 (% of Children 19-35 Months)	CDC	2006	72.0	70.0	103%	
Uninsured Children (%)	Census	2007	12.2	7.3	60%	0.08
Overweight Boys 6-11 Years Old (% of Population)	CDC	2001-2004	17.2	16.9	98%	
Overweight Girls 6-11 Years Old (% of Population)	CDC	2001-2004	24.8	15.6	63%	
AIDS Cases per 100,000 All Children Under 13	CDC	2006	0.4	0.0	4%	0.00
Health Weighted Index					**74.4%**	0.011
EDUCATION (25%)						
Quality (0.25)						
Teacher Quality (0.10)						
Middle Grades–Teacher Lacking at Least a College Minor in Subject Taught (High vs. Low Minority Schools), %	ET	2000	49.0	40.0	85%	
HS–Teacher Lacking an Undergraduate Major in Subject Taught (High vs. Low Minority Schools), %	ET	2000	28.0	21.0	91%	
Per Student Funding (High vs. Low Poverty Districts (Dollars)	ET	2004	5,937	7,244	82%	
Teachers with <3 Years Experience (High vs. Low Minority Schools) (%)	NCES	2000	21.0	10.0	48%	
Distribution of Underprepared Teachers (High vs. Low Minority Schools) (%) (California Only)	SRI	2005-06	8.0	3.0	38%	
Course Quality (0.15)						
College Completion (% of All Entrants)	ET	1999	45.0	73.0	62%	
College Completion % of Entrants with Strong HS Curriculum (Algebra II Plus Other Courses)	ET	1999	75.0	86.0	87%	
HS Students: Enrolled in Chemistry (%)	NCES	2005	63.6	67.1	95%	

The Equality Index of Black America

	Source	Year	Black	White	Index	DIFF ('09-'08)
HS Students: Enrolled in Algebra II (%)	NCES	2005	69.2	71.2	97%	
Students Taking: Precalculus (%)	CB	2007	35.0	55.0	64%	
Students Taking: Calculus (%)	CB	2007	15.0	31.0	48%	
Students Taking: Physics (%)	CB	2007	43.0	55.0	78%	
Students Taking: English Composition (%)	CB	2007	57.0	69.0	83%	0.01
Students Taking: Grammar (%)	CB	2006	51.0	56.0	91%	
Attainment (0.30)						
Graduation Rates, 2-year Institutions (%)	NCES	2002	27.2	33.8	80%	
Graduation Rates, 4-year Institutions (%)	NCES	1999	40.4	58.9	69%	
NCAA Div. I College Freshmen Graduating within 6 Years (%)	NCAA	2001-02	45.0	65.0	69%	(0.03)
Degrees Earned (Assoc) (% of population aged 18-24 yrs)	NCES	2006	2.1	2.7	77%	0.01
Degrees Earned (Bach) (% of population aged 18-29 yrs)	NCES	2006	2.0	3.6	55%	0.01
Degrees Earned (Master) (% of population aged 18-34 yrs)	NCES	2006	0.6	0.9	64%	0.02
Educational Attainment: At Least High School (25yrs. and Over) (% of Population)	Census	2007	82.3	90.6	91%	0.02
Educational Attainment: At Least Bachelor's (25yrs. and Over) (% of Population)	Census	2007	18.5	31.8	58%	(0.01)
Degree Holders (% Distribution by Field)						
Agriculture/Forestry	NCES	2001	0.7	1.2	56%	
Art/Architecture	NCES	2001	3.3	2.9	114%	
Business/Management	NCES	2001	19.5	18.1	108%	
Communications	NCES	2001	3.2	2.4	135%	
Computer and Information Sciences	NCES	2001	3.9	2.2	177%	
Education	NCES	2001	15.3	15.3	100%	
Engineering	NCES	2001	3.6	7.7	47%	
English/Literature	NCES	2001	2.6	3.3	80%	
Foreign Languages	NCES	2001	0.8	0.9	96%	
Health Sciences	NCES	2001	5.4	4.5	120%	

Updated Series ▪ New Series (Index = 0.71)

The Equality Index of Black America

Updated Series   New Series   (Index = 0.71)

	Source	Year	Black	White	Index	DIFF ('09-'08)
Liberal Arts/Humanities	NCES	2001	4.6	6.1	75%	
Mathematics/Statistics	NCES	2001	2.4	1.4	169%	
Natural Sciences	NCES	2001	6.0	5.6	106%	
Philosophy/Religion/Theology	NCES	2001	0.9	1.3	70%	
Pre-professional	NCES	2001	1.6	1.1	146%	
Psychology	NCES	2001	4.9	3.9	126%	
Social Sciences/History	NCES	2001	8.1	4.9	165%	
Other Fields	NCES	2001	13.1	17.2	76%	
Preschool: 10% of Total Scores (0.025)						
Children's School Readiness Skills: Ages 3-5 (% with 3 or 4 skills*)	NCES	2005	44.1	46.8	94%	
*Recognizes all Letters, Counts to 20 or higher, Writes Name, Reads or Pretends to Read						
Elementary 40% of Total Scores (0.10)						
Average Scale Score in U.S. History, 8th Graders	NCES	2006	244	273	89%	(0.00)
Average Scale Score in U.S. History, 4th Graders	NCES	2006	191	223	86%	0.00
Average Scale Score in Math, 8th Graders (Public Schools)	NCES	2005	254	288	88%	(0.03)
Average Scale Score in Math, 4th Graders (Public Schools)	NCES	2005	220	246	89%	(0.01)
Average Scale Score in Reading, 8th Graders (Public Schools)	NCES	2005	242	269	90%	(0.02)
Average Scale Score in Reading, 4th Graders (Public Schools)	NCES	2007	203	230	88%	(0.00)
Average Scale Score in Science, 8th Graders (Public Schools)	NCES	2005	124	160	78%	
Average Scale Score in Science, 4th Graders (Public Schools)	NCES	2005	129	162	80%	
Writing Proficiency at or above Basic 8th Graders (% of Students)	NCES	2002	75	91	82%	
Writing Proficiency at or above Basic 4th Graders (% of Students)	NCES	2002	79	91	87%	
High School 50% of Total Scores (0.125)						
Writing Proficiency at or above Basic 12th Graders (% of Students)	NCES	2002	59	80	74%	
Average Scale Score in Science, 12th Graders	NCES	2005	120	156	77%	
High School GPA's for Those Taking the SAT	CB	2007	3.00	3.40	88%	

The Equality Index of Black America

					Updated Series ■ New Series (Index = 0.71)	
	Source	Year	Black	White	Index	DIFF ('09-'08)
SAT Reasoning Test (Mean Scores)						
Mathematics (Joint)	CB	2008	1,280	1,583	81%	(0.00)
Mathematics (Male)	CB	2008	426	537	79%	(0.01)
Mathematics (Female)	CB	2008	434	555	78%	(0.01)
Critical Reading (Joint)	CB	2008	420	521	81%	(0.01)
Critical Reading (Male)	CB	2008	430	528	81%	(0.01)
Critical Reading (Female)	CB	2008	425	530	80%	(0.01)
Writing (Joint)	CB	2008	433	526	82%	(0.01)
Writing (Male)	CB	2008	424	518	82%	(0.00)
Writing (Female)	CB	2008	412	510	81%	(0.00)
ACT-Average Composite Score	CB	2008	433	526	82%	(0.00)
	ACT	2008	16.9	22.1	76%	(0.00)
Enrollment (0.10)						
School Enrollment: Ages 3-34 (% of Population)	Census	2006	58.1	56.8	102%	0.01
Preprimary School Enrollment	Census	2006	66.7	68.3	98%	0.07
3 and 4 Years Old	Census	2006	59.2	58.2	102%	0.12
5 and 6 Years Old	Census	2006	92.6	95.6	97%	(0.03)
7 to 13 Years Old	Census	2006	97.2	98.6	99%	(0.01)
14 and 15 Years Old	Census	2006	97.5	98.4	99%	0.02
16 and 17 Years Old	Census	2006	93.3	95.9	97%	0.00
18 and 19 Years Old	Census	2006	64.7	67.9	95%	0.08
20 and 21 Years Old	Census	2006	39.1	52.9	74%	0.05
22 to 24 Years Old	Census	2006	27.2	27.4	99%	(0.01)
25 to 29 Years Old	Census	2006	11.8	12.5	94%	0.01
30 to 34 Years Old	Census	2006	8.6	7.4	116%	(0.29)
35 and Over	Census	2006	3.1	1.7	182%	0.13

The Equality Index of Black America

Updated Series | New Series | (Index = 0.71)

	Source	Year	Black	White	Index	DIFF ('09-'08)
College Enrollment (Graduate or Undergraduate): Ages 14 and Over (% of Population)	Census	2006	6.6	6.1	108%	(0.02)
14 to 17 Years Old	Census	2006	1.1	1.1	100%	(0.30)
18 to 19 Years Old	Census	2006	37.7	51.1	74%	0.01
20 to 21 Years Old	Census	2006	34.3	52.0	66%	0.01
22 to 24 Years Old	Census	2006	26.8	26.9	100%	0.03
25 to 29 Years Old	Census	2006	11.1	12.3	90%	(0.00)
30 to 34 Years Old	Census	2006	8.2	7.3	112%	(0.21)
35 Years Old and Over	Census	2006	2.9	1.6	177%	0.21
College Enrollment Rate of Recent High School Graduate (%)	NCES	2006	55.5	68.5	81%	0.05
Adult Education Participation (% of Population)	NCES	2004-05	46.0	46.0	100%	
Student Status & Risk Factors (0.10)						
High School Dropouts: Status Dropouts % (Not Completed HS and Not Enrolled, Regardless of When Dropped)	Census	2005	12.9	11.3	88%	
Children in Poverty (%)	USDC	1999	33.1	9.3	28%	
Children in All Families Below Poverty Level (%)	NCES	2006	33.0	9.5	29%	0.01
Children in Families Below Poverty Level (Female Householder, No Spouse Present) (%)	NCES	2006	49.7	32.9	66%	0.00
Children with No Parent in the Labor Force (%)	USDC	2000	20.3	5.5	27%	
School Age Children (5-15) with a Disability (%)	USDC	2000	7.0	5.7	81%	
Public School Students (K-12): Repeated Grade (%)	NCES	2003	17.1	8.2	48%	
Public School Students (K-12): Suspended (%)	NCES	2003	19.6	8.8	45%	
Public School Students (K-12): Expelled (%)	NCES	2003	5.0	1.4	28%	
Center Based, Child Care of Preschool Children (%)	NCES	2005	66.5	59.1	89%	
Parental Care Only of Preschool Children (%)	NCES	2005	19.5	24.1	81%	
Teacher Stability: Remained in Public School (High vs. Low Minority Schools) (%)	NCES	2005	79.7	85.9	93%	(0.04)
Teacher Stability: Remained in Private School (High vs. Low Minority Schools) (%)	NCES	2005	72.7	82.8	88%	(0.17)
Zero Days Missed in School Year (% of 10th Graders)	NCES	2002	16.5	13.0	127%	
3+ Days Late to School (% of 10th Graders)	NCES	2002	46.1	31.5	68%	
Never Cut Classes (% of 10th Graders)	NCES	2002	64.6	72.9	89%	

The Equality Index of Black America

					☐ Updated Series ▨ New Series	(Index = 0.71)
	Source	Year	Black	White	Index	DIFF ('09-'08)
Home Literacy Activities (Age 3 to 5)						
Read to 3 or More Times a Week	NCES	2005	78.5	91.9	85%	
Told a Story at Least Once a Month	NCES	2005	54.3	53.3	102%	
Taught Words or Numbers Three or More Times a Week	NCES	2005	80.6	75.7	106%	
Visited a Library at Least Once in Last Month	NCES	2005	43.9	44.9	98%	
Education Weighted Index					**78.5%**	(0.001)
SOCIAL JUSTICE (10%)						
Equality Before the Law (0.70)						
Stopped While Driving (%)	BJS	2005	8.1	8.9	110%	
Speeding	BJS	2002	50.0	57.0	114%	
Vehicle Defect	BJS	2002	10.3	8.7	84%	
Roadside Check for Drinking Drivers	BJS	2002	1.1	1.3	118%	
Record Check	BJS	2002	17.4	11.3	65%	
Seatbelt Violation	BJS	2002	3.5	4.4	126%	
Illegal Turn/Lane Change	BJS	2002	5.1	4.5	88%	
Stop Sign/Light Violation	BJS	2002	5.9	6.5	110%	
Other	BJS	2002	3.7	4.0	108%	
Mean Incarceration Sentence (In Average Months)	BJS	2004	40	37	93%	
Average sentence for incarceration (All Offenses) (Male,Months)	BJS	2004	43	39	91%	
Average Sentence for Murder	BJS	2004	256	232	91%	
Average Sentence for Sexual Assault	BJS	2004	104	110	106%	
Average Sentence for Robbery	BJS	2004	101	88	87%	
Average Sentence for Aggravated Assault2004	BJS	2004	51	42	82%	
Average Sentence for Other Violent	BJS	2004	47	43	91%	
Average Sentence for Burglary	BJS	2004	47	44	94%	

The Equality Index of Black America

	Updated Series	New Series			

	Source	Year	Black	White	Index	DIFF ('09-'08) (Index = 0.71)
Average Sentence for Larceny	BJS	2004	23	21	91%	
Average Sentence for Fraud	BJS	2004	25	27	108%	
Average Sentence for Drug Possession	BJS	2004	23	22	96%	
Average Sentence for Drug Trafficking	BJS	2004	38	41	108%	
Average Sentence for Weapon Offenses	BJS	2004	34	32	94%	
Average Sentence for Other Offenses	BJS	2004	25	25	100%	
Average sentence for incarceration (All Offenses) (Female, Months)	BJS	2004	23	24	104%	
Average Sentence for Murder	BJS	2004	231	152	66%	
Average Sentence for Sexual Assault	BJS	2004	55	88	160%	
Average Sentence for Robbery	BJS	2004	80	55	69%	
Average Sentence for Aggravated Assault	BJS	2004	31	31	100%	
Average Sentence for Other Violent	BJS	2004	31	41	132%	
Average Sentence for Burglary	BJS	2004	22	27	123%	
Average Sentence for Larceny	BJS	2004	17	17	100%	
Average Sentence for Fraud	BJS	2004	21	21	100%	
Average Sentence for Drug Possession	BJS	2004	15	16	107%	
Average Sentence for Drug Trafficking	BJS	2004	25	28	112%	
Average Sentence for Weapon Offenses	BJS	2004	20	26	130%	
Average Sentence for Other Offenses	BJS	2004	17	20	118%	
Convicted Felons Sentenced to Probation, All Offenses (%)	BJS	2004	30	26	115%	0.02
Probation Sentence for Murder (%)	BJS	2004	6	5	120%	(0.55)
Probation Sentence for Sexual Assault (%)	BJS	2004	18	17	106%	(0.07)
Probation Sentence for Robbery (%)	BJS	2004	13	11	118%	(0.09)
Probation Sentence for Burglary (%)	BJS	2004	25	22	114%	(0.05)
Probation Sentence for Fraud (%)	BJS	2004	38	40	95%	0.02
Probation Sentence for Drug Offenses (%)	BJS	2004	34	26	131%	0.01

The Equality Index of Black America

Updated Series ▪ New Series (Index = 0.71)

	Source	Year	Black	White	Index	DIFF ('09-'08)
Probation Sentence for Weapons Offenses (%)		2004	25	29	86%	(0.04)
Incarceration Rate: Prisoners per 100,000	BJS	2007	2,142	332	16%	(0.01)
Incarceration Rate: Prisoners per 100,000 People - Male	BJS	2007	3,138	481	15%	(0.01)
Incarceration Rate: Prisoners per 100,000 People - Female	BJS	2007	150	50	33%	0.01
Prisoners as a % of Arrests	FBI, BJS	2007	23.5	8.3	35%	(0.02)
Victimization & Mental Anguish (0.30)						
Homicide Rate per 100,000	BJS	2005	20.6	3.3	16%	(0.01)
Homicide Rate per 100,000: Firearm	NACJD	2003	14.1	2.1	15%	
Homicide Rate per 100,000: Stabbings	NACJD	2003	2.0	0.5	25%	
Homicide Rate per 100,000: Personal Weapons	NACJD	2003	0.9	1.7	197%	
Homicide Rate per 100,000 - Male	CDC	2005	39.7	5.4	14%	(0.01)
Homicide Rate per 100,000 - Female	CDC	2005	6.2	1.9	31%	0.01
Murder Victims (Rate per 100,000)	USDJ	2007	18.9	2.9	15%	(0.04)
Hate Crimes Victims (Rate per 100,000)	USDJ	2005	8.5	0.5	6%	
Victims of Violent Crimes (Rate per 100,000)	BJS	2006	32.7	23.2	71%	0.00
Delinquency Cases, Year of Disposition (Rate per 100,000)	NCJJ	2005	3,059.3	1,342.1	44%	(0.03)
Prisoners Under Sentence of Death (Rate per 100,000)	BJS	2007	4.9	1.1	23%	0.00
High School Students Carrying Weapons on School Property	CDC	2007	6.0	5.3	88%	(0.31)
High School Students Carrying Weapons Anywhere	CDC	2007	17.2	18.2	106%	(0.08)
Firearm-Related Death Rates per 100,000 (Males, All Ages)	CDC	2005	40.1	16.0	40%	(0.02)
Ages 1-14	CDC	2005	2.2	0.9	39%	0.07
Ages 15-24	CDC	2005	90.4	13.9	15%	(0.02)
Ages 25-44	CDC	2005	66.3	17.5	26%	(0.02)
Ages 25-34	CDC	2005	92.8	17.0	18%	(0.01)
Ages 45-64	CDC	2005	40.2	17.8	44%	(0.05)
Ages 45-64	CDC	2005	18.2	20.0	110%	0.06

The Equality Index of Black America

	Updated Series	New Series	(Index = 0.71)

	Source	Year	Black	White	Index	DIFF ('09-'08)
Age 65 and Older	CDC	2005	13.7	28.3	206%	0.23
Firearm-Related Death Rates per 100,000 (Females, All Ages)	CDC	2005	3.8	2.8	73%	(0.03)
Ages 15-24	CDC	2005	6.9	2.2	32%	(0.04)
Ages 25-44	CDC	2005	6.2	4.0	63%	(0.02)
Ages 45-64	CDC	2005	2.7	3.8	141%	0.07
Age 65 and Older	CDC	2005	1.4	2.4	172%	(1.13)
Social Justice Weighted Index					**60.4%**	(0.017)
CIVIC ENGAGEMENT (10%)						
Democratic Process (0.4)						
Registered Voters (% of Total Population)	Census	2006	57.4	69.7	82%	(0.05)
Actually Voted (% of Total Population)	Census	2006	38.6	50.5	76%	(0.09)
Community Participation (0.3)						
Percent of Population Volunteering for Military Reserves (%)	USDD	2006	0.9	0.9	94%	
Volunteerism (% of Population)	BLS	2007	18.2	27.9	65%	(0.03)
Civic and Political (% of Volunteers)	BLS	2007	4.0	5.2	77%	0.04
Educational or Youth Service (% of Volunteers)	BLS	2007	24.3	26.3	92%	(0.06)
Environmental or Animal Care (% of Volunteers)	BLS	2007	0.6	2.1	29%	0.06
Hospital or Other Health (% of Volunteers)	BLS	2007	5.1	8.1	63%	0.01
Public Safety (% of Volunteers)	BLS	2007	0.2	1.5	13%	(0.30)
Religious (% of Volunteers)	BLS	2007	47.9	34.5	139%	0.12
Social or Community Service (% of Volunteers)	BLS	2007	11.6	13.1	89%	(0.04)
Unpaid Volunteering of Young Adults	NCES	2000	40.9	32.2	127%	
Collective Bargaining (0.2)						
Unionism-Members of Unions (% of Employed)	BLS	2007	14.3	11.8	121%	(0.03)
Represented by Unions (% of Employed)	BLS	2007	15.8	13	122%	(0.04)

The Equality Index of Black America

		Updated Series		New Series	(Index = 0.73)
	Source	Year	Black	White	Index	DIFF ('08-'07)
Governmental Employment (0.1)						
Federal Executive Branch (Nonpostal) Employment (%)	OPM	2006	1.2%	0.8	146%	
State and Local Government Employment (%)	EEOC	2003	4.3%	2.5	167%	
Civic Engagement Weighted Index					**96.3%**	(0.040)

EDUCATION

Dear Mr. President:

I know these words are reaching you at a time when our nation's future is met with a cloud of uncertainty. Yet, as it was made clear on November 4, 2008, America has once more reaffirmed its resiliency as a nation and its people were—and are still captivated by the audacity of hope. And an essential part of restoring the American Dream involves improving our education system.

I have been extremely blessed throughout my educational career. I attended the New York public schools where I was able to take advantage of many opportunities. After participating in the National Urban League's Summer Internship Program, I earned my master's degree in Business Administration, and am currently taking courses toward my Ph.D. in Christian Philosophy. I am 24 years old. While my story is one of success, sadly enough, this does not accurately portray the lives of other young Americans, especially in the African-American community.

The high rate of African-American males dropping out of high school and its correlation to the number of African-American males entering prison is a serious indicator that our community is in need of educational resources. Individuals living in poverty often face the toughest challenges when it comes to uplifting themselves out of economic, educational and social hardships because many of us are not able to access the education that helps us make good life decisions.

We must not wallow in the sunsets of yesterday, but boldly embrace the promise of today. America can improve its commitment to education by rededicating itself to one common goal and one-shared belief that, as Dr. Martin Luther King, Jr. once said, "Intelligence plus character—that is the goal of true education."

Sincerely,
Isiah R. Hall

ESSAY 1

The Questions Before Us: Opportunity, Education and Equity

By Hal F. Smith, Ed.D.
National Urban League

> *What can we do? There is only one thing for civilized human beings to do when facing such a problem, and that is to learn the facts, to reason out their connection and to plan the future; to know the truth; to arrange it logically and to contrive a better way.*

W.E.B. Du Bois, 1933[1]

How many is too many? How long is too long? When is it all enough? These are critical questions when examining the issues of African-American educational achievement and success. But these are only the first questions that come to mind once the education and achievement data becomes clear and the consequences observed and experienced. Ultimately though, we are left to mirror the question W.E.B. Du Bois asked decades ago: what can we do?

Seemingly every few years, new data or formulations of data emerge that point to an educational crisis in the African-American community. Whether formulated as an achievement gap problem or a dropout problem, the community is left thunderstruck and overwhelmed wondering when and how we came to such a place?

Over fifty years, after *Brown v. Board of Education*, nearly half of our nation's African-American students, nearly 40 percent of Latino students and 11 percent of white students attend high schools in which graduation is not the norm.[2] In too many ways, by too many measures, we appear to be even further away from realizing the full promise of education than we were on May 17, 1954.[3]

How could we have let it come to this?

The State of Affairs in 2008

Every year more than one million youth leave the school system prior to or during high school. Their failure to graduate has long lasting individual, community and nationally adverse consequences. Dropouts from the class of 2008 alone will cost the United States almost $319 billion in lost wages over their lifetime.[4]

While there is a natural and immediate tendency to attribute educational success chiefly to individual commitment, behavior and work ethic, there remains a large portion of responsibility that must be shared more widely. The motivation, investment and success of individuals partially explain the sorrowful statistics that trouble us today, but a careful examination of the issue raises larger questions of systemic and institutional responsibility and malfeasance.[5] For example, in 1964 a high-school dropout earned 64 cents for every dollar earned by those who held at least a high-school diploma. In 2004, the numbers changed drastically, as the dropout earned only 37 cents for each dollar earned by the graduate and continue to fall even today.[6]

However, an over-preoccupation with the dropout rate obscures the fact that the quality of education outcomes for *all* urban youth and communities has been insufficient for decades. It is increasingly clear that a high-school diploma no longer demonstrates that a graduate—regardless of race, ethnicity and, in some cases, income—has been adequately prepared for higher education or for the world of work.

More damning evidence includes the findings that of the students who took the 2008 ACT, only one in five are prepared for entry-level college courses in English composition, college algebra, social science and biology, while one in four are not prepared for college level coursework in any of the four subject areas.[7]

Clearly, rather than ending when the last high-school student leaves before their expected graduation, the dropout crisis simply extends into college, where many students exit because their prior education has left them underprepared to succeed.[8] For students of all backgrounds, there is a serious and unambiguous disconnect between high-school completion and skills acquisition that severely constrains their options and possibilities for success.

Investments and Opportunities

Recent research and practice strongly suggest that in order to address these and other educational gaps significantly, multi-dimensional approaches are required. In different ways and to different intensities, progress has been made over the past fifty years. Not only have educators performed their jobs; they have been engaged in multiple activities that work, and in some cases, work well.

Given the right interventions and investments, there are things we can do; there are questions we can answer and there are young people who can benefit. In each of the approaches and proposals advanced regarding this situation, there are shortcomings, cautions and incomplete information that should give pause, but only pause. It is worthwhile to investigate each in the singular and in the collective, for it is likely only through compounded impacts that we will make accelerated progress.

In some sense, we will need to fly the plane while we build it, because the need is just that great. The consequences for delayed action, or worse, continued inaction are simply unacceptable. Even given the important policy and practice changes that can be made, meaningful progress is only possible through increased investments in opportunity, a renewed commitment to equity and excellence at scale, and an informed sense of the possible.

High Expectations and Improved Engagement

For many youth, adolescence is a turbulent time full of shifting identity where struggles with autonomy, boundaries and intimacy can overwhelm. Compounding the feelings of disconnection and unease adolescents experience in many urban schools, African-American and Latino students are also beset by lower expectations for both their present and future performance.

Predictably, these students feel unsupported and disconnected from teachers, peers and learning, disengage and disinvest in their learning and success, and tragically embrace these unfortunate and debilitating perceptions with alarming regularity. Lowered and disparate expectations are certainly damaging enough on their own, but expectations alone are not the problem. As they disengage, expectations are made tangible for youth in the condition of their schools and classrooms, in the dearth of learning materials and resources, in the real if often unexpressed sense that somehow these students matter less, if they matter at all.

As children grow throughout the P – 12 age span, there are any number of points where a lack of connectedness can negatively impact learning and development. Whether a struggling student who is attending his/her fourth elementary school in three years, a vulnerable young person in foster care, or the overage and under-credited child who feels pushed out of school by the curriculum or pedagogy, youth require meaningful relationships, high expectations and relevant curriculum in order to thrive. These connections can exist in schools, in a community-based program or in an internship. For the majority of urban youth, their location matters far less than their presence and their quality.

Youth Development / Expanded Opportunities

There has been a great deal of focus over the past two decades on addressing the achievement gap, with somewhat limited impact and success.[9] There are many opportunities available to those who know about them, can access them and can advocate for additional resources. However, this kind of knowledge, time and skill remains unevenly distributed across families and communities. Going forward, it is vitally important to frame and understand how critical a full set of opportunities is to child and youth success and to clarify the relationship between opportunity gaps and achievement gaps.

A careful national examination of the distribution and effects of these programs and supports could help further clarify the correlation between opportunity, supports and achievement. In places such as New York City, Dallas, Chicago and San Francisco, community and municipal leaders have demonstrated that youth opportunities can be constructed that support and accelerate the academic, civic, creative, social, physical and emotional development of young people in an accountable and sustainable system.

Education Partnerships

Valuable education partnerships are constructed through and maintained by high-functioning collaborative relationships and structures that build the capacity to engage and innovate. Developing effective education partnerships requires creating a new covenant between communities and their schools that is explicitly tied to creating an education system that includes but also extends beyond schools. Meaningful partnerships ultimately require forging new relationships, building a multiplicity of connections and developing new capacities to collaborate, all tied to a vision of successful outcomes for children and youth.

Despite the potential for partnership to better provide young people with opportunity and support, blame—directed primarily at teachers, schools and parents—has replaced responsibility at the heart of community–school relationships. Accountability has largely been reduced to test scores rather than the larger sense that somehow everyone has a stake in the success of children and youth. However valuable that notion might be as a guiding vision for change and investment, it is increasingly difficult to fulfill in practice. Complicating relationships and the development of a shared vision are legacies of race, income and gender-based inequities, power differentials (individual and institutional), and competing preconceptions around capacity, skills and appropriate roles.

Large scale education partnerships, such as the Harlem Children's Zone or the Urban League of Greater Miami's Liberty City, demonstrate that community-based organizations can be leaders as well as participants of great consequence in education reform. While each is unique in multiple ways, they provide an important blueprint upon which other place-specific partnerships can develop. Education relationships are not simple to build or maintain, but clearly represent a means to deliver opportunity and improved outcomes in ways not possible for a single institution to accomplish.

Successful Transitions

At each transition point along the P-16 pathway, children and youth can fall behind and become disconnected from schools as they struggle to adapt to changed expectation, supports and learning environments. Ideally, the pathway should emphasize post-secondary success by engaging children and youth beyond the promotion of career and college awareness and preparation toward a focus on readiness, persistence and success beyond high school. Post-secondary success orientation necessitates the creation of robust supports at the P-K, elementary to middle school, middle school to high school and high school to post-secondary transition points in order to positively impact the dropout and achievement gaps.

For example, studies note that while retention in any grade has a negative impact on a student's odds of making it through the ninth grade, retention in the middle grades is particularly problematic and is a contributing factor to a student's chances of dropping out later in their academic career. [10] In addition to a hopeful focus on success in the future, strong transition programs also properly orient parents and youth to the current environment, providing opportunities for children and youth to orient themselves properly with the new environment and setting and include opportunities for educators and administrators to develop coherence between the curricula, pedagogy and desired outcomes.

Multiple Pathways to Success

From the time students enter schools in pre-k, kindergarten and first grade, too many urban students lose additional educational ground every year, ultimately ending up with three or four years' difference between their expected academic skill and content knowledge and their actual age. To create a bridge to post-secondary success, it is necessary to create an alternative framework for public education that encompasses the range of abilities, interests and skills necessary for the 21st century. While others have successfully argued for multiple pathways as an addition to current education models, perhaps it is time to develop a multiple pathways concept that opens opportunity for all students.

Thoughtful multiple pathway programs maximize choice, as they promote student engagement and prepare students for the full range of post-secondary options. Intentionally connecting career/technical knowledge with academic knowledge, skills and perspective opens possibility to all students, more fully realizing the promise of education.[11] The shift to a multiple pathways formulation can disrupt educational policy and practices that inevitably disadvantage groups underserved and under-supported by traditional schooling models and practices.[12] However, the multiple pathways concept is simply an organizing frame that can include numerous constituent parts and varied models. A list of additional models to be considered in an expansive pathways portfolio includes charter schools, community schools, early college programs, alternative schools and carefully-managed credit recovery programs.

Effective use of data

For all the numerous and varied reasons to find fault with the No Child Left Behind Legislation (NCLB) and implementation, it is abundantly clear that it has made an important contribution in the area of data. The accountability provisions in NCLB have proven to be an invaluable tool for engaging communities around education reform and accountability. While far from perfect, the current data requirement for subgroup and regular reporting are invaluable foundational steps toward a more comprehensive, responsive and useful accountability system.

Accurate and timely data is necessary to allow thoughtful teachers to apply their knowledge and insight in innovative ways nearer to the point of potential failure and disconnect. Data should better inform how educators work with the students in front of them so they can alter the pace of instruction, create additional supports and generally better educate their students.[13] Ideally, the accountability measures would function as an early warning system to alert educators and parents when the learning gaps are far smaller and more manageable. For example, what do we know about the kinds of experiences and measures that are predictive of dropouts prior to high school?

A 2006 Philadelphia study found that there are four powerful factors, both individually and in combination, that can predict which 6th graders will ultimately fall behind and off-track:

- Attending school 80 percent or less of the time
- Receiving a poor final behavior mark
- Failing Math
- Failing English

A sixth grader with any of the four indicators has only a 10 - 20 percent chance of graduating with his/her peers.[14] Researchers have begun to label these students as "early dropouts." Although some students may stay in school until legally required to do so, many simply do not have the skills necessary to transition to the next grade or educational setting successfully.

In most cases, students who struggle early in their academic careers find it incredibly difficult to recover in time to graduate, due to absent high-quality intervention. Policy makers and administrators have long argued that what gets measured gets done; similarly, if what we want to accomplish is to better prepare all students for post-secondary success, we need a fuller array of measures and indicators that better capture progress, impact and outcomes. As early as elementary school and middle school, there is enough information available to intervene in the educational lives of students, before they fall so far behind that dropping out is nearly inevitable.[15]

Conclusion

Within a landscape of stunted progress and deferred dreams, education must provide the necessary attitudes, capacities and aptitudes in young people that effectively prepare youth to take advantage of opportunities to thrive. For African Americans and other communities of color, the potential of education exists in the spaces between promises of equity and justice made manifest, and those kept in abeyance. The act of an African-American child learning to read and achieving at the highest levels unfortunately remains a political statement and a bold and resolute declaration of possibility. As each young person comes to believe in their inherent ability and in their full humanity and worth, the struggle for civil rights is similarly furthered. No matter the specifics of a particular set of questions about the state of African-American education, current conditions need not be permanent. Rather than remaining despondent over where we are, the times and conditions demand that we pragmatically construct an education of possibility, rather than proscription.

In each promising example outlined herein there is great potential and promise on which to build, but only if we are willing to work differently and collectively, invest abundantly and pragmatically and innovate thoughtfully and flexibly, can we expect to dramatically change the data and circumstances that now confront us. What we require, what we must build together is an education in both philosophy and practice that intentionally widens opportunity and expands possibility as it connects the will to know with the will to become. [16]

NOTES

[1] Foner, Philip S. (1991). W.E.B. Du Bois Speaks: Speeches and Addresses 1920-1963. 7th Ed. Pathfinder. New York.

[2] Balfanz, Robert. Legters, Nettie. (2004). Locating the Dropout Crisis: Which High Schools Produce the Nation's Dropouts? Where Are They Located? Who Attends Them? Report 70. Center for Research on the Education of Students Placed At Risk (CRESPAR). Johns Hopkins. Baltimore.

[3] A majority minority high school is five times more likely to promote 50% or fewer freshmen to senior status on time than a majority white school. However, poverty appears to be the key correlate in that majority minority high schools with more resources (e.g., selective programs, higher per pupil expenditures, suburban location) successfully promote students to senior status at the same rate as majority white schools. Orfield, G., Losen, D., Wald, J., & Swanson, C., (2004). Losing Our Future: How Minority Youth are Being Left Behind by the Graduation Rate Crisis, Cambridge, MA: The Civil Rights Project at Harvard University. Contributors: Advocates for Children of New York, The Civil Society Institute.

[4] Understanding High School Graduation Rates. (2008). Alliance for Excellent Education. http://www.all4ed.org/files/Sources_wc.pdf

[5] In 2004, research suggested that only an estimated 68% of all students, regardless of race or ethnicity, who enter 9th grade graduate with a regular diploma in 12th grade . Orfield, G., Losen, D., Wald, J., & Swanson, C., (2004). Losing Our Future: How Minority Youth are Being Left Behind by the Graduation Rate Crisis, Cambridge, MA: The Civil Rights Project at Harvard University. Contributors: Advocates for Children of New York, The Civil Society Institute.

[6] Rouse, Cecelia Elena. "The labor market consequences of an inadequate education." Paper presented at the Symposium on Social Costs of Inadequate Education, Teachers' College, Columbia University. Routledge, NY. (2005).

[7] ACT (2008). The Forgotten Middle: Ensuring That All Students Are On Target for College and Career Readiness Before High School. Iowa City.

[8] Similarly, data suggests that almost thirty percent of all entering under-graduate students required remedial courses in their first year of college, with sixty-five percent of those needing to take more than one remedial course. Nearly four out of five undergraduate remedial students had a high school grade point average of 3.0 or higher. Strong American Schools. Diploma to Nowhere. Strong American Schools. Washington, D.C..

[9] DeShano da Silva, Carol, James Philip Huguley and Zenub Kakli, and Radhika Rao (Eds). The Opportunity Gap: Achievement and Inequality in Education (2007). Cambridge. Harvard Education Press.

[10] Balfanz, Robert, Herzog, Lisa & Mac Iver, Douglas J. (2007). "Preventing Student Disengagement and Keeping Students on the Graduation

Path in Urban Middle-Grades Schools: Early Identification and Effective Interventions". 42 Educational Psychologist. Philadelphia.

[11] Ibid.

[12] Saunders, M., & Chrisman, C. A. (2008). Multiple Pathways: 21st Century High Schools that Prepare All Students for College, Career and Civic Participation. Boulder and Tempe: Education and the Public Interest Center & Education Policy Research Unit. Retrieved 12/29/08 from http://epicpolicy.org/publication/multiple-pathways

[13] Gleason, P. and Dynarski, M. (2002). "Do We Know Whom to Serve? Issues in Using Risk Factors to Identify Dropouts". Journal of Education for Students Placed at Risk 7, no. 1 . University of Louisville. Lousiville.

[14] Balfanz, Robert. Herzog, Liza. (2006). Keeping Middle Grades Students On Track to Graduation: Initial Analysis and Implications. PowerPoint presentation. http://www.philaedfund.org/powerpoint/dropoutresearch_4.06.pdf

[15] Achievement levels attained by eight grade appear to be more impactful on readiness for post-secondary success than anything that happens academically in high school. ACT.(2008). The Forgotten Middle: Ensuring That All Students Are On Target for College and Career Readiness Before High School. Iowa City.

[16] hooks, bell [Gloria Watkins] (2004), Teaching to Transgress: Education as the Practice of Freedom

ESSAY 2

Needed: Equality in Education

By Congressman Chaka Fattah

I n nearly fifty-five years since the Supreme Court's landmark *Brown v. Board of Education* decision, much has changed in the education of African-American students. *De jure* segregation has been abolished and many avenues for opportunity have opened in the best educational institutions across the country. Civil rights laws have criminalized blatant discrimination in housing and employment, granting increasing numbers of families access to the social and economic capital critical to full participation in American life. These accomplishments, and the generations of struggle that created them, should not be ignored.

Yet in the five decades plus of official desegregation, much has not changed at all. The visible and codified tools of disenfranchisement and oppression have given way to far more devious and subtle forms of discrimination. Nowhere is this more evident or outrageous than in elementary and secondary education. This foundation for civic participation, economic opportunity and social integration is corrupted by the inequity in both educational resources and student performance.

Today, African-American children are far more likely to find themselves in front of an inexperienced teacher, they are less likely to have access to up-to-date instructional technology and staff trained in its use, more likely to attend buildings in disrepair, less likely to have access to rigorous and engaging curricula, more likely to face over-crowded classrooms and less likely to meet with counselors and other pupil services personnel. When our students face so many obstacles in obtaining the resources crucial to academic development, it is no wonder that so many of them fail to meet the ambitious standards we as parents and as a society set for them.

Recently, we have seen a renewed interest in educational equality at the federal level, after decades of debate on these issues was confined to state legislatures and courthouses. The much maligned (and flawed) No Child Left Behind Act made the radical step of expecting that *all children* regardless of their race, income, language of birth or disability would perform on the same level as their more privileged peers. To expect anything else of any child does a great injustice to them and our society. We have enshrined in law the principle held by parents of generations of underserved children: that every child has the potential to be successful. It is our only hope as a society to take full advantage of the mental power of every one of our children, from the inner city of Philadelphia, to the Mississippi Delta and to the suburbs of Chicago.

We have been debating a false choice for far too long. On the one hand, there are those who argue that the injustice our children battle is limited to the inequity in educational performance. That we must simply expect more of our children and schools and they will rise to meet the challenge. This argument fails to acknowledge what it takes to improve student performance: better qualified and supported teachers and greater access to educational resources. The focus is limited to what our children and schools are able to do without regard for the tools necessary to advance educational outcomes.

There is also some support for a similarly limited philosophy which asks only for increased resources believing that alone can be a measure of equity. There is no reason to choose between these standards of equality. We must simultaneously demand that each of our students be expected to meet the highest academic standards, while holding those same systems responsible for providing the tangible tools of instruction and academic preparation accountable. As the new President has said time and again, accountability is a two-way street.

This change in expectations, no longer lazily predicting the failure of children based on zip code, creates a new, powerful and historic opportunity for African-American children.

However, *No Child Left Behind* has left a critical piece of the student performance puzzle unaddressed. While we should never use a child's own lack of resources as justification for expecting less of them, we are foolish to ignore the gross inequity in resource distribution. It is as if we are teaching students in many of our urban and rural school districts to swim in pools without water, then lamenting their inability to compete with Michael Phelps.

In order to address this gross inequity in educational resources, I have authored the Student Bill of Rights (SBOR), which mandates the collection of resource equity data at the state and local level in order to hold these officials accountable for providing students and teachers the opportunity to be successful. SBOR, however, is about much more than data collection. It will build the irrefutable and compelling case for federal action that will fill that pool with resources to level the field of opportunity for all our children.

Just as states are required to demonstrate how they will teach all children to grade-level performance, they will need to show how they intend to provide the *resources* necessary for classroom teachers and school leaders to make that happen. Given irrefutable evidence that fewer and lower-quality educational resources are available to students demonstrating the lowest academic performance, administrative funds will be withheld from the states responsible for the discrepancies and delivered directly to the schools and districts in need.

If the United States is to remain the economic and technological superpower of the world, as well as a strong, vibrant and diverse democracy, we must make use of the knowledge, skills and creativity of each of our citizens. Knowledge is power. Who knows what great American novel, what cure to a devastating disease or what secret to alternative energy is currently trapped in the mind of a child in Detroit, Mich. or Bullock County, Ala., who has not been taught to read well, cipher through complicated math formulas or navigate the intricacies of a computer?

It is only through a quality education that he or she will be properly prepared for full civic, social and economic participation in our American society. Success should not be limited to the arbitrary accident of skin color, family income or the address of a child's school.

These advances are long overdue, but the prospects have never been brighter. The historic election in 2008 has ushered in the hope-filled administration of Barack Obama, perhaps the most education-savvy and urban-friendly president our nation has ever known. We have an opportunity to make real and tangible the goals of the civil and human rights movements that have preceded us. The lynchpin of America's greatness is education, which can only be achieved by equal educational opportunity for all. The time is right. The time is now. We must seize the day!

From Miracle to Movement: Mandating a National Opportunity to Learn

By John H. Jackson Ph.D.
Schott Foundation

O
On January 16, 2009, Flight 1549 took off from LaGuardia Airport on a charted course with 155 passengers from various racial, ethnic, geographic and socio-economic backgrounds. Less than five minutes into the flight, unexpected system failures, caused by a flock of birds, led to a highly skilled emergency landing by the aircraft's pilot. The 155 passengers would find themselves in the middle of the Hudson River amid frigid waters, and miraculously, they all survived. What is now called "The Miracle on the Hudson" was the emblematic illustration of the type of highly skilled decisions, asset investments and collaboration needed to address the challenges facing our country.

Like Flight 1549, America's history is one that started on a bright course, both economically and politically. During America's early years as a nation, one of the major factors that separated the United States from its international peers and allowed its economy and democracy to flourish was the country's significant investments in education. The United States was one of the first industrialized nations to make education compulsory.

During World War II, President Franklin Roosevelt made a significant investment to increase access to higher education through the G.I. Bill. Since 1944, when the first G.I. Bill was enacted, the Department of Veteran Affairs reports that the United States has provided more than $72 billion in benefits to more than 21.3 million veterans, service members and family members. A decade later, following the recommendation of economist Milton Friedman, the first federal student loans were provided under the National Defense Education Act of 1958 and were direct loans subsidized with U.S. Treasury funds. For nearly 200 years, America built its globally leading infrastructure based on making significant investments in human capital through advancing opportunities in public education.

In 1954, the Supreme Court through its most significant piece of jurisprudence of the 20th century, *Brown v. Board of Education*, positioned the country to expand those opportunities and investments.[1] *Brown* launched America on a course to augment the growth of our nation, civil society and economy by providing equitable educational opportunities to those the law had for centuries denied. A decade later, the passage of the 1964 Civil Rights Act, along with the 1965 Elementary and Secondary Education Act (ESEA), as a part of President Lyndon B. Johnson's "War on Poverty" would provide additional federal fiscal and policy support for the expansion of opportunities to U.S. citizens. The ESEA outlined a clear federal role in education and doubled federal aid for public schools. The ESEA was designed as both a federal implementation and enforcement mechanism for providing equitable educational opportunities as well as desegregation incentives for Southern school districts, as *de jure* districts were barred from funds. The *Brown* decision, coupled with the impact of the 1964 Civil Rights Act and 1965 ESEA, placed the United States on a course toward sustaining its position as a global leader of opportunity and democracy.

America's educational investments during the 1950s and 1960s caused a major reduction in the black-white achievement gap, large increases in high school graduation and college enrollment levels for black students, as well as increasing desegregation that occurred in many Southern states during the period.[2]

Like Flight 1549 however, the promising journey America was on would also stall. A flock of federal court decisions that challenged, and in some cases contradicted, the interpretation of the *Brown* decision damaged the country's course. Although the federal government in *Brown* and ESEA outlined a federal role in education, when the Supreme Court was asked in the 1973 *San Antonio v. Rodriguez* decision whether the federal government should protect an American's right to an education, they responded with an alarming "no."[3] In the wake of *Brown*, many advocates pursued similar equal protection arguments in efforts to equalize school funding and hold states responsible for the gross inequities in education spending found in poor urban racially isolated districts.[4] When the states failed to protect the articulated rights under *Brown*, the advocates sought federal redress. In *San Antonio v. Rodriguez*, the Supreme Court held that there was no right to an education protected by the U.S. Constitution.[5] With *Rodriguez*, the opportunity for challenging educational inequity as a matter of federal constitutional law was curtailed severely.

In 1974, the Supreme Court rendered another blow in *Milliken v. Bradley*.[6] In this desegregation case, the Court shielded the suburbs from participating in the remedy to unlawful urban segregation. All suburban metropolitan districts that could not be proven to have engaged in acts of intentional racial discrimination were not liable and were excluded from the remedy. This decision meant little could be done to stem the fact that many sought to relocate from urban schools under desegregation orders to the mostly white suburban rings where the high prevalence of housing discrimination against blacks prevented them from entering. *Milliken* left racially-isolated schools in urban districts stranded for a remedy.[7]

Following a series of similar cases in the 70s, by the early 1980s, the nation was clearly on a trend of racial re-segregation.[8] The racial achievement gap and drug usage in urban communities, as well as the 1981-1982 economic recession, all indicated that the country's education, economic and social altitudes were decreasing.[9]

Brace for Impact!

Forty-five years since *Rodriguez* and *Milliken*, parent and community advocates in over forty states have brought demands for adequate and equitable resources to extend educational opportunities to their children; however, few have had significant results.[10] Fifteen-year-old students in the United States now rank 20th among 29 OECD (Organization for Economic Co-operation and Development) member countries in reading and 23rd in math.[11] The United States also ranks high in inequitable educational outcomes.[12] According to the National Center for Education Statistics (NCES), it is estimated that less than 47 percent of black males in the United States graduate from high school.[13]

The implication of poor performance impacts not only education, but domestic corporate growth, health coverage and even national security. As John A. Powell, an internationally recognized authority in the area of civil rights and civil liberties, once stated, "Segregation negatively affects not only our students but also our democratic structure, reifying racial subordination in employment, health, wealth access, and political participation. . .and remains today a reality imposed by those with power and privilege on those without."[14]

America now faces the first generation of blacks who will earn less than their parents. The first generation of all children who are less likely to go to college than their parents. The first generation whose life expectancy is less than their parents.

The Rescue Plan

The year 2009 has shepherded in a new era for the United States, both historically and politically. Central in this new era is the reality that like those on Flight 1549, our destinies as a nation of people are consolidated and now is the time to consolidate our opportunities.

In a thriving society, race, ethnicity, gender, native language or disability status should not dictate educational opportunity or outcomes. The persistence of such structures works against the national interest of maintaining an economically and civically thriving union. Current gross inequalities in educational opportunities for urban and rural children—specifically for African-American males—lie in stark contrast to the ascendance of the first African-American president both in performance and opportunities.

Dismantling these barriers of educational opportunities must once again become one of the primary roles of the federal government. The federal government must seek to protect every citizen's right to an opportunity to learn. Where states seek the resources to guarantee all of their students a fair and substantive opportunity to learn, the federal government must provide the support in order to bring this ideal into fruition. Far too often today, the federal government finds itself in a posture of issuing mandates without support or presenting barriers without opportunities. Unlike the board of education in Topeka that sought to preserve their *de jure* segregation, today local school board members, as was the case in the *Seattle* and *Louisville* rulings and colleges and universities in *Gratz* and *Grutter*, are fighting for greater outcomes and diversity in their schools. The nation's military and corporations are stressing the need for high-skilled graduates and diversity.[15]

Far too often over the past forty-five years, the federal government's rulings and limited educational appropriations often served as the major barriers for states seeking to expand opportunities for all students. The United States needs to respond immediately to the fact that because of a lack of bureaucratic capacity, political will or economic constraints, states currently are at best only capable of providing U.S. children their own systems of separate and unequal education with *limited opportunity*. In this climate, leaving the protection of a child's opportunity to learn primarily in the hands of the states creates systems which are inherently unequal and that lack the type of opportunities necessary to protect our national interest. America must seize this moment and insist that all of its children have an equitable opportunity to learn. A child's opportunity to learn must be protected as a federal and human fundamental right.

Building an "Opportunity-to-Learn" Nation

When evaluating opportunity, access to the resources needed to seize the desired-end product—in this case high educational standards—is the most logical place to start. Research commissioned by The Schott Foundation for Public Education, and supported by numerous other studies, indicates that providing a child a fair and substantive opportunity to learn means substantively giving the students access to four core resources:

1. Early childhood education
2. Access to highly effective teaching
3. College preparatory curriculum
4. Equitable instructional expenditures

The Opportunity-to-Learn (OTL) framework focused on how equitable access to resources generates public benefits and brings a new level of federal involvement in education reform. In the interest of yielding a greater return on a substantially larger investment in the public educational system, the federal government would more aggressively hold states accountable for reaching resource-equity benchmarks, as well as targeting resources to building on what works to allow the students to meet high standards.

The Opportunity-to-Learn resource accountability approach also does not rely on a program where a corrective response is only triggered after children have experienced a high level of school failure. Rather than wait for large numbers of students to perform poorly in school or drop out, a school or district would be subject to intervention by the state or federal government when the resource shortage was noticeable and persistent, even if the test scores were currently good. Good performances are not indicators of maximized opportunities.

We will know we have built an Opportunity-to-Learn nation when students from the poorest communities have the same opportunity to access early childhood education, a highly effective teacher, a college-bound curricula and equitable instructional expenditures as those students in public schools in the wealthiest districts. The Opportunity-to-Learn framework is an independent assessment as to whether by the very nature of attending a U.S. public school we have extended the necessary OTL resources to the student, and, by extension, the opportunity to fully participate in our democracy, thereby protecting the child's "pursuit of happiness."

Across the nation, we are able to identify high-poverty, high-minority individual schools where the students are, on average, achieving higher than predicted outcomes. Yet we are unable to identify a single high-poverty, high-minority district and/or state where the students, on average, are achieving lower outcomes. Saving a few thousand students through individual school-based reforms is admirable, but not nearly what is needed to protect the national interest of providing an opportunity to learn to children who are currently locked in state and local educational *systems* that are failing them by the millions. Systemic levels of reform and resource accountability are needed to protect these students.

The federal government should more specifically work to ensure equitable educational opportunity in three important ways:

1) By implementing a "resource-focused" (Opportunity to-Learn Resource Index) accountability system to generate better returns on the investment of federal and state funding;

2) By increasing appropriations to ensure that states have the means to provide equitable opportunities to learn; and

3) By active use of federal powers of guidance, oversight and enforcement to ensure that each state does in fact provide every child with an equitable "Opportunity to Learn."

While Congress focuses on the proposed $819 billion "American Recovery and Investment Act of 2009" (ARIA), it is important to note that this effort, while needed, is part of a "search and rescue" funding plan designed to fill gaps in a timely, targeted and temporary fashion. Even with the proposed $142 billion dedicated to education, ARIA will not provide an opportunity to learn to all students nor heal the country's macro-economic challenges. When we consider that over the past several years the United States has spent over $1 trillion in war spending that has failed to stimulate the economy, it is unlikely that additional spending alone will do the job without renewing the American core strategy that placed the nation as a global leader—significant investments in human capital through advancing opportunities in public education.

According to OECD, the United States will need at least 60 percent of its population to possess a postsecondary college degree by 2025 to remain globally competitive. At present, roughly 39 percent of Americans hold a two-year or four-year college degree and that attainment rate has held steady for the past four decades. To achieve the OECD goal, the United States will need to produce 16 million more graduates than the current total. With the country's changing demographics, this means the educational trajectory for a significant number of black and brown children will have to change to meet this goal. America must be forward thinking and place their educational investments on a trajectory to:

(a) Ensure all Americans have a fair and substantive opportunity to learn by accessing a 21st century high quality public education by 2020;

(b) Ensure America is workforce competitive in the global market in 2020;

(c) Ensure the American citizenry is substantively engaged as good stewards of their communities, environment, democratic values and collective opportunities;

(d) Ensure that the economic liabilities related to deficiencies and disparities in the public educational system are substantively reduced;

(e) Ensure that any current or potential national security threats related to deficiencies and disparities in the public education system are substantively minimized.

Human and education rights advocates—and other Americans as well—must act and continue their level of pre-election engagement to demand a federally-protected Opportunity to Learn for all students. Let us not forget the lesson learned from the "Miracle on the Hudson."

It was individual citizens whose destinies were consolidated that acted first. It was their movement from the shelter of the plane stepping out onto the wings and into the light of day that engaged the private sector ferrys, the local city police and fire departments, and eventually the federal support. Our message from the "Miracle on the Hudson" is that whether the grounding of America's flight is a story of triumph or tragedy, it will not be defined by the President, the Democrats or the Republicans, but by "We the People."

NOTES

[1] See *Brown v. Board of Education*, 347 U.S. 483 (1954).

[2] Gary Orfield and Erica Frakenberg, Reviving *Brown v. Board of Education:* How Courts and Enforcement Agencies Can Produce More Integrated Schools, in BROWN AT 50: THE UNFINISHED LEGACY, at 187, Rhode and Ogletree eds., American Bar Assoc. (2004).

[3] *San Antonio Independent School District v. Rodriguez*, 411 U.S. 1 (1973).

[4] See e.g., Michael Rebell, *Educational Adequacy, Democracy, and the Courts*, available on line at http://www.schoolfunding.info/ [hereinafter Educational Adequacy]. (Citing Peter Enrich, *Leaving Equality Behind: New Directions in School Finance Reform*, 48 Vand. L. Rev. 101, 120-121 (1995).

[5] *San Antonio Independent School District v. Rodriguez*, 411 U.S. 1 (1973).

[6] Milliken v. Bradley 418 U.S. 717 (1974).

[7] This is a widely held view among civil rights advocates. See generally, E. Cherinsky, *The Segregation and Resegregation of American Public Education* in School Resegregation: Must the South Turn Back? At 34 Boger and Orfield eds., (2005).

[8] See Gary Orfield, Reviving the Goal of an Integrated Society: A 21st Century Challenge, January 16 2009 available at www.civilrightsproject.ucla.edu.

[9] National Bureau of Economic Research, Inc., Historical Poverty Tables-Periods of Recession 2008.

[10] The actual number is subject to change, but one organization, "Access", tracks state lawsuits regarding methods of funding public schools. See www.schoolfunding.info/states/state_by_state.php3. Last visited on February 3, 2009.

[11] Organization of Economic Cooperative Development—2003 PISA Results, NCES (2005).

[12] NCES, 2005, International Outcomes of Learning in Mathematics Literacy and Problem Solving PISA Results NCES (2005).

[13] "Given Half a Chance: The Schott 50 State Report on Public Education and Black Males", The Schott Foundation for Public Education (2008).

[14] John A. Powell, *A New Theory of Integrated Education: True Integration in* School Resegregation: Must the South Turn Back? A 283 Boger and Orfield eds., (2005).

[15] See *Grutter v. Bollinger,* 539 U.S. 306 (2003). The majority opinion cited amici briefs filed by the U.S. military (Brief for Julius W. Becton Jr., et al., and the nation's leading corporations (3M et al., and General Motors Corp.) each stressing the value of diversity.

HEALTH

Dear Mr. President:

My name is Erica Marie Williams. I am 29-years old and have sickle cell anemia. I was born with this disease, and it affects my body and my life in the worst way. Some days my pain is so bad that I can't even get out of bed. I am forced to stay in bed all day, and my bed becomes a terrible prison for me. And since I was seven, I've had constant seizures and have suffered strokes.

Throughout my life, I have had to seek medical treatment constantly and make regular visits to the hospital. But at times, I get very frustrated by the medical service I get when I visit certain hospitals. Because I suffer seizures, I need emergency treatment when I arrive at the hospital. But a lot of times, the personnel at the hospital don't seem to know how to properly and promptly treat victims with my disease. And oftentimes when I am admitted to the hospital for emergency service, I have to wait longer than I should before a doctor or another medical person will see me.

Also, I need to take medication on a regular basis to treat this disease. But the cost of the prescribed medication that I need is steadily increasing. Because of my illness, I never could hold down a job, and during adulthood, I have to depend on my husband for support. I'm struggling financially and I am also a parent of a seven-year-old daughter. There is still no cure for sickle cell anemia, so I need medication to treat this illness in order to survive.

Mr. President, I ask for you to help improve the health care system in this country, so that people like me can get the sufficient health care we need and are able to purchase the medication we need at an affordable cost.

Sincerely,
Erica Marie Williams

ESSAY 4

Improving African Americans' Access to Quality Healthcare

By Darrell J. Gaskin, Ph.D.
University of Maryland

A lthough the United States has a nationwide healthcare delivery system, unfortunately, not all Americans have equal access to it. Many Americans, particularly minorities, face socioeconomic, geographic, cultural and language barriers to care that prevent them from receiving the best healthcare America has to offer, and such barriers adversely affect African Americans in particular. These barriers result in unmet healthcare needs, delayed and denied medical treatment, and the delivery of sub-standard quality care. Because African Americans have less access to care, they have poorer health status, higher rates of morbidity and mortality, and greater economic hardship. In 2006, African Americans were 87 percent more likely to report they were in fair or poor health, in comparison to whites. They were also 29 percent more likely to die and had higher rates of hypertension, diabetes and stroke.[1] While African Americans have similar rates of cancer in comparison to whites, they were more likely to die from the disease because their cancer was diagnosed at later stages, and they received less care. On average, African Americans spent 16.5 percent of their income on medical care, compared to whites who spent 12.2 percent.[2] However, despite spending a larger share of their income on medical care, African Americans face healthcare disparities.

Racial disparities in healthcare are well-documented.[3] For the most part, African Americans receive less care and lower quality treatment than whites, and the problems that African Americans experience in the healthcare marketplace are due to patient, provider and health system barriers to care. Patient factors include treatment preferences and refusals, medical mistrust, and health literacy and provider factors include prejudice and bias, clinical uncertainty and miscommunication, stereotyping, and cultural incompetence. In addition, health system factors include lack of universal health care coverage, geographic barriers of care, poorly functioning referral networks, and under-resourced minority-serving and safety-net institutions.

Much attention has been paid to addressing patient and provider-related factors. To address patient-related factors, health literacy programs, culturally sensitive health education materials and patient-decision making tools have been developed and implemented in healthcare settings.[4] To address provider-related factors, cultural competency-training curriculum have been developed and implemented in medical schools, hospitals and health systems.[5] In addition, researchers have studied physician-patient encounters to develop interventions to improve communication during the office visit.[6] Also, scholars have developed surveys and evaluation tools that determine whether physicians have implicit racial biases that affect patient care.[7] While these efforts are laudable, they will not alone remedy the problems African Americans experience when accessing the healthcare delivery system. To improve access to care, system-level barriers must be addressed.

African Americans' Problems Accessing Quality Healthcare

Although some progress has been made, African Americans still face problems accessing primary care.[8] Compared to whites, African Americans were 12 percent less likely to have a usual primary care provider and 26 percent less likely to have a provider visit during the year after controlling for age, gender, socioeconomic status and location. According to a medical study, African-American children were less likely to have a physician visit, more likely to have an emergency room visit, less likely to have a preventative dental visit and less likely to use prescribed medication, when compared to white children.[9] Other studies have found that racial differences in health insurance coverage, the availability of physicians and income have been identified as major contributors to disparities in primary care.[10]

Exacerbating this current dilemma in healthcare confronting African Americans is that certain studies have also indicated that black Americans face significant barriers to preventive care.[11] Data from the 2000 National Health Interview Survey found that whites have higher rates of influenza vaccination, pneumococcal vaccination, colorectal cancer screening and mammography than African Americans. Similar to other studies, it was concluded that African Americans' higher poverty rates, lower rates of health insurance coverage and lack of a usual source of care partially explained their lower rate in the use of preventive services.[12]

Despite efforts to improve overall patient safety and quality care in hospitals, race disparities still persist. Several studies have presented empirical evidence suggesting that African Americans receipt of lower quality hospital care was due to variations in quality of care across the hospitalization system rather than variations in quality of care within specific hospitals.[13] Prior studies have found that African Americans were concentrated in a relatively small number of hospitals that provided lower quality care.[14] This disparity in performance was due to a lack of financial resources.[15]

African Americans also face barriers to care for chronic conditions, such as heart disease, cancer and stroke, the leading causes of death in the United States. Furthermore, numerous studies have documented that African Americans receive lower quality cardiovascular care.[16] Most studies in fact show racial differences in the delivery of cardiac revascularization, medications and therapies in hospital-based settings.[17] Compared to whites, African Americans were also less likely to receive diagnostic angiography, coronary artery bypass graft (CABG), percutaneous transluminal coronary angiography (PTCA) and thrombolysis, with odds ratios ranging from 0.23 to 0.87.[18]

In addition, African Americans suffer from higher cancer death rates and lower cancer survival rates, because of lower cancer detection rates at early cancer stages and disparities in the quality of treatment. For example, the odds of being diagnosed with late stage prostate cancer for African-American men were 2.6 times that of whites.[19] Similarly, African-American women with breast cancer were less likely to be identified at an early stage.[20] In addition, a national study showed that African Americans were more likely to have uncontrolled and untreated hypertension.[21]

The Fundamental Problem with the U.S. Healthcare System

The U.S. healthcare system is a market-based system with a large public component that operates primarily on free-market principles. However, markets cannot yield desirable results when all willing buyers and sellers are unable to freely participate in it, and unfortunately, inequities in our society produce inequities in healthcare. The fundamental problem with the U.S. healthcare system is the lack of universal coverage, high rates of Medicaid coverage and poverty among many African Americans that limits their access to quality health care.

The lack of healthcare providers in predominately African-American communities is also a barrier to care. The inability of physicians who serve African Americans to obtain referrals for specialty care hinders their patients' ability to navigate a fragmented healthcare system. As a result, African Americans reliance on financially stressed and under-resourced providers limits their access to high quality healthcare.

In 2007, almost one in five African Americans did not have health insurance and about one in four were covered by Medicaid. African Americans were almost twice as likely as whites to be uninsured and 2.5 times more likely to be covered by Medicaid. Of the 45.6 million persons lacking health insurance in 2007, 16.1 percent were African Americans. Health insurance is a major determinant of access to care and quality of care. A comprehensive review of the literature found that persons without health insurance were less likely to receive primary care and preventative services also had limited access to specialty services. Also, they were more likely to have an avoidable hospital stay.[22]

Although Medicaid coverage is better than not having any health insurance at all, it is a far cry from being an easily accessible and comprehensive healthcare coverage system. Persons who enter the healthcare marketplace covered by Medicaid do not have the same purchasing power as privately-insured Medicare patients. On average, Medicaid fees for physician services were 57 percent of commercial fees and 69 percent of Medicare fees.[23] This differential in reimbursement along with routine delays in payments makes Medicaid patients less attractive to serve, compared to other patients.[24] In a national survey, only 57 percent of physicians reported that they would accept new Medicaid patients.[25]

African Americans reliance on Medicaid coverage and greater propensity to be uninsured makes it difficult for their communities to attract healthcare providers. The economic reality of lower Medicaid reimbursement and greater charity-care need makes it difficult for physicians and other healthcare providers to maintain fiscally viable practices in African-American communities. Physicians with over 70 percent of minority patients received a third of their revenues from Medicaid.[26] This was almost three times more than physicians with less than 30 percent of minority patients. Physician incomes in these minority-serving practices were 13 percent lower than incomes in practices with physicians whose minority patients were fewer than 30 percent.

Residential segregation compounds the effects of this economic reality, because of the geographic concentration and isolation of impoverished African Americans. A recent study found that physicians were less likely to participate in Medicaid where impoverished patients were nonwhite and racially segregated.[27] Moreover, other studies have shown that residential segregation reduced African Americans' access to physician care,[28] and it was also discovered that physician participation in Medicaid was lower in communities with large minority populations.[29] Given these access problems, it is not surprising that, when compared to whites, African Americans were more reliant on community health centers, hospital outpatient departments and emergency rooms for their usual source of care.[30]

This is not due to choice but rather inequities in the healthcare marketplace.

The fragility of the market for physician services in African-American communities is probably the root cause of racial differences in primary, preventative and specialty-care use. Studies have shown that physicians serving African Americans reported difficulty referring their patients to high-quality specialists, accessing diagnostic imaging services, obtaining ancillary services, admitting their patients for elective hospital services and communicating with other providers about their patients.[31] The referral problems of physicians serving African Americans are probably due to their payer mix. Minority-serving physicians may find their colleagues are reluctant to receive their referrals, because they are more likely to refer a "low pay" or "no pay" patient than other physicians.

Residential segregation also negatively affects availability of hospital care. Similar to segregation in education, housing and employment, segregation in healthcare resulted in African Americans receiving less care and lower quality care than whites. Despite federal efforts through the Hill Burton Act and Medicare to integrate hospitals, segregation in hospital care still persists.[32] Hospital care remains somewhat segregated, with African Americans more depended on urban public, safety-net and major teaching hospitals.[33] Care for African Americans was concentrated among relatively few hospitals and physicians. Twenty-five percent of the hospitals serve over 90 percent of elderly African-American patients, and 22 percent of physicians administer medical care to over 80 percent of elderly African Americans.[34] Similar to physician services, hospitals that serve predominately African American patients do not generate the same revenues as other hospitals, because African Americans were more likely to be uninsured or covered by Medicaid. Some hospitals that serve high proportions of African Americans are under substantial financial stress and thus are unable to make capital investments to upgrade and improve facilities, acquire new technologies, develop training programs, and acquire additional and qualified staff that would allow them to provide better quality of care to their patients.

Policy Recommendations

To eliminate the barriers to quality healthcare for African Americans, we need to implement three significant changes in the U.S. healthcare system. First, we must implement universal healthcare coverage to ensure that all Americans receive adequate medical treatment. The best way to achieve universal coverage is to implement a single-payer system similar to the current Canadian healthcare system. This could be achieved by expanding Medicare to the entire population, and we should finance this system through a progressive Medicare payroll tax, general revenues and individual premiums. Premiums should be progressive, based on income and family size.

While others have argued that healthcare reform should be built on the existing employer-based system, I disagree. I am of the belief that the employer-based healthcare system should be dismantled. American business has lost its competitive edge globally in part due to ever-increasing healthcare costs, and healthcare costs have grown faster than inflation for the last few decades. These costs are embedded in the price of American products, and rising healthcare costs are putting American workers and their products out of the global marketplace. Because employers are no longer paying for healthcare benefits, it's reasonable to expect that unions and individual workers will bargain for higher salaries and wages to compensate for the loss of employers' contributions to health insurance premiums. This increase in salaries and wages should offset increases in payroll and income taxes.

Second, if universal coverage through Medicare is not politically feasible, and we must settle for reform that builds on the current employer-based system, then we should adopt the coverage expansion outlined in the Obama healthcare plan. However, it is imperative that we increase Medicaid funding to eliminate the disparities in reimbursement rates with other payers. This will reduce the access to care problems of under-insurance for the poor. Potential monetary sources to use to subsidize this funding include taxes on tobacco, alcohol, snack foods and health plans.

And finally, in an effort to address the geographic imbalance in healthcare providers, we should reward providers located in underserved communities with higher reimbursement rates from Medicare and Medicaid, with grants and subsidies to support capital improvements and training. This would enable physicians, hospitals and other health professionals who serve African Americans and other underserved populations to provide better care. This could be best achieved by improving the targeting and expanding of existing subsidy programs, including Medicare and Medicaid disproportionate share payments, to maximize their impact in underserved communities.

Improving the healthcare system will have a profound impact on African Americans, their families and communities and bringing down barriers to quality care would benefit their health, social well-being and the nation's economy.

NOTES

[1] Pleis JR, Lethbridge-Cejku M, "Summary Health Statistics for U.S. Adults: National Health Interview Survey," 2005. National Center for Health Statistics. Vital Health Stat 10(235). 2007

[2] 2005 Medical Panel Expenditure Survey

[3] Mayberry, R.M., F. Mili, and E. Ofili. 2000. "Racial and Ethnic Differences in Access to Medical Care." *Medical Care Research Review* 57 Suppl 1: 108-145. Institute of Medicine (IOM). 2003. Unequal Treatment: Confronting Racial and Ethnic Disparities in Health Care. Brian D. Smedley, A. Y. Stith, and A. R. Nelson, Editors. Washington, DC: National Academy Press. Agency for Healthcare Research and Quality (AHRQ) 2007 National Healthcare Disparities Report.

[4] Gibbons MC. A historical overview of health disparities and the potential of eHealth solutions. 2005. J Med Internet Res. Oct 4;7(5):e50. Review. Dohan D, Schrag D. 2005. Using navigators to improve care of underserved patients: current practices and approaches. *Cancer* 104(4):848-55. Calhoun

EA, Whitley EM, Esparza A, Ness E, Greene A, Garcia R, Valverde PA. 2008 A National Patient Navigator Training Program. *Health Promot Pract.* Dec 30 (Epubl).

[5] Beach MC, Price EG, Gary TL, Robinson KA, Gozu A, Palacio A, Smarth C, Jenckes MW, Feuerstein C, Bass EB, Powe NR, Cooper LA. 2005. Cultural competence: a systematic review of health care provider educational interventions. *Med Care.* 43(4):356-73. Beach MC, Rosner M, Cooper LA, Duggan PS, Shatzer J. 2007. Can patient-centered attitudes reduce racial and ethnic disparities in care? *Acad Med* 82(2):193-8. Paez KA, Allen JK, Carson KA, Cooper LA. 2008. Provider and clinic cultural competence in a primary care setting. Soc Sci Med. 66(5):1204-16. Saha S, Beach MC, Cooper LA. 2008. Patient centeredness, cultural competence and healthcare quality. *J Natl Med Assoc.* 100(11):1275-85.

[6] Ghods BK, Roter DL, Ford DE, Larson S, Arbelaez JJ, Cooper LA. 2008. Patient-physician communication in the primary care visits of African Americans and whites with depression. *J Gen Intern Med.* 23(5):600-6.

[7] Green AR, Carney DR, Pallin DJ, Ngo LH, Raymond KL, Iezzoni LI, Banaji MR. 2007. Implicit bias among physicians and its prediction of thrombolysis decisions for black and white patients. J Gen Intern Med. 22(9):1231-8. Sabin JA, Rivara FP, Greenwald AG. 2008. Physician implicit attitudes and stereotypes about race and quality of medical care. *Med Care* 46(7):678-85.

[8] Agency for Healthcare Research and Quality (AHRQ) 2007 National Healthcare Disparities Report.

[9] Flores G, Tomany-Korman SC. (2008) Racial and Ethnic Disparities in Medical and Dental Health, Access to Care, and Use of Services in US Children. Pediatrics 121; e286-e298.

[10] Lillie-Blanton, Marsha and Hoffman, Catherine. The Role of Health Insurance Coverage in Reducing Racial/Ethnic Disparities in Health Care. *Health Affairs*, (2005), 24(2):398-408. Hargraves, Lee and Hadley, Jack. The Contributions of Insurance Coverage and Community Resources in Reducing Racial/Ethnic Disparities in Access to Care. Health Services Research, (June 2003), 38(3): 809-829. Weinick, Robin and Zuvekas, Samuel. Racial and Ethnic Difference in Access to and Use of Health Care Services, 1977 to 1996. 2000. *Medical Care Research and Review* 57:36-54.

[11] Lee KA, Wortley PM, Coughlin SS. Comparison of racial/ethnic dispari-

ties in adult immunization and cancer screening. American Journal of Preventive Medicine, 2005; 29(5), 404-411. Chen, J.Y., Diamant, A., Pourat, N., & Kagawa-Singer, M. (2005). Racial/ethnic disparities in the use of preventive services among the elderly. American Journal of Preventive Medicine, 29(5), 388-395. Sambamoorthi U, McAlpine DD. Racial, ethnic, socioeconomic, and access disparities in the use of preventive services among women. *Prev Med.* 2003 Nov;37(5):475-84. Corbie-Smith G, Flagg EW, Doyle JP, O'Brien MA. Influence of usual source of care on differences by race/ethnicity in receipt of preventive services. J Gen Intern Med. 2002 Jun;17(6):458-64. Herbert PL, Frick KD, Kane RL, McBean AM. The Causes of Racial and Ethnic Differences in Influenza Vaccination Rates among Elderly Medicare Beneficiaries. Health Services Research 2005;40(2):517-537.

[12] Chen, J.Y., Diamant, A., Pourat, N., & Kagawa-Singer, M. (2005). Racial/ethnic disparities in the use of preventive services among the elderly. American Journal of Preventive Medicine, 29(5), 388-395. Fiscella K, Holt K. (2007) Impact of Primary Care Patient Visits on Racial and Ethnic Disparities in Preventive Care in the United States. J Am Board Fam Med 20:587-597. Corbie-Smith G, Flagg EW, Doyle JP, O'Brien MA. Influence of usual source of care on differences by race/ethnicity in receipt of preventive services. J Gen Intern Med. 2002 Jun;17(6):458-64. DeLaet DE, Shea S, Carrasquillo O. Receipt of preventive services among privately insured minorities in managed care versus fee-for-service insurance plans. J Gen Intern Med. 2002 Jun;17(6):451-7. Schneider EC, Cleary PD, Zaslavsky AM, Epstein AM. 2001. Racial disparity in influenza vaccination: does managed care narrow the gap between African Americans and whites? *JAMA.* 286(12):1455-60.

[13] Gaskin DJ Spencer CS, Richard P, Anderson G, Powe NR, and LaVeist TA., 2008. "Do hospitals provide lower quality care to minorities compared to whites?" *Health Affairs 27(2): 518-527.* Barnato A.E., F.L. Lucas, D. Staiger, D.E. Wennberg, and A. Chandra. 2005. "Hospital-Level Racial Disparities in Acute Myocardial Infarction Treatment and Outcomes." *Medical Care* 43:308-319. Blustein J., and B.C. Weitzman BC. 1995. "Access to Hospitals with High-Technology Cardiac Services: How Is Race Important?" *American Journal of Public Health* 85:345-351. Bradley E.H., J. Herrin, Y. Wang, R.L. McNamara, T.R. Webster, D.J. Magid, M. Blaney, E.D. Peterson, J.G. Canto, C. V. Pollack, and H.M. Krumholz. 2004. "Racial and Ethnic Differences in Time to Acute

Reperfusion Therapy for Patients Hospitalized With Myocardial Infarction." Journal of the American Medical Association 292:1563-1572. Hasnain-Wynia R, D.W. Baker, D. Nerenz, J. Feinglass, A.C. Beal, M.B. Landrum, R. Behal, and J. Weissman. 2007. "Disparities in Health Care are Driven by Where Minority Patients Seek Care." Archives of Internal Medicine 167:1233-1239. Jha AK, Orav EJ, Li Z, Epstein AM. "Concentration and quality of hospitals that care for elderly black patients," *Arch Intern Med.* 167, no.11 (2007):1177-82. Skinner J, A. Chandra, D. Staiger, J. Lee, and M. McClellan. 2005. "Mortality after Acute Myocardial Infarction in Hospitals that Disproportionately Treat Black Patients." Circulation 112:2634-2641.

[14] Skinner J, A. Chandra, D. Staiger, J. Lee, and M. McClellan. 2005. "Mortality after Acute Myocardial Infarction in Hospitals that Disproportionately Treat Black Patients." Circulation 112:2634-2641. Jha AK, Orav EJ, Li Z, Epstein AM. "Concentration and quality of hospitals that care for elderly black patients," *Arch Intern Med.* 167, no.11 (2007):1177-82.

[15] Hasnain-Wynia R, D.W. Baker, D. Nerenz, J. Feinglass, A.C. Beal, M.B. Landrum, R. Behal, and J. Weissman. 2007. "Disparities in Health Care are Driven by Where Minority Patients Seek Care." Archives of Internal Medicine 167:1233-1239. Meyer JA, S Silow-Carroll, and T Kutyla. 2004. Hospital Quality: Ingredients for Success: Overviews and Lessons Learned. New York, NY: Commonwealth Fund.

[16] Institute of Medicine (IOM). 2002. Insuring Health: Care with Coverage Too Little, Too Late. Wilhelmine Miller and Dianne M. Wolman, Editors. Washington, DC: National Academy Press. Peterson ED, Shaw LK, DeLong ER, Pryor DB, Calif RM, Mark DB. Racial Variation in the Use of Coronary-Revascularization Procedures: Are the Differences Real? Do They Matter?" *New England Journal of Medicine* 1997; 336: 480-486. Lillie-Blanton, M., O. Rushing, S. Ruiz, R. Mayberry, and L. Boone. 2002. Racial Differences in Cardiac Care: The Weight of the Evidence. Washington, DC: Kaiser Foundation and the American College of Cardiology Foundation.

[17] Epstein AM, Weissman JS, Schneider EC, Gatsonis C, Leape LL, Piana RN. Race and gender disparities in rates of cardiac revascularization: do they reflect appropriate use of procedures or problems in quality of care? Medical Care. 2003;41(11):1240-55. Rathore SS, Mehta RH, Wang Y, Radford MJ, Krumholz HM. Effects of age on the quality of care provided to older

patients with acute myocardial infarction. *Am J Med.* 2003 Mar;114(4):307-15. Petersen LA, Wright SM, Peterson ED, Daley J. 2002. "Impact of Race on Cardiac Care and Outcomes in Veterans with Acute Myocardial Infarction." *Medical Care* 40 (1Suppl): I-86 – I-96. Bell PD, Hudson S. Equity in the diagnosis of chest pain: race and gender. *Am J Health Behav.* 2001 Jan-Feb;25(1):60-71. Okelo S, Taylor AL, Wright JT Jr, Gordon N, Mohan G, Lesnefsky E. 2001. Race and the decision to refer for coronary revascularization: the effect of physician awareness of patient ethnicity. *J Am Coll Cardiol.* 38(3):698-704. Hannan E.L., H. Kilburn Jr, J.F. O'Donnell, G. Lukacik , E.P. Shields. 1991. "Interracial Access to Selected Cardiac Procedures for Patients Hospitalized with Coronary Artery Disease in New York State." Medical Care 29: 430 441. Escarce JJ, Epstein KR, Colby DC, Schwartz JS. (1993) Racial differences in the elderly's use of medical procedures and diagnostic tests. *Am J Public Health* 83 no. 7:948-54.

[18] Lillie-Blanton, M., T.M Maddox, O. Rushing, and G.A. Mensah. 2004. "Disparities in Cardiac Care: Rising to the Challenge of Healthy People 2010." *Journal of the American College of Cardiology* 44(3):503-508. Kressin N.R. and L.A. Pestersen. 2001. "Racial Differences in the Use of Invasive Cardiovascular Procedures: Review of the Literature and Prescription for Future Research." Annals of Internal Medicine 135 (5):352-366.

[19] Clegg LX, Reichman ME, Miller BA, Hankey BF, Singh GK, Lin YD et al. (2008). Impact of socioeconomic status on cancer incidence and stage at diagnosis: selected findings from surveillance, epidemiology, and end results: National Longitudinal Mortality Study.

[20] Lantz PM, Mujahid M, Schwartz K, Janz NK, Fagerlin A, Salem B, Liu L, Deapen D, Katz SJ. The Influence of Race, Ethnicity, and Individual Socioeconomic Factors on Breast Cancer Stage at Diagnosis. AJPH 2006 Dec;96(12):2173-8. Clegg LX, Reichman ME, Miller BA, Hankey BF, Singh GK, Lin YD et al. (2008). Impact of socioeconomic status on cancer incidence and stage at diagnosis: selected findings from surveillance, epidemiology, and end results: National Longitudinal Mortality Study.

[21] Deswal A, Petersen NJ, Urbauer DL, Wright DL, Wright SM, Beyth (2006). Racial variations in quality of care and outcomes in an ambulatory heart failure cohort. The American Heart Journal 152 (2):348-354.

[22] Institute of Medicine (IOM). 2001. Insuring Health: Coverage Matters Insurance and Health Care.

Wilhelmine Miller and Dianne M. Wolman, Editors. Washington, DC: National Academy Press. Institute of Medicine (IOM). 2002. Insuring Health: Care with Coverage Too Little, Too Late. Wilhelmine Miller and Dianne M. Wolman, Editors. Washington, DC: National Academy Press. Gaskin DJ, and Hoffman C., 2000. "Race and Ethnic Differences in Preventable Hospitalizations Across Ten States" *Medical Care and Review* 57 (Supp. 1):85-107.

[23] Zuckerman S, McFeeters J, Cunningham P, Nichols L. Changes in medicaid physician fees, 1998-2003: implications for physician participation. 2004. *Health Affairs*. Jan-Jun;Suppl Web Exclusives:W4-374-84. Hogan C. 2003. Medicare Physician Payment Rates Compared to Rates Paid by the Average Private Insurer, 1999-2001. MedPAC August 2003 No. 03-06.

[24] Cunningham PJ, O'Malley AS. Do Reimbursement Delays Discourage Medicaid Participation by Physicians? Health Affairs 28, no. 2009:w17-w28.

[25] Cunningham PJ, O'Malley AS. Do Reimbursement Delays Discourage Medicaid Participation by Physicians? Health Affairs 28, no. 2009:w17-w28.

[26] Reschovsky JD, O'Malley AS. Do primary care physicians treating minority patients report problems delivering high-quality care? *Health Affairs*. 2007;26(3): w222-231.

[27] Greene J, Blustein J, Weitzman BC. 2006. Race, Segregation and Physicians Participation in Medicaid. The Milbank Quality 84(2):239-272.

[28] Fossett, J., H. Chang, and J. Peterson. 1991. Hospital Outpatient Services and Medicaid Patients' Access to Care. Medical Care 29(10):964-976. Fossett, J.W., J.D. Perloff, P.R. Kletke, and J.A. Peterson. 1991. Medicaid Patients' Access to Office-based Obstetricians. Journal of Health Care for the Poor and Underserved 1(4):405-21

[29] Mitchell, J.B. 1991. Physician Participation in Medicaid Revisited. Medical Care 29(7):645-53. Perloff JD, Kletke PR, Fossett JW, Banks S. 1997. Medicaid Participation among Urban Primary Care Physicians. *Medical Care* 35(2):142-57. Bronstein, J.M., E.K. Adams, and C.S. Florence. 2004. The Impact of S-CHIP Enrollment on Physician Participation in Medicaid in Alabama and Georgia. Health Services Research 39(2):301-17.

[30] Gaskin DJ, Arbelaez JJ, Brown J, Petras H, Wagner F, and Cooper LA. 2007. "Examining Racial and Ethnic Disparities in Site of Usual Source of Care." *Journal of National Medical Association 99(1):22-30.* Lillie-Blanton M, Martinez RM, Salganicoff A. 2001. Site of medical care: do racial and ethnic differences persist? *Yale J Health Policy Law Ethics* 1:15-32.

[31] Bach PB, Pham HH, Schrag D, Tate RC, and Hargraves JL. 2004 Primary Care Physicians Who Treat Black and Whites. *New Engl J Med* 351:575-584. Reschovsky JD, O'Malley AS. Do primary care physicians treating minority patients report problems delivering high-quality care? *Health Affairs.* 2007;26(3): w222-231.

[32] Jha AK, Orav EJ, Li Z, Epstein AM. "Concentration and quality of hospitals that care for elderly black patients," *Arch Intern Med.* 167, no.11 (2007):1177-82. Smith DB. 1998. The racial segregation of hospital care revisited: Medicare Discharge Patterns and Their Implications. *AJPH* 88(3):461-463. Smith DB. Health Care Divided: Race and Healing in a Nation (Ann Arbor, Michigan: University of Michigan Press, 1999).

[33] Smith-Bindman R, Miglioretti DL, Lurie N, Abraham L, Barbash RB, Strzelczyk J, Dignan M, Barlow WE, Beasley CM, Kerlikowske K. 2006. Does utilization of screening mammography explain racial and ethnic differences in breast cancer? *Ann Intern Med.* 144(8):541-53. Gaskin DJ. "The Hospital Safety Net: A Study of Inpatient Care for Non-Elderly Vulnerable Populations" in Access to Health Care: Promise and Prospects for Low-Income Americans, Lillie-Blanton M., Martinez R.M., Lyons B., and Rowland D., eds. (Washington D.C.: The Henry J. Kaiser Family Foundation), 1999 pp. 123-138.

[34] Jha AK, Orav EJ, Li Z, Epstein AM. "Concentration and quality of hospitals that care for elderly black patients," *Arch Intern Med.* 167, no.11 (2007):1177-82. Bach PB, Pham HH, Schrag D, Tate RC, and Hargraves JL. 2004 Primary Care Physicians Who Treat Black and Whites.

ESSAY 5

Health Is Where the Home Is: The Relationship Between Housing, Neighborhoods and Health Status

By Eboni Morris and Lisa Bland Malone
National Urban League Policy Institute

R esearch has begun to unravel the relationship between where we live and our health. A community's social, economic and physical environment has a direct impact on individual behavior and neighborhood characteristics can be linked to mortality, disability, birth outcomes, chronic conditions and disease, reproductive behaviors, and mental health problems.[1] This relationship—combined with factors such as income, race, ethnicity, type of employment, and education—forms the social determinants of health that must be addressed, if racial and ethnic health disparities are to be eliminated in the United States.

Racial and ethnic health disparities are evident in all major health indicators tracked by the federal government. According to the Centers for Disease Control (CDC), the ten major causes of death for African Americans are heart disease, cancer, stroke, unintentional injuries, diabetes, homicide, chronic lower respiratory disease, nephritis- nephrotic syndrome and nephrosis, HIV/AIDS, and septicemia. In their 2007 report on the nation's health, the National Center for Health Statistics reported the following statistics:

- The average life expectancy of a black male is almost 10 years less than a white female;

- A black female's average life expectancy is almost 5 years less than a white female's, and a black male's life expectancy is almost 5 years less than a white male's;

- 12.7 percent of African Americans rate themselves in fair or poor health, and 12.3 percent have limitations due to chronic health conditions;

- 66 percent of African-American men and 79 percent of African-American women, 20 years or older, are over-weight;

- 18 percent of African Americans aged 65 years and younger do not have health insurance and 26.6 percent receive Medicaid as the primary form of medical coverage.[2]

These grim health statistics are an example of the racial health disparities that exist between blacks and whites in America.

Neighborhood and Community Effects on Health

There is growing evidence of a link between the neighborhood we live in and our health. For instance, one-fifth of all Americans live in neighborhoods where at least 20 percent of the residents are poor.[3] And nearly half of all blacks—46.1 percent—live in poor neighborhoods, compared with only one in ten whites.[4] Because such neighborhoods suffer from harmful environmental factors—poor air quality, poorly maintained older homes, lack of healthy food options, and the lack of clean open spaces for physical activity and social gatherings—and tend to have an abundance of liquor stores, fast food restaurants, adverse traffic conditions and vandalism. These residents are exposed to adverse health conditions to a greater degree than residents of higher-income areas. As a result, even after controlling for individual characteristics, individuals that reside in a disadvantaged community have poorer health outcomes than those in less disadvantaged communities.[5]

The infrastructure of a neighborhood can impact the health and quality of life of its residents. For example, the quality of educational facilities in a neighborhood affects children for a number of reasons beyond the quality of teaching and learning. Older school buildings in need of basic substantive repairs, the lack of adequate heat and air conditioning, poor ventilation, less nourishing meals, fewer opportunities for physical activity, and the presence of environmental contaminants, such as asbestos, corroded pipes that contaminate drinking water and lead paint, can all cause health hazards for children attending these schools.[6]

There are obvious health issues associated with living in communities with high rates of crime. In crime-ridden neighborhoods, parents may be reluctant to allow children to play outdoors, substantially reducing a child's opportunity for healthy play and physical activity. Obesity and the health maladies that accompany a lack of physical activity already plague the African-American community.[7]

The development and the current disinvestment occurring in some of our nation's central cities or "first-ring suburbs" have contributed to poor health outcomes in residents. The occurrence of spatial mismatch, where individuals may reside in areas that do not offer access to high paying entry-level jobs, has left many in urban communities with little or no employment opportunities.[8] Unemployment often leads to the loss of healthcare coverage for an individual and their family.[9] The loss of healthcare coverage can potentially exacerbate existing chronic conditions, causing new health issues to arise.[10] Also, families without health insurance and limited resources for everyday necessities can plunge even deeper into financial hardship due to healthcare costs.

In addition to high unemployment, these areas also have high numbers of low-income housing units built near major highways and other toxic sites, contributing to high levels of respiratory ailments and other chronic conditions.[11] Dumpsites are often located in low-income, rural and minority communities where land costs were typically low and the surrounding residents have little to no political clout.[12] These residents are frequently unaware of the toxins present around them and aside from toxic industrial sites and dumping, there is illegal "roadside" hazardous waste dumping, which is another contaminate affecting the residents' health.[13]

Ultimately, the geographic proximity to healthy opportunities is crucial, and can make it easier for residents to adopt a healthy lifestyle. Quality, yet affordable, grocery stores are essential to a vibrant community; in addition to providing nutritious food options for neighborhood residents, the outlets can also serve as an anchor for other businesses. In addition, access to healthy foods can reduce obesity rates and other related diseases, such as diabetes and high-blood pressure. However, low-income neighborhoods are more likely to have fewer supermarkets and more fast food chains, as compared to wealthier neighborhoods, making it more difficult for individuals to adopt a healthy diet and lifestyle.[14]

Housing Quality and Health Outcomes

Sub-standard housing is common in poor and neglected neighborhoods where blacks and Hispanics are more likely to live, and thus exacerbates already existing racial and ethnic health disparities.[15] Homes that are poorly constructed and poorly-maintained may contain lead, mold, dust, water leaks, poor ventilation, dirty carpets, or other allergens and pest infestations that can trigger chronic disease, unintentional injuries and unhealthy child development.[16]

Lead

Lead poisoning is the number one environmental problem and is a pollutant currently impacting our children. Even in small doses, lead can have irreversible damaging effects. Such effects include lower intelligence, impaired-attention span, hyperactivity, and other key learning and behavioral disabilities. By 1978, the government had banned the use of lead in homes.

Nearly four million homes in the United States contain some form of lead paint and dust.[17] It is estimated that 310,000 children between the ages of 1 and 5 have elevated blood-lead levels.[18] A recent study on lead levels in drinking water in the District of

Columbia concluded that hundreds of young children in the District experienced potentially damaging amounts of lead in their blood when lead levels were dramatically rising in the city's tap water due to a new chemical that was added to the water treatment starting in 2001. In some high-risk neighborhoods, the number of toddlers and infants with blood-lead concentrations that can cause irreversible IQ loss and developmental delays more than doubled.[19]

Asthma

Asthma, one of the most common chronic diseases among children, is associated with exposure to allergens, such as mold, dust mites, cockroaches and other pest infestations. Tobacco smoke and other pollutants can trigger and/or exacerbate asthma. The highest-level of cockroach allergens were in older neighborhoods, urban areas and low income households, which also have high numbers of children already affected by asthma.[20]

Unintentional Injuries and Disease

Unintentional injuries from sub-standard housing can occur because of numerous problems in a poorly-maintained home, including exposed heating sources, unprotected high-story windows, slippery surfaces, inadequate lighting, electrical wiring and poorly designed stairs.[21]

Residential crowding has also been linked to infectious disease.[22] Children who live in crowded conditions experience poor cognitive and psychomotor development.[23] Indoor temperatures can affect health as well, and cold indoor conditions can contribute to poor cardiovascular health.[24]

Culture and Social Norms

The culture of the community also affects health status. Individuals who live among those with unhealthy habits are more likely to also engage in similar behaviors.[25] Communities with high levels of social capital can have mortality rates that are ten times lower than a neighborhood of similar income but with less social capital.[26]

Healthcare Access

The inequitable distribution of healthcare resources has a tremendous negative impact on the health of its residence in under-served areas; not only does the lack of affordable health care affect health outcomes, but the limited emergency services—police, fire, EMT within close proximity—further plagues these communities.[27] In addition, the failure of many neighborhood health facilities to incorporate the ideals of cultural competence, where health professionals understand the cultural needs of the community it serves and incorporates this into their service delivery, reduces residents' ability to obtain the quality health care they need.[28]

Affordability

Research has also shown a positive correlation between housing affordability and health outcomes among children ages 6 to 17 whose family's income is at or below the poverty line.[29] Low-income families are more likely to live in sub-standard housing and unsafe neighborhoods. In addition, the costs of housing can prevent families from putting limited resources toward nutrition and other preventative health measures.[30] Low- income individuals who have difficulty paying rent, mortgage or other household expenses are less likely to have medical coverage and are more likely to use emergency room treatment.

Homeownership also has benefits for health. Neighborhoods with high levels of home ownership have higher rates of stability and wealth. The individual health benefits include improved self-efficacy and self-esteem, lower blood-pressure and better mental health. Balfour and Smith (1996) found that homeownership led to increased personal security and self-esteem among clients of a lease-purchase program.[31] Homeownership in low-income neighborhoods also lowers the rate of unintentional injury. In a 2004 edition of *American Journal of Public Health*, Edmond Shenassa, along with two other colleagues, found that low-income rental housing is more likely to have inadequate maintenance.[32]

Housing instability—foreclosure, eviction, and/or homeless-ness—also affects health, both physically and mentally. Researchers Mason Haber and Paul Toro found that children who are homeless experience higher rates of mental health problems. Even though the impact of the current foreclosure crisis on health has yet to be stud-ied, it can be safely predicted that neighborhoods with excessive rates of foreclosure will see greater health detriments as a result in the coming months and years.[33]

Conclusion and Recommendations

Because neighborhoods and the conditions therein do not func-tion in a vacuum, a holistic approach is needed to address health issues caused by housing conditions in the United States. There are many areas where further policy is needed to improve housing con-ditions and the neighborhoods of the underserved. Addressing unhealthy homes and unhealthy neighborhoods is a critical compo-nent in eradicating health disparities. Implementing effective solu-tions is essential to ensuring the future health of the underserved.

- A major economic investment in infrastructure improve-ment and neighborhood stabilization as called for in the National Urban League's *Opportunity Compact* is neces-sary, as well as modernizing and expanding mass transit in communities so residents have access to education, employment and healthcare opportunities. The American Recovery and Reinvestment Act, signed into law in February 2009, is a step in the right direction, but it does not go far enough. Additional investments must be made.

- Communities need to be designed with health in mind, because these basic components of urban infrastructure can promote a healthy lifestyle in the community. For example, a community's "built environment" needs to be structured in a way that allows children to walk to school or have outdoor recess. Better air quality can reduce the incidence of asthma in children, and reliable and safe transportation can provide the means for residents to reach education and job opportunities, contributing to a healthier lifestyle.

- Policies that encourage major retail food stores to move into poor neighborhoods—including the use of tax incentives and increasing the use of farmers' markets in urban areas—can improve health outcomes in underserved neighborhoods while also promoting economic growth. Brownspace redevelopment, the development of abandoned and open infrastructure, is an integral part of the economic redevelopment in a blighted community, and it also improves public health.

- Healthy neighborhoods need thriving positive social relationships, also referred to as "social capital," which are the links between people and institutions in a neighborhood. When communities become close knit, they are able to rally together to bring about positive changes to their environment. This can also help turn regular citizens into local leaders who can advocate for additional resources for their community. Close-knit communities also have the ability to produce successful children who are less likely to be involved in unhealthy behaviors, such as smoking, drinking, illicit drug use and gang activity.[34]

- Investing in "smart growth" techniques in underdeveloped communities is another part of economic development. Smart growth refers to a model of planning that involves building housing near economic centers, such as shopping areas, transportation and employment opportunities. Developing more "green" and sustainable building techniques in the public and private sectors that focus on building "healthy" structures is also necessary. There must also be more attention to "environmental justice," which works to reduce the hazardous materials that exist in the physical environment of poor and low-income communities.

- The reduction of residential segregation, primarily through the enforcement of the Federal Fair Housing Act, is another important factor in improving the health of communities. Housing discrimination remains a problem in America, as do unfair mortgage lending practices, and research has documented the disparate treatment received by minorities when looking to rent or purchase a home. Federal enforcement of fair housing laws has been modest at best, but increased funding and resources directed toward the enforcement and awareness of housing discrimination is crucial. In addition, there must be increased cooperation and coordination between the various entities involved in the enforcement of the Federal Fair Housing Act, including federal, state and local governments, and community organizations.

- The expansion of the Healthy Homes Initiative (HHI) at all levels of government and in local communities can also play a key role in improving health outcomes of minorities and the underserved. HHI was launched by the U.S. Department of Housing and Urban Development (HUD) to protect children and their families from housing-related health and safety hazards. HUD is currently working on a strategic plan for this initiative due out later in 2009.

- Involving the local community is key to any successful solution. Building the capacity of local residents to advocate for themselves and educate their fellow neighbors to promote public awareness regarding the potential health and environmental problems that exist in homes and in neighborhoods is the most direct approach. An important piece of legislation has been introduced this year by Congressman Frank Pallone (D-NJ) titled, The *Toxic Right-to Know-Protection Act* H.R. 776. This legislation empowers residents by arming them with the necessary information about chemical dumping to protect their communities.

NOTES

[1] Robert Wood Johnson Foundation. Commission to Build a Healthier America. *Issue Brief 3: Neighborhoods and Health.* September 2008.

[2] National Center for Health Statistics. *Health, United States: 2007 – with Chartbook on Trends in the Health of Americans.* Hyattsville, MD 2007.

[3] Ibid.

[4] Bishaw A. *Areas with concentrated poverty: 1999.* Washington, D.C.: U.S. Department of Commerce, Economics and Statistics Administration, U.S. Census Bureau; 2005.

[5] Robert Wood Johnson Foundation. Commission to Build a Healthier America. *Issue Brief 3: Neighborhoods and Health.* September 2008.

[6] Ibid.

[7] The CDC reports that between 2001 and 2004, 17 percent of African American boys and 24 percent of African American girls between the ages of 6 and 19 were overweight.

[8] McCart, Michael, R.; Smith, Daniel W.; Saunders, Benjamin E.; Kilpatrick, Dean G.; Resnick, Heidi; Ruggiero, Kenneth. Do Urban Adolescents Become Desensitized to Community Violence? Data from a National Survey. *American Journal of Orthopsychiatry* 2007; 77(3): 434-442.

[9] Ibid.

[10] Ibid.

[11] Ibid.

[12] Alternative Police Institute of the Center for Third World Organizing

Toxics and Minority Communities Issue Pac # 2

[13] Ibid.

[14] McCart, Michael, R.; Smith, Daniel W.; Saunders, Benjamin E.; Kilpatrick, Dean G.; Resnick, Heidi; Ruggiero, Kenneth. Do Urban Adolescents Become Desensitized to Community Violence? Data from a National Survey. *American Journal of Orthopsychiatry* 2007; 77(3): 434-442.

[15] Krieger, James and Higgins, Donna. Housing and Health: Time Again for Public Health Action. *American Journal of Public Health*. May 2002, Vol 92, No. 5: 758-768.

[16] Ibid.

[17] Lubell, Jeffrey; Crain, Rosalyn; Cohen, Rebecca. Framing the Issues – the Positive Impacts of Affordable Housing on Health. *Center for Housing Policy.* July 2007.

[18] Ibid.

[19] Leonnig, Carol D. High Lead Levels Found in D.C. Kids. Washington Post. Tuesday January 27, 2009.   Page A01

[20] Ibid.

[21] Krieger, James and Higgins, Donna. Housing and Health: Time Again for Public Health Action. *American Journal of Public Health*. May 2002, Vol 92, No. 5: 758-768.

[22] Ibid.

[23] Ibid.

[24] Ibid.

[25] Ibid.

[26] Ibid.

[27] McCart, Michael, R.; Smith, Daniel W.; Saunders, Benjamin E.; Kilpatrick, Dean G.; Resnick, Heidi; Ruggiero, Kenneth. Do Urban Adolescents Become Desensitized to Community Violence? Data from a National Survey. *American Journal of Orthopsychiatry* 2007; 77(3): 434-442.

[28] Ibid.

[29] Krieger, James and Higgins, Donna. Housing and Health: Time Again for Public Health Action. *American Journal of Public Health*. May 2002, Vol 92, No. 5: 758-768.

[30] Ibid.

[31] Balfour, Danny L. and Janet L. Smith. 1996. Transforming Lease

Purchase Housing Programs for Low Income Families: Towards Empowerment and Engagement. Journal of Urban Affairs 18(2): 173-188.

[32] Shenassa, Edmond D., Amy Stubbendick, and Mary Jean Brown. 2004. Social Disparities in Housing and Related Pediatric Injury: A Multilevel Study. American Journal of Public Health 94(4): 633-639.

[33] Haber, Mason G. and Paul A. Toro. 2004. Homelessness, Mental Health, and Economic Justice. PsyACT Policy Brief. Detroit, MI: Wayne State University, Research Group on Homelessness and Poverty.

JOBS

Dear Mr. President:

I grew up in the inner city of Atlanta, and like many young black men in urban communities, I couldn't find a job and got "caught up," as the boys on the street say, with the wrong crowd and ended up doing time in jail.

When I came out of jail, I had trouble re-adjusting and getting myself back into the mainstream, as many ex-offenders do. However, my father told me about the National Urban League's Ex-Offender's Program, and I enrolled in the program through the Urban League affiliate in Atlanta.

Through the program, I received extensive job training and coun-seling on how to search for employment. In the Ex-Offender's Program, I learned practical job skills, such as classes on computer lit-eracy, and the program trained me on how to develop a resume and prepare for job interviews. The training I received built my confi-dence, and it made me more marketable in the workforce. I was eventually hired for a job, and I have been employed ever since.

Mr. President, we need to provide more job training and employ-ment to people living in urban communities. Although we are cur-rently going through tough economic times, and Americans of all races are unemployed, I think that it is especially important that we provide employment opportunities to black youth, who have much higher unemployment rates. Also, many ex-offenders are unaware of programs that can help them make a successful return to society, and many become repeat offenders and return to jail.

Providing employment opportunities is not only beneficial to these young African Americans, but also beneficial to American society in general.

Sincerely,
Sam Gordon III
Atlanta, GA

ESSAY 6

Infrastructure and Job Creation — A Priority for Urban America

By Senator Christopher J. Dodd

> *"The state of the economy calls for action, bold and swift, and we will act — not only to create new jobs, but to lay a new foundation for growth."*

– President Barack Obama in his inaugural address, January 20, 2009

T he events of Inauguration week were, without question, an inspiration to millions, here at home and across the world, signaling an era of new beginnings for America and the end of another defined all too often by what President Obama called "petty grievances and false promises" that have prevented us from accomplishing big things for our country.

As fate would have it, our new President arrives at the most perilous moment for America in memory, with our economy mired in what some believe could be the deepest and most severe economic downturn since the Great Depression, and more than a half million jobs lost each month.

While none of us are immune to recessions, minorities are especially vulnerable during this particular downturn. As of January, unemployment had risen to 7.2 percent and unemployment for African Americans was over 11 percent. Our healthcare system leaves 47 million people to fend for themselves, and is largely responsible for America having the dubious distinction of being a leader among industrialized nations in infant mortality, with African-American children twice as vulnerable.

Nine to 10 thousand homes are entering foreclosure every day, and some say this crisis will result in a net loss in homeownership rates for African Americans, wiping out a generation of wealth and progress. As a result of all this, many Americans today doubt our ability to create opportunities here at home for generations to come.

But to question our ability to overcome seemingly insurmountable obstacles would be to ignore our history during difficult moments. When our continued prosperity has been doubted and our place in the world questioned, we have always had the wisdom to seek new thinking about the foundations of our country's strength—and the courage to embrace it.

And we have always drawn strength from all of our people from every corner of society. Indeed, from iconic structures like the United States Capitol and the White House to our railroads and the subways in major cities such as New York City, which we still use today. Yet, it was African-American workers who in so many respects designed and built so much of this country.

When Leland Stanford drove the final "golden spike" into the ground at Promontory Summit, Utah, on May 10, 1869, joining the rails of the first transcontinental railroad, travel from coast to coast in the United States was reduced from six months or more to a single week, binding our Union and again transforming the very notion of American commerce. It was an historic moment to which we owe countless black workers—many of whom gave their lives in this endeavor.

Many of us are probably too young to remember, but at the height of the Great Depression, President Roosevelt created the Works Progress Administration, which put more than a million African Americans to work constructing infrastructure projects. One of the crowning achievements was the Alaska Highway, a 1,500-mile military supply route between Fairbanks, Alaska and Dawson Creek, British Columbia that cost $135 million and was completed in just eight months. Central to that effort were three black regiments of the Army Corps of Engineers—the 93rd, 95th and 97th—totaling nearly 4,000 troops in all.

Architects, engineers and builders of all races and ethnicities have been at the core of our country's greatest achievements and with our challenges so great, they must be again.

A Decaying Infrastructure

Indeed, for all our problems, Americans are more willing than ever to think differently about making long-overdue investments in our infrastructure. The American Society of Civil Engineers recently handed out a report card grading 15 aspects of our infrastructure—from our roads to our levees to our transit systems. Only four of the 15 received grades higher than a D and nothing rated higher than a C-plus. Like any parent, if one of my daughters came home with a report card like that, it would certainly get my attention.

We all remember the greatest infrastructure failure of our lifetimes:

The breached levees in New Orleans. Many have forgotten that just before the nightmare in Louisiana that exposed so many problems in our country came the blackout across the Northeast that left 40 million Americans without power in 2003.

But those are only the most noticeable problems. The bridges in my state of Connecticut are an average of fifty years old—the oldest in the nation. There are wastewater systems in major urban areas that are over a century old, many in the Northeast. We have a digital divide that leaves large swaths of our population behind—shamefully, the United States ranks 15th in the world in broadband deployment. As we struggle to raise academic standards in our schools, many of the buildings themselves are literally crumbling. And for most of our country, the transportation system is inefficient and responsible for a third of our carbon footprint and deteriorating air quality, which is connected to rising asthma rates in our children.

In all, we are told by our best minds that America needs an estimated $2.2 trillion simply to maintain the infrastructure we have.

The Possibilities for Job Creation

But for all the challenges posed by our neglected infrastructure, addressing them in a comprehensive way offers a once-in-a-generation opportunity for change and job creation, if we have the wisdom and will to grab it.

The Department of Transportation estimated that for every billion dollars invested in transportation, some 35,000 transportation construction jobs are created—jobs that on average pay nearly $1,000 per week. At a time when we are losing 20,000 jobs a day, we can't overstate the importance of noting these are jobs that cannot be outsourced. In my state of Connecticut, the average annual pay of our construction workers is $56,000.

That's one reason infrastructure investment is at the heart of our $787 billion economic recovery plan, signed into law in February 2009. It will likely include some $100 billion to restore our transportation, energy and water infrastructure. When finalized, the stimulus is expected to create or maintain between 3 and 4 million jobs.

But once we've fixed all our roads and bridges—no small task in itself—we have to make sure people are working in sustainable jobs. We need to leverage this moment to not only get our economy moving again in the short term, but begin making the kinds of investments we need to be competitive as communities, as regions and as a nation in the 21st century.

Infrastructure investment can help here as well. To understand how, you only need look at one of the most promising trends in recent years: "transit-oriented development"—innovative economic development projects that integrate housing and commercial developments with public transportation to encourage smart land-use, creating vibrant communities where people can live, work and get to and from easily while using less energy.

Transit-oriented development not only helps us deal with big problems like congestion and unstable gas prices; it is a big job creator as well. In addition to jobs created during construction—building the office and retail space, the rail stops, and housing—transit-oriented development creates sustainable, permanent jobs. It creates new opportunities for the people we need to drive the buses and operate the rails and work at the banks, coffee shops, dry cleaners and news-stands that are staples of every healthy community.

But to encourage transit-oriented development, we need to make transit a priority.

A friend recently told me that for years, transit—that is, local public transportation—has been regarded as a "necessary evil," not something we thought about much. But even as we discuss the need for big new ideas, in so many ways, the moment has arrived for one we've had kicking around for a century.

Today, the number of transit riders is growing and reaching levels we have not seen in decades. In 2007, as gas prices soared, Americans took over 10 billion trips on public transit, the highest number in half a century. I expect those numbers to have remained strong in 2008, despite a deep recession and lower gas prices. Public transit saves over 4 billion gallons of gasoline annually and reduces carbon emissions by some 37 million metric tons a year – that's equivalent to the electricity used by almost 5 million house-holds. And according to a 2004 United States Department of Transportation analysis, public transportation creates 19 percent more jobs than the same investment in building roads or highways.

A "necessary evil" a generation ago, today transit's just plain necessary.

Congress is scheduled to write a new surface transportation law later this year. As chair of the Senate Banking, Housing and Urban Affairs Committee, which will be responsible for the transit provi-sions in that bill, I believe we have a unique opportunity to make growth opportunities like transit a priority in America and lay the ground work for an integrated transportation system that can be the foundation for job creation in our country.

One of the most promising areas for sustainable job creation in the coming years will be good-paying, green collar jobs that make America more energy independent. The economic recovery package dedicates some $4.5 billion to modernize the electrical grid. Indeed, for all the optimism about our ability to create a fleet of plug-in hybrid cars and buses that run on electricity, the current grid simply isn't capable of handling the load. Many people think the grid would simply shut down.

Our electrical grid needs to be capable of handling what our people and our country want to accomplish and build.

In addition to reducing our dependence on fossil fuels, projects like modernizing the grid mean we have an opportunity to create millions of new jobs in the green energy sector for years to come. I'm pushing for training programs within Job Corps and elsewhere to help create a new generation of professionals—not simply ready to build these technologies, but to install, repair and maintain them.

The time has come to ensure our mechanics, electricians, plumbers and construction workers have the skills and tools they need to pioneer the first wave of green technologies.

A New Way to Fund America's Priorities

But to fund these big initiatives now and into the future, we need to start thinking big as well. It's been fifteen years since I testified before a House congressional committee advocating for a capital budget to begin making tomorrow's investments today. Well, tomorrow is here. And we're still not making the necessary investments.

That is why one of my top priorities is creating a National Infrastructure Bank—a bipartisan idea I developed over the course of several years with Senator Chuck Hagel from Nebraska, who has since retired, former New Hampshire Senator Warren Rudman and financier Felix Rohatyn, who helped prevent New York City from falling into bankruptcy during the 1970s.

The need was obvious. Only hours after we proposed this legislation in August of 2007, the bridge carrying Interstate 35 over the Mississippi River in Minneapolis buckled and broke, killing 13 people and injuring more than 100. For those in my state of Connecticut who remember the Mianus River Bridge collapse in Greenwich 25 years ago, this type of tragedy is all too familiar.

The National Infrastructure Bank will not prevent tragedy. But it would ensure that important projects receive funding. It creates a new funding stream and competitive process for wastewater systems or any other project that offers the greatest economic and environmental benefits that no community can afford to build or rebuild on its own.

The Infrastructure Bank would encourage regional approaches to infrastructure needs, encouraging private sector participation to fund big projects important to our communities. That's why Governors and Mayors across the partisan divide support the National Infrastructure Bank, from Pennsylvania Governor Ed Rendell to New York Mayor Michael Bloomberg, to California Governor Arnold Schwarzenegger. President Obama co-sponsored our infrastructure bank legislation as a senator and endorsed the idea during his campaign. So, I'm hopeful to see action on the bill this year.

Finding new ways to create jobs by funding infrastructure projects is a priority for me and the Banking Committee I chair, because at a time of great economic challenges, it's a priority for our cities and our country.

A Defining Moment for Urban America

For all the talk about funding infrastructure projects as quickly as possible right now, we have an opportunity to focus our resources on projects that are not only "shovel-ready," but also "future-ready"—that prepare our cities and our people for the challenges to come.

Whether it was the Erie Canal that connected the Great Lakes and the eastern seaboard, the rural electrification effort that brought electricity to some two million farms in 45 states within twenty-four months, or the Interstate Highway System that connected every community in the country, America has always recognized that when we invest in our infrastructure, we invest in our metropolitan communities and in our future.

And the long-term infrastructure investments we need to make for the decades to come will have the added benefit of creating much-needed jobs right now.

We need leadership—and not just from our President—that will ask a nation as good ans as great as ours to live up to our history, our expectations, our hopes and dreams—to appeal to the common aspirations we share as Americans.

When people talk about this period in history, as they surely will, you and I want them to talk about how, together, we turned a challenge into an opportunity for our communities and our families.

At this defining moment, as we have so many times before, let us once again seek the wisdom and the will to make that possible. As our new President has said, "This is the moment." Let us seize it.

ESSAY 7

Why Reduce African-American Male Unemployment?

By William M. Rodgers, III, Ph.D
Rutgers University

J ust one year into the current recession that began December 2007, the U.S. economy lost over 2.6 million private-sector jobs. The job losses have been widespread, but largest in construction, manufacturing, retail trade, and professional business services.[1] The alarming observation is that the bulk of the recession's job losses occurred in the final quarter of 2008, signaling a dramatic acceleration in the labor market's deterioration.

What have been the consequences of the job losses? Between December 2007 and December 2008, the Bureau of Labor Statistics' (BLS) "official" U.S. unemployment rate jumped from 4.9 to 7.2 percent. Over 11.0 million Americans are now unemployed, compared to 7.7 million at the recession's start. The number of Americans working part-time for economic reasons more than doubled from 3.4 million to 8.0 million. Marginally attached individuals, people who "want a job" but are not actively searching, increased from 1.3 million to 1.9 million. If the part-time workers and marginally attached individuals are added to the calculation of the BLS's "official" unemployment rate, the jobless rate jumps from 7.2 to 13.5 percent.[2]

Shifting to the experience of African-American men reveals that at the start of the recession their jobless rate was 9.7 percent (compared to the nation's rate of 4.9 percent), and had increased to 14.3

percent after twelve months. This 4.6 percentage point growth is double the increase in the nation's jobless rate. In terms of actual people affected, the number of unemployed African-American men increased from 808,000 to 1,199,000, a 48 percent increase.

A consequence of the recession is that public awareness and policy conversations have shifted from addressing the economy and African Americans' long-term challenges to saving an economy in peril. The immediate goals are to bailout and restructure financial and housing markets, and provide temporary, targeted and timely economic stimulus. Because of the delayed impact of economic stimulus, it is important in the short-term to structure a stimulus-recovery package that minimizes the increase in African-American male unemployment. Doing so will not only help the economy recover, but it will also reduce the "scaring" effects that the recession will have on future opportunity, especially for young African Americans who are the most sensitive demographic group to economic change.

This essay's primary goal is to highlight some of the important economic and fiscal benefits associated with minimizing the increase in African-American male unemployment over the next three years. To do this, I first estimate the statistical relationship between U.S. and African-American male unemployment rates. I then use this statistical relationship and forecasts of the U.S. unemployment rate to construct estimates of the African-American male unemployment rate for the period 2009-2012. Based on the African-American male unemployment rate forecasts, I then develop forecasts for African-American childhood poverty, Unemployment Insurance (UI) and food stamp usage. The latter two are key components of the stimulus-recovery package. A scenario with a stimulus-recovery package of $750 billion is compared to a scenario without a package. According to a report by Mark Zandi at Moody's Economy.com (see note 4), $750 billion is a good benchmark because it is consistent with estimates of the "direct economic costs of the financial panic," representing five percent of the nation's gross domestic product (GDP). The actual amount of the stimulus-recovery bill signed by President Obama on February 17, 2009 was $787 billion. Therefore, the estimates and forecasts presented in this essay represent lower limits of the potential effects of the economic stimulus-recovery package.[3]

Over the forecast period from 2009 to 2012, compared to no stimulus, a $750 billion package spent equally in 2009 and 2010 will:

- Keep the African-American male unemployment rate from surpassing 20 percent, though the jobless rate will still rise to 18 percent,

- Keep approximately 2.0 million African-American children out of poverty,

- Lead to 13.2 million fewer Americans utilizing the regular UI program, generating a savings of $32 million and

- Generate 16.7 million fewer Americans utilizing the food stamp program, a $23 million dollar savings.

Albeit modest, the savings from increased labor force participation and less need for temporary support should be used to complement existing investments in job development, academic achievement, early childhood education, and prisoner re-entry strategies. Use of the savings in these areas will have a positive multiplier effect, increasing tax revenue and health insurance coverage, lowering African-American childhood poverty, reducing the usage of food stamps, and slowing the growth in incarceration expenditures.

An additional benefit of the stimulus-recovery package's temporary income support, aid to state infrastructure investments and expenditures on health care and education will be to help minimize the long-term "scaring" effects that today's recession will have on all Americans, but especially young African Americans that are out-of-school, or will be graduating from high school and college in the next few years. When the next economic expansion starts, it will make addressing the historical challenges that African Americans face a bit easier.

How Bad is Today's Recession?

The media, economic forecasters, and most policymakers characterize the economy as the worst since the Great Depression. Credit markets are frozen, consumers have cut back significantly on purchases and consumer confidence is at historical lows. Although the facts support these statements, the length of the current recession still has not surpassed the 16-month recession from July 1981 to November 1982 as being the worst on record since WWII. Nor has the unemployment rate risen to levels seen during the 1981-82 recession, when it peaked at 10.8 percent.

The reason for these extreme characterizations and demand for quick policy responses are largely due to the dramatic acceleration in the economy's erosion during the 4th quarter of 2008. From October to December, private sector job losses accelerated, accounting for almost two-thirds (61 percent) of the total lost since December 2007. Also, growth in long-term unemployment during the 4th quarter accounts for 42 percent of the recession's total growth (868,000).

What Does the Future Have to Hold?

Moody's Economy.com estimates that without a stimulus package, the U.S. unemployment rate could rise to over 10 percent in the third quarter of 2009.[4] With a $750 billion stimulus package ($372 billion in 2009, $378 billion in 2010), the unemployment rate would peak at 9.0 percent in the 1st and 2nd quarters of 2010 and fall to 8.5 percent in the 2nd half of 2010.[5] If these forecasts prove to be accurate, the current recession will set a record for the longest post-WWII recession although the unemployment rate would remain below the peak rate of 10.8 percent reached during the 1981-82 recession.[6] However, even without setting a record for the highest post-WWII recession unemployment rate, this forecast of the U.S. unemployment rate has major implications for African-American men.

To support this claim, I build on estimates in Rodgers (2006), where first I utilize the historical relationship between the U.S. and African-American unemployment rates to forecast the latter.[7] One word of caution with interpreting the forecasts, due to the unique nature of the downturn, past trend relationships may provide little ability to accurately predict the future. Table 1 reports forecasts of the unemployment rate for African-American men between 2009 and 2012. Two scenarios are provided—the African-American unemployment rate with and without a stimulus package. Based on data from 1972 to 2008, a 1 percentage point decline in the U.S. unemployment rate is associated with a 15.4 percent decrease in the African-American male unemployment rate.[8] Given this relationship, in the absence of economic stimulus, the African-American male unemployment rate would rise from 11.4 percent in 2008 to 17.7 percent in 2009, continue to increase to 22.6 percent in 2010 and begin to fall in 2011 to 21.4 percent. As the national unemployment rate begins to drop in 2011 and 2012, the African-American male jobless rate would fall to 15.8 percent. Assuming Moody's Economy.com's $750 billion stimulus package, the unemployment rate of African-American men would jump to 15.6 percent in 2009, increase to 17.5 percent in 2010, fall to 14.0 in 2011, and end at 10.7 percent in 2012.[9] The stimulus-recovery package could potentially lower African-American male unemployment by 2.0 percentage points in 2009, 5.1 percentage points in 2010, a full 7.4 percentage points in 2011, and 5.1 percentage points in 2012; albeit, these rates are still far from acceptable.

What are some of the economy-wide benefits of the stimulus-recovery plan's ability to lessen the probability that the unemployment rate of African-American men rises to over 20 percent? To answer this question, I estimate the relationship between African-American male unemployment, African-American childhood and adult poverty, and a variety of program usage and fiscal indicators for the UI, food stamp, and the Earned Income Tax Credit (EITC) programs. I use these estimated relationships to generate forecasts of improved conditions for African-American children and general program savings based on an economic recovery package of $750 billion. Tables 2 - 5 present estimates for selected outcomes. The choice of these indicators was largely determined by the availability of extended time series data on an outcome.

As Table 2 shows, a $750 billion package would lead to 238,000 fewer African-American adults in poverty in 2009, 663,000 fewer in 2010, almost 1.0 million fewer in 2011, and just over one-half million fewer in 2012. With respect to African-American children, a major benefit from lowering African-American men's unemployment is the reduction in African-American childhood poverty. Over the 2009 to 2012 forecast period, a lower African-American male unemployment rate will keep approximately 2.0 million African-American children out of poverty. These children will be healthier, perform better in school, and live in safer neighborhoods. The broader long-term impacts will be to improve their life chances of contributing to the economy and their communities, and a lower likelihood of becoming involved with the criminal justice system. However, it is important to note that Table 2 also reports that our work to improve the life chances of African-American children doesn't stop with the stimulus-recovery package. At the end of the forecast period in 2012, one-third of African-American children remain in poverty.

There are a variety of fiscal benefits to minimizing the increase in African-American male unemployment via the stimulus-recovery package. African-American men comprise a disproportionate share of UI claimants, either because of their education, skill, working in weak industries and living in weak local labor markets, or discrimination. As such, a stimulus-recovery measure will reduce the number of UI claims, the number and amount of weekly benefits paid, the number of exhaustees, and UI employer taxes. Table 3 illustrates that from 2009 to 2012, a $750 billion stimulus package could lead to 13.2 million fewer Americans utilizing the program, 3.6 million fewer exhaustees, and $32 million fewer dollars in regular benefits being paid. Table 3 also shows that employer UI taxes would be lower during the 2009 to 2012 period as a result of lower unemployment rates.

Finally, Tables 4 and 5 report the savings associated with Food

Stamp (Supplemental Nutritional Assistance) and EITC programs. For Food Stamps, the reduction in African-American male unemployment will generate 1.7 million fewer participants in 2009, 4.7 million fewer participants in 2010, 6.7 million fewer participants in 2011, and 3.6 million fewer participants in 2012. The smaller number of participants translates into a $2.3 million savings in the first year of the stimulus-recovery package. The estimated savings would rise to $6.6 million and $9.5 million in 2010 and 2011. As the economy recovers in 2012, the reduction in African-American male unemployment via the stimulus-recovery package could generate $5.1 million in savings.

The Earned Income Tax Credit's results are counter intuitive. The benefits of lower African-American unemployment via the stimulus-recovery package are to generate 1.8 million fewer claims and over $740,000 more paid out in 2009. What is happening here is that the stimulus-package is bolstering the incomes of lower and middle-income families such that they are no longer eligible for the credit, but payments go up because the stimulus-recovery package provides (directly and indirectly) jobs for low-wage workers, who on average receive larger credits.

A Final Word

As I mentioned earlier, the purpose of these forecasts is to provide an economy-wide sketch of some of the benefits to minimizing the potential surge in African-American male unemployment. Relative to the stimulus-recovery package's total price tag, the estimated short-term benefits are definitely modest.[10] These benefits are based on the implementation of a hypothetical $750 billion stimulus-recovery package that equally splits expenditures across 2009 and 2010. The actual package, signed into law in February 2009, carries a price tag of $787 billion with $575 billion in new spending and $212 billion in tax cuts for individuals and businesses. Seventy-four percent of the bill's appropriations are to be spent by the end of fiscal 2010.

Further, largely due to data availability, this essay highlights only two major sources of potential programmatic benefits and savings: the UI and food stamp programs. *The State of Black America 2007* introduced the Equality Index, a weighted average of the following sub-indices: Economics, Health, Education, Social Justice and Civic Engagement. Each of the sub-indices contains a variety of indicators that generate benefits when the African-American unemployment rate is low.[11] The "bang per buck" will be larger if more dollars are allocated (absolute and relative) toward urban communities for UI and food stamps, job creation, and education and training.

Along with the short-term economic benefits, keeping African-American male unemployment as low as possible during the recession will have long-term benefits for the economy. A temporary, targeted, and timely stimulus-recovery package that invests in areas that both indirectly and directly impact urban communities, such as direct job creation, education and training, unemployment insurance and food stamps, will reduce the long-term "scaring" effect on all Americans, but especially young African-American men that are out-of-school, or will be graduating from high school and college in the next few years.[12] This would place us in a slightly better position to address the historical challenges that African-American males face when the next expansion starts. We are yet again confronted with the opportunity to take the sage advice of the auto technician in the Phram oil filter commercial. "You can pay me now, or pay me later."

Table 1: Forecasts of the U.S. and African American Unemployment Rates[13]

U.S. Unemployment Rate	Actual	Forecasts			
	2008	2009	2010	2011	2012
No Stimulus	5.74	9.31	11.11	10.77	9.07
$750 Billion Stimulus	5.74	8.15	8.91	7.62	6.1
Difference	0.00	-1.16	-2.2	-3.15	-2.97
African American Male Unemployment Rate					
No Stimulus	11.4	17.7	22.6	21.4	15.8
$750 Billion Stimulus	11.4	15.6	17.5	14.0	10.7
Difference	0.00	-2.04	-5.10	-7.39	-5.07

Table 2: Forecasts for African-American Poverty[14]

Black Adult Poverty (%)	Actual	Forecasts			
	2008	2009	2010	2011	2012
No Stimulus	19.8	22.7	25.3	24.6	21.4
$750 Billion Stimulus	19.8	21.8	22.7	20.8	19.3
Difference	0	-1	-3	-4	-2
Black Adult Poverty (Thousands)					
No Stimulus	4,742	5,474	6,135	5,957	5,135
$750 Billion Stimulus	4,742	5,236	5,473	5,005	4,601
Difference	0	-238	-663	-952	-534
Black Child Poverty (%)					
No Stimulus	33.6	37.6	41.0	40.1	35.9
$750 Billion Stimulus	33.6	36.3	37.5	35.1	32.9
Difference	0	-1	-4	-5	-3
Black Child Poverty (Thousands)					
No Stimulus	4,106	4,680	5,191	5,054	4,423
$750 Billion Stimulus	4,106	4,493	4,677	4,315	4,000
Difference	0	-186	-514	-739	-423

117

Table 3: Forecasts for the Unemployment Insurance (UI) Program[15]

	Actual	Forecasts			
Initial Claims	**2008**	**2009**	**2010**	**2011**	**2012**
No Stimulus	23,042,200	27,098,968	30,826,397	29,803,577	25,117,926
$750 Billion Stimulus	23,042,200	25,780,803	27,105,521	24,464,890	22,214,200
Difference	0	-1,318,166	-3,720,876	-5,338,687	-2,903,726
Average Weekly Benefit Amount					
No Stimulus	$288	297	305	303	294
$750 Billion Stimulus	$288	294	297	292	287
Difference	0.0	-3.1	-7.9	-11.4	-7.5
Average Employer Tax					
No Stimulus	0.66	0.88	1.10	1.03	0.73
$750 Billion Stimulus	0.66	0.81	0.88	0.72	0.60
Difference	0.00	-0.07	-0.22	-0.31	-0.13
Average Employer Tax Rate					
No Stimulus	2.44	3.27	4.14	3.88	2.70
$750 Billion Stimulus	2.44	3.00	3.30	2.68	2.20
Difference	0.00	-0.27	-0.84	-1.20	-0.50
Number of Exhaustees					
No Stimulus	2,670,579	3,752,963	4,941,330	4,563,896	2,912,098
$750 Billion Stimulus	2,670,579	3,401,264	3,803,598	2,950,568	2,325,687
Difference	0	-351,699	-1,137,732	-1,613,328	-586,412
Benefits Paid					
No Stimulus	30,524,891	40,059,670	49,835,736	46,902,023	33,819,445
$750 Billion Stimulus	30,524,891	36,961,534	40,331,125	33,360,199	27,915,157
Difference	0	-3,098,135	-9,504,611	-13,541,824	-5,904,288

Table 4: Forecasts for the Supplemental Nutritional Assistance (Food Stamps) Program[16]

	Actual	Forecasts			
Total Benefits (Millions)	**2008**	**2009**	**2010**	**2011**	**2012**
No Stimulus	34,611	41,688	48,346	46,484	37,997
$750 Billion Stimulus	34,611	39,388	41,739	37,017	33,062
Difference	0	-2,299	-6,608	-9,467	-4,935
Total Costs (Millions)					
No Stimulus	37,533	44,686	51,340	49,496	41,072
$750 Billion Stimulus	37,533	42,362	44,718	40,002	36,018
Difference	0	-2,324	-6,622	-9,494	-5,054
Average Participation (Thousands)					
No Stimulus	28,408	33,522	38,236	36,939	31,001
$750 Billion Stimulus	28,408	31,860	33,534	30,194	27,354
Difference	0	-1,662	-4,702	-6,745	-3,647
Administrative Costs (Millions)					
No Stimulus	2,921	3,138	3,319	3,273	3,056
$750 Billion Stimulus	2,921	3,067	3,134	3,005	2,889
Difference	0	-70	-186	-268	-168

Table 5: Forecasts for the Federal EITC Program[17]

Amount	Actual	Forecasts			
	2008	2009	2010	2011	2012
No Stimulus	44,387,566	42,097,311	40,400,330	40,793,180	42,672,736
$750 Billion Stimulus	44,387,566	42,841,484	42,196,338	43,401,071	44,571,215
	0	744,172	1,796,009	2,607,891	1,898,478
Number of Returns					
No Stimulus	23,042,200	28,470,023	33,709,524	32,213,031	25,436,950
$750 Billion Stimulus	23,042,200	26,706,361	28,542,422	24,822,051	21,766,739
	0	-1,763,663	-5,167,102	-7,390,980	-3,670,210

NOTES

[1] The only broad industry sector that has not shed jobs during the recession is education and health care and social assistance. Even in the December 2008 Employment Situation when payroll employment fell by 524,000, educational services added 7,000 jobs and health care and social assistance added 37,500 jobs. Social assistance added 5,900 jobs. Within health care, ambulatory health care services add 14,200 jobs, hospitals added 11,900, and nursing and residential care facilities added 5,500 jobs.

[2] The group that causes the biggest jump is the inclusion of individuals working part-time for economic reasons. They live in areas that have weak demand for workers.

[3] This essay was written prior to the signing of a $787 billion stimulus package on February 17, 2009.

[4] See Mark Zandi, "The Economic Impact of a $750 Billion Fiscal Stimulus Package," January 6, 2009. www.Moodys.com. In 2009, $231 billion of the $372 billion would be in the form of business and payroll tax credits. In 2010, the composition would shift from tax cuts to government spending, with infrastructure receive $129 billion. In 2009 UI program would receive $10 billion and $16 billion in 2010. Food stamps would receive $26 billion, spread equally across both years.

[5] The incoming Administration estimates that a $775 billion package would cause the unemployment rate to peak at 8 percent during 2009, while

at 9.0 percent without a recovery package. See Christina Romer and Jared Bernstein, "The Job Impact of the American Recovery and Reinvestment Plan," January 9, 2009, Chair, Nominee, Designate, Council of Economic Advisors and Office of the Vice President.

[6] CBO anticipates that the current recession, which started in December 2007, will last until the second half of 2009, making it the longest recession since World War II. If the recession continues beyond June, it would last at least 19 months. The recession has the potential of being the severest deepest recession since WWII. CBO estimates that economic output in 2009 and 2010 will average 6.8 percent below its potential. Potential is the level of output that would be produced if the economy's resources were fully employed. The downturn may not result in the highest unemployment rate. The CBO's forecast of 9.2 percent in early 2010 is still below the 10.8 percent observed close to the end of the 1981–1982 recession. Source: Statement of Robert A. Sunshine, Acting Director The Budget and Economic Outlook: Fiscal Years 2009 to 2019 before the Committee on the Budget United States Senate

January 8, 2009 http://www.cbo.gov/ftpdocs/99xx/doc9958/01-08-Outlook_Testimony.pdf.

[7] See Ronald B. Mincy, Editor, "Black Males Left Behind," The Urban Institute Press. Washington, DC: 2006.

[8] Monthly time series data generates a similar estimated relation.

[9] Some might argue that these are too high. After 16-20 months of deep recession, African Americans may begin to become discouraged, stop searching and leave the labor force. This may not be the case or at least not that large. I estimated similar relations between the U.S. unemployment rate and the labor force participation rate of African-American men and found that a 1 percentage point increase in the national unemployment rate is associated with a 0.22 percent decline in African-American male's labor force participation ratio.

[10] These savings are non-trivial. For example, the savings could be used to help fund Job Corps FY09 budget request of $110,000,000 for facility construction, rehabilitation, and acquisition. http://www.dol.gov/dol/budget/2009/PDF/CBJ-2009-V3-04.pdf. The savings could cover a major portion of the funding the recent Community Based Job Training Grants that the Department of Labor Awarded.
http://www.dol.gov/opa/media/press/eta/eta20090068.htm.

[11] Some of the indicators are household income, home and car ownership, measures of substance abuse, access to care.

[12] In research on the black-white wage gap from 1979 to 1992, I show in William M. Rodgers III, "Male Black-White Wage Gaps: A Distributional Analysis, 1979-1994," Southern Economic Journal, April 2006, v. 72, issue 4, pp. 773-93, that young African-American men who attempted to enter the labor market during and shortly after the 1981-82 recession suffered scaring effects. Their earnings were very slow to recover.

[13] Forecasts of the U.S. unemployment rate come from Moody's Economy.com. The actual figures come from www.bls.gov. The forecasts for African-American men are developed as follows. I first estimate the relationship between the African-American male unemployment rate and the U.S. unemployment rate using a two-year polynomial in the first degree with the coefficient on the third year set to zero. The model contains a time trend and has been corrected for first-order serial correlation. I then use this estimated relationship and the U.S. unemployment rate forecast to construct the African-American male forecast.

[14] The actual figures come from a variety of sources. The forecasts for each indicator are developed as follows. I first estimate the relationship between the indicator and the African-American male unemployment rate using a two-year polynomial in the first degree with the coefficient on the third year set to zero. The model contains a time trend and has been corrected for first-order serial correlation. I then use this estimated relationship and the African American unemployment rate forecast to construct the forecast for each indicator.

[15] See note 14.

[16] See note 14.

[17] See note 14.

ESSAY 8

Nothing Trickles Down: How Reaganomics Failed America

By William E. Spriggs, Ph.D.
Howard University

A midst the excitement of President Obama's historic election is a sobering dose of reality. He has inherited an economy in a recession that stands to go on record as the worst, some are saying, since the Great Depression. Up to now, this dubious distinction has been held by the Reagan Administration which saw unemployment rates jump to the highest level on record during the early 1980s. The principles and policies President Reagan proposed to address the economic downturn—more tax cuts (especially for the wealthy) and less government spending—became the basis of what we now know as "trickle-down" economics or Reaganomics.

In the face of the mounting economic challenges of 2007 and 2008, the George W. Bush Administration sought to reapply the principles of Reaganomics by refusing to offer a substantial economic stimulus plan. Although they finally gave in to a modest tax cut at the beginning of 2008, it proved insufficient to turn the economic tide. The economy lost nearly 2 million jobs over the last quarter of 2008, home foreclosures continued to mount, consumer confidence plummeted and credit markets tightened as banks and other major corporations continued to fold. In this economic environment, President Obama's proposal of an economic stimulus plan that would include a substantial amount of new spending as well as tax cuts was perfectly logical, or so it seemed to everyone except Congressional Republicans who, with the exception of three, refused to vote in support of President Obama's plan. Instead they have opted to hearken back to their "fundamentals" of pursuing the Reaganomic policies of minimal direct government intervention. In spite of this clear drawing of Congressional battle lines, President Obama signed the *American Recovery and Reinvestment Act* into law on February 17, 2009, thus winning the battle in his first step toward addressing the economic crisis.

So, what went wrong with Reaganomics and why would repeating these policies take us on the wrong path? Or, are African Americans and others who tend to have less fond memories of the Reagan years on the wrong side in this policy debate? This essay explores the lessons learned from the experience of the 1980s, why they are important to understanding the potential course of the economic recovery to come and the pitfalls that should be guarded against.

The Best of Times and The Worst of Times

Though many Americans continue to revere Ronald Reagan, history casts doubt upon the economic legacy of his administration. When Reagan was first elected, the economy was struggling with high inflation and rising unemployment, but he rejected a role for the government in the economy, famously noting in his first Inaugural address, "In this present crisis, government is not the solution to our problem; government is the problem." He went on to say:

Well, this administration's objective will be a healthy, vigorous, growing economy that provides equal opportunities for all Americans, with no barriers born of bigotry or discrimination. Putting America back to work means putting all Americans back to work. Ending inflation means freeing all Americans from the terror of runaway living costs. All must share in the productive work of this "new beginning," and all must share in the bounty of a revived economy. With the idealism and fair play which are the core of our system and our strength, we can have a strong and prosperous America, at peace with itself and the world.

Unfortunately, that was not the reality lived by African Americans during his administration. While Reaganomics did not end bigotry or discrimination in the economy, did not put all Americans back to work and did not distribute the bounty of a revived economy, the worst of the Reagan legacies was that African Americans were blamed for the failure of the Administration's policies. Notions of "a culture of poverty" and black social pathologies continue to be used to explain setbacks endured by African Americans during bad economic times. Such rhetoric only hurts policy development by diverting resources away from removing the greater barriers of discrimination and lop-sided policies to address so-called pathologies, a strategy that is only moderately effective at generating African-American and indeed American advancement.

To understand the impact of Reagan's legacy, it is necessary to look back at how economic policy worked before Reagan and to then look at how economic policy worked after Reagan. I evaluate the Reagan record in the context of what happened before he took office, and by comparison, what happened under Bill Clinton. Examining the damage that Reaganomics did to African Americans and to the American economy can help us better understand the implications of longer-run economic policy outcomes and to develop more effective policies as we struggle to emerge from the current economic crisis.

The Kennedy-Johnson Era and the War on Poverty

In 1965, 65.6 percent of black children lived below the poverty line.[1] But by 1969, the poverty rate fell to 39.6 percent, reducing the number of black children in poverty by almost 40 percent. Such remarkable changes over the span of four years could not have resulted from changes in black families alone, but required changes in economic policies as well. For example, payrolls grew 18 percent during those years as the labor force grew more slowly by 11 percent. This reduced the African-American unemployment level to record lows. During this time period, several increases in the federal minimum wage also helped the bottom earners of the economy.

For example, the minimum wage increased three times during that period, raising its value in today's dollars from $7.56 an hour to $8.31 an hour, a figure much higher than the current minimum wage of $6.14.[2] While child poverty was shrinking due to increased employment and wages, public support for poor children also increased. The number of children helped by the former Aid to Families with Dependent Children (AFDC) grew from 3.2 million to 4.9 million, and the value of their benefits grew 31 percent from 1965 to 1969.[3] As discrimination in hiring was reduced, particularly in Southern industries, African Americans were given greater access to middle-class jobs from which they had been barred before the passage of the 1964 Civil Rights Act.[4] Increasing access to jobs for African Americans through anti-discrimination policies rapidly lowered African-American poverty in just five years—far more than was accomplished by increasing the educational attainment of African Americans, in absolute levels and relative to whites, during the next 25 years.[5]

The federal government also increased its commitment to investing in the future of the American people through education, training, health and income security by increasing spending from what amounted to 5.3 percent of GDP (the sum of the nation's resources) in 1965 to 7 percent by 1969, an increase of over 30 percent.[6] From 1967 to 1970, the average income for the bottom 20 percent of Americans climbed almost 10 percent, while for the richest 20 percent, it climbed 7 percent.[7] This put America on a path such that if the economy continued to grow and poverty declined with that same relationship to growth, by the mid-1970s poverty in America would have been eliminated. Instead, America veered from that path of shared prosperity to one of growing inequality; hence, poverty became a fixture in America.

Once the commitment to ending discrimination and raising the wages of those at the bottom ended, the poverty rate for African Americans changed little from 1969 to 1981. Ronald Reagan had a simple interpretation for the failure to reduce poverty in those years—"Liberals fought poverty and poverty won."[8] However, the evidence shows that Reagan was clearly wrong. The Kennedy-Johnson Administration and President Johnson's War on Poverty dramatically lowered poverty levels and created a period where both rich and poor did better. More aptly, liberals lost and the war on poverty ended, but the war on the poor began.

The Reagan Effect

A hallmark of Reaganomics was the idea that the federal government overtaxed Americans. In 1965, the lowest federal income tax bracket began at $23,210 (in today's dollars) for a married couple with two dependent children and the maximum rate was 70 percent for income above $1,365,300. When Reagan took office in 1981, the lower tax bracket began at $17,515 for a married couple with two children, and the maximum rate was applied to income over $519,305. Inflation resulted in higher tax rates on inflation-adjusted incomes, because the tax brackets were not adjusted as quickly as prices were rising.[9] A cornerstone of Reagan's policy was to lower the maximum marginal tax rate from 70 percent to 50 percent and the lowest tax rate from 14 to 11 percent. But, early in his administration, a compromise was reached on handling Social Security that greatly increased the Federal Insurance Contribution Act (FICA) tax that funds Social Security. In 1980, 47.2 percent of federal revenue came from individual income taxes, and 30.5 percent came from the FICA tax. However, when Reagan left office in 1989, the percentages had changed to 45 percent from individual income and 36.3 percent from FICA.[10] Since the FICA tax is capped, so that workers above given income levels do not pay more, the result was that Reagan made the federal tax burden less progressive, giving much greater tax relief to those with high income than to those with low income.

The "Reagan effect" was more a matter of the distribution of the burden than the tax burden itself. During the "liberal tax and spend" 1960s, the federal government received between 17 and 19.7 percent of GDP. During Reagan's term, the federal government's share fell from 19 percent to 18.4 percent—with less reliance on income and corporate tax and greater reliance on the surplus generated by Social Security. Government spending became less progressive as well, with the federal efforts on behalf of American people in education, health, training and income support falling from 11.5 percent of GDP in 1980 to 10.5 percent by 1989 when Reagan left office.

While Reaganomics lowered tax burdens for those with high incomes, it simultaneously lowered America's investment in its people. Ronald Reagan became the first elected president since the passage of the federal minimum wage not to increase it, resulting in the greatest decline in purchasing power for minimum wage workers. Therefore, although Reagan voiced great concern for the effect of inflation on income tax brackets, he showed no concern for the drop in living standards of low-wage workers. When he took office, the minimum wage was worth $7.67 an hour, and when he left office, it was worth $5.59 an hour. By doing nothing for low-wage workers, and de-investing in the American people, it is not surprising that the poverty rate for American children was at 17.9 percent in 1980, but stood at 19 percent when Reagan left office in 1989.[11]

The Effect of Reaganomics on Black America

For African Americans, Reagan's record was far worse. For example, in 1980, median black family income was $30,439. When Reagan left office in 1989, it had increased to $32,628, only to fall back to $30,439 by the end of the Reagan-Bush Administration in 1993. That is a stunning figure when compared to the 1975 median income of $30,762 for black families, and the progress that was made over the previous 12 years—in 1967 the median family income of blacks was $26,461. It is even more astonishing given that only 31 percent of African Americans over age 25 were high-school graduates in 1970, and by 1990 the figure had climbed to 63.1 percent. Thus, while the educational attainment of African Americans doubled, African-American incomes remained unchanged.[12]

The fact that economic gains failed to keep pace with gains in the educational attainment of African Americans is attributable to the fact that pay rates for African Americans at given levels of education did not remain constant relative to whites. During the Reagan years however, pay rates for African Americans, especially young African-American men, deteriorated dramatically compared to whites with the same level of education; this was especially true for blacks with a college education.[13] Similarly, there was deterioration in the relative unemployment rates for African Americans when compared to whites with the same level of education. Thus, despite dramatic gains in education relative to whites, the ratio of black-to-white unemployment remained a steady 2-to-1 ratio.[14] These legacies of the Reagan era are directly related to the administration's hostility toward the affirmative action and anti-discrimination policies of the Kennedy-Johnson era.

The failings of Reagan's economic policies were also compounded by a deliberate effort on the part of the Federal Reserve, under Paul Volcker, to squeeze inflationary pressures out of the economy. This was accomplished by dramatically raising interest rates, strictly controlling the growth of the money supply and allowing unemployment rates to sky-rocket. President Reagan agreed to ride this dangerous roller-coaster, convinced by Federal Reserve Chairmen Volcker that the economy would be much better with moderate rather than uncontrolled inflation. The result indeed was modest inflation, compared to the 1968-1980 period, but it also resulted in prolonged high unemployment rates. At the height of the Fed-induced recession, black unemployment peaked at 21.2 percent in January 1983. In fact, the black unemployment rate remained in double digits during Reagan's entire term. In March 1980, the black unemployment rate was at 12.9 percent and when Reagan left office in January 1989, it was at 11.8 percent. To understand how severe the experience was for African Americans, it is important to note that the highest monthly unemployment rate for whites (since 1954 when the data was first collected) was the 9.7 percent it reached in December 1982. African Americans endured unemployment rates above 9.7 percent for every month from May 1974 to July 1997; a higher rate of unemployment than the worst that white America ever endured, and only for one month. It would be unfair to blame the Federal Reserve policy on Reagan; however, in light of the consequences of prolonged periods of high unemployment on discrimination in the labor market, the Reagan Administration was too lax in preventing the effects of a weak labor market from compounding the situation for African Americans.

Economic Policy Under the Clinton Administration

Clear evidence of the failure of the Reagan-Bush legacy was revealed during the term of Bill Clinton. From January 1998 to October 2001, the black unemployment rate remained below 9.7 percent and reached a record low of 7 percent in April 2000. Median black family income broke records each year from 1997 to 2000, peaking at its current record of $40,547 in 2000.[15] The poverty level for black children fell every year from 1993 to 2001, reaching its record low of 30 percent in 2000. The gains in income and employment that would have been expected from the gains in education began to manifest during the Clinton Administration and policy clearly contributed to improved outcomes for African Americans. In part, the Federal Reserve helped the Clinton Administration by not overreacting when the unemployment level fell to lower levels than it did during the 1980s. The success of African-American workers during the Clinton Administration was also the result of an economy that was much more affected by the world economy and technological change than during the Reagan years.

Policy Recommendations

Government cannot solve all problems. Still, clearly, Ronald Reagan was wrong. It isn't the case that "government is the problem;" more correctly, "bad government is the problem." Shifts in the economy that are certain to follow the current turmoil will create new winners and new losers. Good government must ensure equity in the new course, not a repeat of the growing inequality that followed the 1980s. Government must guard against the reemergence of inequality along the old fault lines of race, gender, ethnicity and class that let some easily become winners while trapping others into being losers. Good government will insure a recovery that indeed shows a rising tide lifts all boats by taking the following steps:

- Protect wages by restoring balance to labor relations, reinforcing America's labor laws through such legislation as the Employee Free Choice Act, and insuring that the minimum wage rises with productivity;

- Resolve the instability of having unemployment and Medicaid operate as state-run programs by converting them into federal programs with federally set eligibility and benefit levels;

- Intensify civil rights safeguards by appropriating more funds to the Equal Employment Opportunity Commission and the Department of Labor's Office of Contract Compliance to enforce anti-discrimination in hiring, especially for projects funded by federal dollars;

- Facilitate transparency in the hiring of workers on federally funded projects by insisting that the U.S. Employment Service, through the network of Wagner-Peyser funded state employment services, be the sole employment entry point to newly created jobs. This will ensure that everyone has equal knowledge and an equal chance at landing a job.

Conclusion

In the end, perhaps one of the most lasting legacies of the Reagan Administration will be his influence on subsequent presidents and what this will mean for generations of American children to come. Despite the headway in lowering the federal debt made during the Clinton Administration, the Reagan legacy of running up the federal debt by lowering taxes for the wealthy and running up huge deficits on military spending was revived by George W. Bush. Under Bush, the federal debt increased to record levels for our children to resolve and as was the case at the end of the Reagan-Bush Administration, we face another collapse of financial markets; this

time, fueled by unregulated investment banking and insurance financial sectors that over-speculated in real estate loans.[16] Once again,
the Reagan approach of lowering taxes for the wealthy and running
up huge deficits on military spending have not benefited African
Americans and a repeat of those economic policies under George W.
Bush have shown how dangerous they are to the entire American
economic system.

Ironically, the only viable option left to President Obama for getting the country out of this mess is to further increase the debt by
implementing the spending necessary to create jobs and get the
economy moving again. Could it be any more obvious? Nothing trickles down.

NOTES

[1] http://www.census.gov/hhes/www/poverty/histpov/hstpov3.xls

[2] http://www.epi.org/page/-/old/issueguides/minwage/table4.pdf

[3] http://www.socialsecurity.gov/policy/docs/statcomps/supple-
ment/2003/9g.pdf

[4] Heckman, JJ. And B. Payner,"Determining The Impact of Federal Anti-
discrimination Policy on The Economic Status of Blacks: A Study of South
Carolina," (with B. Payner), American Economic Review, (March 1989),
79(1), 138-17[7] and Darity, William A., Jr. and Patrick L. Mason, "Evidence on
Discrimination in Employment: Codes of Color, Codes of Gender," pp. 63-90.

[5] http://www.census.gov/population/socdemo/education/p20-158/tab-
04.pdf , http://www.census.gov/population/socdemo/education/p20-194/tab-
01.pdf , http://www.census.gov/population/socdemo/education/p20-
462/tab01.pdf

[6] http://www.whitehouse.gov/omb/budget/fy2006/pdf/hist.pdf page 52

[7] http://www.census.gov/hhes/www/income/histinc/p60no231_tablea3.pdf

[8] http://en.wikiquote.org/wiki/Ronald_Reagan

[9] http://www.irs.gov/pub/irs-soi/histab23.xls

[10] http://www.whitehouse.gov/omb/budget/fy2006/pdf/hist.pdf page 35

[11] http://www.census.gov/hhes/www/poverty/histpov/hstpov3.xls

[12]http://www.census.gov/population/socdemo/education/phct41/table3.xls

[13] Bound, John and Richard Freeman, 1992, "What Went Wrong? The Erosion of the Relative Earnings and Employment among Young Black Men in the 1980s," *Quarterly Journal of Economics, 107*:201-232; and Gyimah-Brempong, Kwabena and Rudy Fichtenbaum, 1993. "Black-white wage differential: The relative importance of human capital and labor market structure," *Review of Black Political Economy, 21* (March): 19-52.

[14] William E. Spriggs and Rhonda M. Williams, "What Do We Need to Explain About African American Unemployment," in Robert Cherry and William M. Rodgers, III (eds.), *Prosperity for All? The Economic Boom and African Americans* (New York: Russell Sage, 2000): 188-207.

[15] http://www.census.gov/hhes/www/income/histinc/f07B.html

[16] During the Reagan-Bush era, the problems were more confined to the Savings and Loan industry that collapsed and forced the bailing out of depositors who would have otherwise lost their money.

ESSAY 9

The Coming Green Economy

By J. Phillip Thompson Ph.D.
Massachusetts Institute of Technology

There are numerous reasons why "green" issues are rising to the forefront of national discussion and public policy. Rising levels of carbon emissions are blanketing the earth and raising the earth's temperature, leading to ice melting in the polar caps and raising ocean levels as well as changes in weather patterns.[1] Moreover, climate change throughout the world will also have direct effects on humans and human habitats, making food and water shortages more likely to occur.[2] Throughout many urban communities, buildings will need more energy for cooling, and cities will experience declining air quality. Climate change will also increase rising ocean levels that may pose dangers for cities situated on coasts. Reducing energy consumption is also essential in resolving critical problems such as rising fuel costs, wasteful energy use in developed countries and declining supplies of oil and natural gas.

Buildings themselves—overwhelmingly concentrated in cities—are the largest single contributor to annual greenhouse gas emissions. About 60 percent of electricity generated at U.S. power plants goes to commercial and residential buildings.[3] Furthermore, buildings account for about 40 percent of carbon (CO_2) emissions in the United States. To reduce carbon emissions and energy costs, government authorities will have to modify policies in U.S. cities with respect to energy consumption.

Other factors pertaining to urban energy consumption must also be taken into consideration. Transportation, particularly motor vehicles, contributes another 30 percent of carbon emissions. The United States consumes 25 percent of the world's energy and generates 25 percent of global warming pollution, despite having only 5 percent of the world's population.[4] Continued population growth requires greater amounts of energy to keep cities—the hubs of economic activity—running. If government officials do not take action, greenhouse gas emissions will continue to grow, and the energy burden will increase the costs of living for everyone.

The "Greening" Effect on Social Issues

Individuals from low-income urban communities, with the least resources to adapt to climate change, may suffer the most, and the effect of global warming has many implications for African-American communities. Traditionally, African Americans have been concentrated in cities, and black-elected officials can play a definitive role in shaping programs designed to reduce carbon emissions and conserve energy.

Greening cities will require paradigm shifts in how we think about development and think about issues pertaining to social equity. New development in many cities—such as luxury condominiums, restaurants and shopping areas—will be more concentrated in urban metropolitan areas and near public transit, prompting suburbanites to relocate back to the metropolis. Unless new ways are found to finance, build and maintain affordable housing, increases in population will likely exacerbate gentrification and raise housing costs for urban black populations, given the limited space in such areas.

Historically, institutionalized racism has created concentrated poverty in urban areas, and large swaths of cities disconnected from parts of the downtown and the suburbs. Poor public transportation options isolated many low-income areas from jobs and quality supermarkets, while also imposing high transportation costs for low-income people. It is estimated that working families earning under $50,000 tend to spend nearly 30 percent of their disposable income on transportation—more than on housing. Yet impoverished citizens spend nearly 40 cents of every dollar they earn on transportation.[5] To avoid a whole new phase of energy-induced poverty, it is essential that cities be developed in an integrated and equitable manner.

How "Greening" Creates Job Opportunities in Urban America

The new Obama Administration has said that retrofitting the nation's building stock for energy efficiency will be a high priority, and over 900 mayors have already pledged to "green" their cities. The most immediate implication of this is the need for the creation of a new green workforce, particularly in the construction trades where nearly one-in-two unionized workers are expected to retire in the next five years. In Germany, a program to perform energy retrofits on 200,000 homes saved or created 140,000 construction jobs during an industry downturn.[6] In addition, New York City's green-city plan calls for the retrofitting of 980,000 buildings, and hundreds of thousands will be needed to perform the work. This demand for a multitude of workers will far exceed the current supply of construction workers in the area. In Chicago, the green-city plan also calls for retrofitting 600,000 buildings, and similar to New York City, the undertaking will require a massive labor construction force, thereby creating an abundance of job opportunities. By and large, retrofitting the nation's four million commercial buildings and 230 million residential units will call for a workforce development program of unprecedented magnitude.

Public policy has vitally shaped demand for green building by mandating the Leadership in Energy and Environmental Design (LEED) rating system for green building compliance in their buildings. For example, California mandates that all new and renovated state-owned facilities paid for by state funds meet LEED standards. In 2001, the city of Los Angeles authorized $1.2 billion dollars for upgrading nine of its community college campuses in accordance with LEED standards and recently approved an ordinance requiring all private sector buildings over a certain threshold to be LEED certifiable. In the near future, state-level emissions caps are likely to increase green demand, as businesses offset carbon emissions with energy efficient office space improvements.

Local hiring provisions can be built into publicly-supported development projects to provide openings for minority inclusion in large construction projects. The Los Angeles Community Redevelopment Agency (CRA) recently adopted the Construction Careers Policy (CCP) and Project Stabilization Policy, requiring projects receiving large subsidies from the CRA to reserve at least 30 percent of apprentice-level jobs for residents of high unemployment neighborhoods and at least 10 percent for low income or hard-to employ members of the workforce. In addition, the CCP requires project developers to submit local hiring plans that must be approved prior to construction.

To oversee its implementation of the CCP, the CRA will hire a jobs coordinator whose responsibilities include networking with local recruitment organizations, providing information about available opportunities and developing an up-to-date list of residents, qualified for hire on projects (UCLA Center for Research and Education 2008, p.13). Also, a built-in Project Labor Agreement (PLA) component requires projects receiving CRA subsidies above a certain threshold to collaborate with the building trades to jointly administer apprenticeship programs. This places workers under the protection of collective bargaining agreements, ensuring that projects will deliver high-paying career path jobs with health benefits.

Other Green Economic Opportunities

Additional green economic opportunities exist in producing renewable energy—including sources such as hydropower, solar, wind, geothermal and bio-energy—or in local community clean energy production. For example, some cities have rivers or tidal canals that can be used to power electrical generators, providing low-cost energy over time and can serve as a magnet for attracting businesses. Community-scale wind power generation is utilized in some states and some local governments even subsidize loans to small businesses or co-operatives to construct wind turbines for renewable energy generation. Also, diesel fuel can be made with minimal processing from used vegetable oil and has become yet another "green" opportunity for business growth in urban areas. And during recent years, cooperative businesses in low-income communities have sprung into life collecting used vegetable cooking oil and delivering it to plants that convert the oil to diesel fuel.

Through the process of renewing energy, many urban communities can also substantially reduce expensive utility costs. Geothermal energy, for instance, emanates from underground heat of the earth and can serve as an invaluable renewable energy source. The steam and hot water produced inside the earth can be used to heat buildings or generate electricity at minimal cost over time. In addition, the process of producing geothermal energy requires expertise and manpower, which in turn can create potential, lucrative business opportunities.

Similar to geothermal energy, electric co-generators can also reduce heating costs significantly for urban infrastructure. These co-generators, roughly the size of a refrigerator, serve as small modular generators to produce the power for home or commercial building use. Fueled by natural gas or hydrogen, they generate both electricity and heat by capturing excess heat from the electrical generator and distributing it to local residential and commercial buildings. Co-generators are clean, relatively inexpensive, pay for themselves quickly and operate much more efficiently than large power plants.

Certain states and cities across the United States have the option to allow local community energy producers to sell energy back to the grid, providing numerous opportunities for community wealth generation. For example, if a low-income housing development conserves electricity by only allowing laundry machines to run after 6:00 pm and runs an energy generator during the day, when energy prices are highest, the housing development could save money. In this way, energy can be an economic engine for low-income communities, not just for big energy companies. States and cities must make other big choices about their energy future that have major economic implications.

Nuclear plants have already been proposed in roughly 30 different areas across the country at astronomical costs, yet this energy conservation approach is cheaper, safer and produces many more jobs. A nuclear reactor costs at least $7 billion, however, conservation and renewal energy alternatives frequently save or provide comparable amounts of energy at a fraction of the cost and distribute the economic growth opportunities and benefits toward small and labor intensive businesses and consumers.

The latter point bears emphasis, because African Americans, being disproportionately low income, endure relatively high-energy costs. Although low-income households use less energy than upper income households overall, they tend to live in poorly maintained buildings and therefore pay more for energy per square foot of living space than do wealthier households. Lower-income households are situated in poorly insulated buildings and also have less-energy-efficient appliances and heating systems.[7] Emphasizing energy conservation through building improvements over high-cost power plants is especially important for African-American families who tend to pay proportionally more for energy.

Conclusion

Although the emphasis of this essay has been on energy, "greening" cities will require substantial changes in public transportation, open space, urban agriculture and vegetation, conservation of water, and sewage reuse. Urban agriculture, for example, increases accessibility of locally grown food while reducing transportation costs for food.[8] Urban greening projects, such as green roofs and urban parks, reduce urban heat island effects, improve water usage and air quality in urban areas and lessens detrimental storm water run-off that can indirectly contaminate rivers and oceans. In urban areas, reclaimed brownfields, abandoned industrial land most often polluted from previous uses, offer prime land for redevelopment for open green spaces, housing and commercial facilities. All of these opportunities serve as areas for job and business growth in the green economy.

Last, there are other immediate equity issues with major economic implications. The "green lease" issue is being debated in cities initiating building retrofit programs. In some cases, the government is helping landlords retrofit their buildings with low-interest loans, tax-breaks and assistance in obtaining certified contractors and discount prices on bulk-purchased appliances. In other cases, when money is loaned to the customer for a home retrofit, utility companies are being asked to add a charge on their customer's utility bill to funnel back the cost of retrofits to lenders. Sometimes utilities are also asked to allow use of their transmission lines for the sale of energy back to the electrical grid from individual homes or buildings. The beauty of retrofitting is that a reduction in building energy costs produces savings that can be used to pay back the initial cost of the retrofit in a short period of time.

However, the question is what happens then? Do landlords maintain rents at their pre-retrofit level, and realize higher profits as a result of a publicly-supported retrofit program or do tenants get a "green lease" rent reduction as well? Or, does the public recoup some of the savings to fund other programs needed to green the city? Similarly, how much should utility companies be compensated for collecting retrofit payments or for permitting the use of their transmission lines, also developed with substantial public support? The sums under discussion are substantial, and state and local officials will have to negotiate the terms.

In short, the newly emerging green economy promises to shift in our economy and way of life as much as the industrial revolution did more than a century ago. However, unlike the industrial revolution, African Americans today, have the capacity to become full participants of the revolutionary movement and reap the financial benefits and rewards.

NOTES

[1] Intergovernmental Panel on Climate Change. www.ipcc.ch. Accessed June 2008.

[2] Ibid.

[3] Energy Information Administration. http://www.eia.doe.gov/. Accessed August 2008.

4 Green Communities. http://www.greencommunitiesonline.org/. Accessed July 2008.

5 Ibid.

6 Ibid.

7 Ibid.

8 See San Francisco's Foodshed Report as an example. http://www.farmland.org/programs/states/ca/Featurepercent20Stories/San-Francisco-Foodshed-Report.asp. Accessed

HOME OWNERSHIP

Dear Mr. President:

My name is Malinda Dokes, and I am a 19-year veteran of the U.S. Army. Like so many Americans across the country, I was recently in jeopardy of losing my home, due to foreclosure.

I financed my house through a mortgage company and because of a communication breakdown between the mortgager and the military finance office where I am stationed, I went two months behind in payments. Through constant letters and phone calls, the finance company threatened to foreclose on my home.

I tried to get help, but experienced a great deal of difficulty. Although I had served in the U.S. Army for nearly 20 years, I was unable to find anyone in the military that could offer the counseling I needed in helping me resolve my dilemma. I even sought help from my church and, although I was grateful for their generosity, the amount of money ($300) they gave me was not enough to cover the past due mortgage payments. Also, they didn't have the knowledge to offer the housing counseling I needed to handle my situation.

I learned about the Urban League's Prevention Program, and through the program I received expert counseling on how to avoid foreclosure of my home. Representatives from the program served as an intermediary between me and the finance company and were able to mediate renegotiation on my mortgage payments, which enabled me to keep my house.

Like the many millions of people across the country facing foreclosure, I had little knowledge of laws regarding mortgage financing, as well as the credit counseling services that were available that could have helped me avoid these problems. Please increase funding for housing counseling services to assist the many Americans across the country who are in danger of losing their most prized possession—their home.

Sincerely,
Malinda Dokes
Sgt 1st Class, U.S. Army

ESSAY 10

What Must Be Done?
The Case for More Homeownership and
Financial Education Counseling

By Cy Richardson
National Urban League

P romoting homeownership has been a policy priority in America since the Great Depression, and a number of policy efforts at the federal, state and local level have been directed toward this end. Homeownership is thought to benefit not only individuals and families but also communities and the nation as a whole. For most Americans, homes are their greatest assets, and homeownership is the strategy by which most Americans are able to build wealth.

The National Urban League (NUL) has long championed the key themes of "*preparation*" and "*readiness*" with regard to its programs that assist clients in making the leap from renting to owning and taking on the responsibilities and realities of ownership. NUL's pre-purchase counseling programs, for example, have long been a way of preparing and qualifying prospective homeowners—particularly those who have low income, inadequate savings or impaired credit histories—for the financial responsibility of a mortgage. In addition, most Urban League affordable housing programs also include a financial literacy component, with such training generally addressing debt management, budgeting, and techniques to maximize saving. Within the community development arena, pre-purchase homebuyer counseling has been a fundamental strategy for increasing homeownership among disadvantaged households in distressed communities. As a catalyst for neighborhood stabilization, community organizations, such as the Urban League, provide training to develop "bankable" borrowers who can qualify for a mortgage and appropriately manage their debt. The Urban League was an early advocate and facilitator of this practice and typically provides homebuyer training, both before and after purchase, to nearly 75,000 individuals each year.

While the achievements of the housing education and counseling industry are exemplified by the steady increase in the number of low-income and minority first-time homebuyers over the last decade, the increasing threat posed by predatory lending, and the recent trend of increasing foreclosures clearly indicates that a strong housing counseling industry is needed to sustain the gains made in homeownership among low-income and minority consumers. By promoting homeownership education and a dual emphasis on basic financial literacy, the retrenchment in minority homeownership rates seen in recent years can be overcome and the full promise of the "ownership society" can be realized for those underserved communities historically left behind from public and private wealth creation initiatives.

While the issues of foreclosure are certainly capturing center stage at the moment, now more than ever, a strong housing counseling industry is needed to sustain the gains made in homeownership among low-income and minority consumers. This essay addresses many of the issues critical to the non-profit housing counseling industry as outlined below:

- A strong homeownership education and counseling industry can benefit consumers but must be sustained in both a pre- and post-purchase context.

- The Urban League and other national intermediaries have long track records of accomplishment by actively facili-

tating counseling to promote responsible homeownership and avoid foreclosures.

• A deeper public/private commitment must be made to
post-purchase education and counseling.

• More resources are needed to support nonprofit organizations and to stimulate research within the industry.

Homeownership education and counseling must be an irreplace-
able requirement for affordable loan products aimed at low-income
and minority consumers. An effective counseling and education program can offer many benefits to consumers and the lending industry.
Pre-purchase education and counseling has been credited with
expanding homeownership in underserved communities, in part, by
producing informed borrowers knowledgeable about the lending
process and better prepared to accept the responsibilities of homeownership. Pre-purchase education and counseling has also been
found to lower the risk of default. [1]

An important part of the pre-purchase counseling process is
working with potential borrowers to remove barriers to homeownership. The most often cited barriers are affordability and credit problems.[2] The Urban League and many other community-based nonprofit agencies work with potential homeowners to build or repair credit. Others may offer financial assistance to supplement down payments, closing costs or monthly payments. Without such assistance
the barriers to homeownership may be insurmountable for many
low-income individuals.

Post-purchase education and counseling can stabilize homeownership in underserved communities. Post-purchase education and
counseling refers to a range of services—from instruction on home
maintenance, budgeting and foreclosure prevention, to crisis intervention for delinquent borrowers, or counseling to prevent or assist
victims of predatory lending. The intensive, one-on-one default and
delinquency counseling most often provided by nonprofit agencies

such as the Urban League, reduces the incidence of foreclosure among low-income households. Urban League counselors work closely with borrowers to help them understand their options and act as intermediaries in negotiating between borrowers and servicers to put the best workout in place. Moreover, if a workout is not feasible or unsuccessful, these agencies ease the homeowner's transition to other affordable housing options.

Although good counseling may potentially reduce the incidence of predatory lending in low-income and minority communities, counseling in and of itself will not stop predatory lending. Only by changing the laws governing mortgage lending—to stop lenders from financing high points and fees, charging exorbitant prepayment penalties, refinancing special loan programs for first-time buyers into high-cost credit—can we fully address the problem of unscrupulous predatory mortgage lending. Clear prohibitions to stop the most egregious practices, coupled with assignee liability is what is needed to tackle this problem.

Importantly, while the Urban League privileges both pre- and post-purchase counseling, only a fraction of the organizations that provide pre-purchase housing counseling and education also provide assistance to established homeowners. That assistance will most likely take the form of group instruction on maintenance and other issues related to owning a home. Due to the dearth of available funding, very few organizations are able to provide pre-refinance counseling or assistance to victims of predatory lending. Many of the homeowners most at risk—particularly the elderly—are long-time homeowners with substantial amounts of equity accrued in their homes. They are not the traditional clients of housing counseling organizations who often focus on first-time homebuyers, and they are not likely to seek assistance prior to signing a loan. Aggressive outreach and effective public education campaigns are necessary to get these potential victims to seek help before crisis strikes.

The capacity of nonprofits to offer default and delinquency counseling or predatory lending assistance must be expanded to stem the alarming increase in the foreclosure rate over the past several years.

The homeowners who are most at risk of foreclosure are low-income consumers, suffering the effects of the downturn in the economy and targeted by predatory lenders. HUD is mandated under program guidelines to reduce defaults and foreclosures.[3] However, there is much more that HUD can do to fulfill this mandate.

The homeownership education and counseling industry has evolved over the last thirty years to address the needs of traditionally underserved populations in the housing marketplace. At its inception, industry efforts were focused on reducing the substantial number of defaults under HUD's *Section 235* program through post-purchase counseling aimed at delinquent borrowers. However, with the advent of affordable loan products, encouraged and supported by federal policy and designed to increase homeownership rates among traditionally underserved populations, the industry's focus shifted dramatically to pre-purchase homeownership education.[4] The result has been a marked increase in homeownership among low-income and minority Americans. Unfortunately, the demand for default and delinquency counseling and predatory lending counseling has also exploded over the last few years.

The barriers to providing effective default and delinquency counseling are numerous. Default and delinquency counseling is time intensive and expensive. To provide effective assistance, counselors must meet with homeowners face-to-face, review relevant paperwork—such as letters from the lenders, foreclosure notices, and the like—discuss their budgets thoroughly, help them apply for public assistance, and provide other services to increase their income or decrease expenses. Then the counselor will work with the homeowner and the lender or servicer to craft an appropriate workout. As most cases are referred after months of default, counselors deal with the most difficult cases. This type of counseling cannot be performed effectively from afar by telephone counseling only.

Even fewer nonprofit agencies provide any type of pre-refinance counseling or services to assist victims of predatory lending.[5] The agencies that provide this service most often provide it after the person has been victimized by a predatory lender. To provide effective service, counselors must be skilled and adequately trained to review mortgage documents that may contain complex or hidden terms disadvantageous to the homeowner. The demand for counseling to prevent foreclosure or assist victims of predatory lending has clearly outstripped the capacity of nonprofit and other agencies to provide such assistance. Given the susceptibility of low-income borrowers to predatory lending and foreclosure, HUD must encourage the growth of default and delinquency and predatory lending counseling programs in the industry. Providing these services is more expensive, as it takes more time to assist homeowners and counselors must be well-trained.

It is also important that HUD funding be targeted to legitimate nonprofit organizations that provide the most effective types of services to low-income consumers. Community-based, nonprofit housing agencies such as the Urban League have consistently been found to provide the most successful—but the most time intensive—types of education and counseling services.[6] The League also provides a broad range of services either directly or through referral to other organizations. However, nonprofit housing counseling agencies are competing with more organizations—both nonprofit and for-profit—for the small pool of funding and resources available to conduct this work.

The situation has changed in recent years as credit counseling agencies have increasingly begun to offer housing counseling services as well. However, there are many types of credit counseling agencies, some good and many not. Legitimate, honest credit counselors are often uniquely qualified to help consumers. They are already working with consumers to address unsecured debt, and when properly trained, can provide a holistic service by assisting consumers with delinquent secured and unsecured debt.

Unfortunately, aggressive firms masquerading as nonprofit organizations have been among the credit counseling agencies that are most likely to deceive or to gouge consumers. Massive cuts in creditor funding for agencies has exacerbated this trend, leaving many well-intentioned organizations without sufficient funding to provide appropriate services.

To make up these funding deficits, traditional credit counseling agencies have increasingly sought out housing counseling dollars. Some of these agencies have done so with the best of intentions and are developing quality housing counseling programs. Others are only chasing available dollars.

In addition to questions surrounding the credit counseling industry, there are many questions outstanding about the nonprofit housing counseling and education industry in general. Despite the industry's long history, there are only a handful of studies documenting the types of services provided, the effectiveness of counseling at reducing default, or other issues of interest to lenders and policymakers. The scarcity of rigorous analysis is particularly stark with respect to post-purchase programs. While homeowners are turning in increasing numbers to credit and housing counseling organizations for default and delinquency counseling and predatory lending assistance, little is known about how these services are delivered, the numbers of homeowners served, and whether the agencies that provide these services have sufficient resources and funding to meet the need.[7] There are many reasons for the lack of research on this industry. However, one of the main hurdles is funding. Given the reliance of HUD on this industry to assist low-income homeowners, HUD must fund more research, and encourage the private sector to sponsor exploratory studies and make data available for review and analysis.

Likewise, it would also be useful to fund an analysis of how best to take advantage of Earned Income Tax Credit (EITC) outreach and free-tax preparation to promote financial and homeownership education. At present, there is much talk about the need to do this, and experimentation is going on in many urban communities. But it is not clear whether the most effective models have been documented and promoted.

Moving beyond these initial observations, explicitly, then, what must be done?

As a first step, there is a need to develop new strategies that help low-income borrowers—particularly those that may not have extensive financial knowledge—make better and more informed credit choices. Additional investments in financial education and home-ownership counseling must be a key component of this strategy. Financial education has been shown to help households manage their finances more prudently, especially in decisions concerning credit, saving and investment, and it has been shown to reduce the likelihood of default. Calling for more financial education is not a new idea, but challenges remain in funding educational programs and developing appropriate curricula and delivery channels for diverse audiences.

Second, we need to expand access to affordable homeownership opportunities. The gap in homeownership affordability—especially in states like New York and California—is as high as it has ever been. As long as an adjustable rate, interest-only or high LTV subprime loan is the only way to afford a house, low-income families will continue to take on loans that they cannot sustain over the long term, and may be at greater risk of falling prey to unscrupulous lending practices. In stark contrast to the results we are seeing in the subprime market, the vast majority of new homeowners who have gone through affordable homeownership programs—which often involve pre- and post-purchase counseling as well as a savings component such as an Individual Development Account—have not defaulted on their loans.

This evidence also speaks to a much greater need for savings options for low-income families, both owners and renters. Helping families save for a downpayment, and ensuring that they have a savings buffer to help them weather adverse economic times or life events, may lead to better outcomes overall than mortgages that make homeownership affordable only through risky loan terms. In addition, strategies to increase the supply of affordable homes are also needed. For example, we must be more proactive in thinking about innovative ways to convert foreclosed properties into affordable rental or homeownership opportunities. Other potential strategies, such as the establishment of housing trust funds and community land trusts, can serve as mechanisms for creating long-term housing affordability.

Third, to be successful, policies that help low-income and minority households enter homeownership must be linked with broader community development strategies. Low-income households, and particularly low-income minority households, may be especially vulnerable to buying homes in disadvantaged neighborhoods, where job opportunities are limited, schools are often subpar, and the financial benefits of homeownership may be more limited. Much of the work that the nonprofit community development sector already does to stimulate neighborhood economic development, increase local employment opportunities and wages, and improve neighborhood-linked amenities such as schools and transportation options, are critical in transforming the opportunities available to low-income and minority households.

Finally, we need to think more broadly about how homeownership fits into the overall asset-building landscape for low-income and minority households, and what other programs or policies are necessary to ensure that homeownership is affordable and sustainable. In one study of low-income homeowners, researchers found that two-thirds of households that refinanced their homes did so to pay down other debt, including higher cost credit card debt. Others borrowed against the equity in their homes to pay for medical and educational expenses.[8] It should be troubling to us all that so many low-income families are having to use home equity to help manage their overall debt load, or to bridge a gap in health care insurance. We need to help households learn how to manage their finances and to create safety nets that offer protection against economic shocks, so that low-income and minority families are less vulnerable to losing their homes.

The housing counseling and education industry provides invaluable assistance to low-income and minority consumers. While many questions linger about funding and the efficacy of some of the services provided by the industry, it is incontrovertible that a strong counseling industry has the potential to benefit all consumers and therefore must be considered for deeper public and private commitment in conjunction with other solutions to stabilize and shore up the economy from Main Street to Wall Street and the places in between.

NOTES

[1] Abdighani Hirad and Peter M. Zorn, *A Little Knowledge Is a Good Thing: Empirical Evidence of the Effectiveness of Pre-Purchase Homeownership Counseling* May 2001. For example, borrowers who received any form of pre-purchase counseling (classroom style, by telephone, or individually) as part of Freddie Mac's Affordable Gold lending program had a 19 percent lower delinquency rate than those who received no counseling. Borrowers who received one-on-one counseling had a 34 percent lower delinquency rate.

[2] See George W. McCarthy and Roberto G. Quercia, *Bridging the Gap Between Supply and Demand: The Evolution of the Homeownership Counseling Industry*, Report No. 00-01, Research Institute for Housing America, 2000.

[3] See the HUD Housing Counseling Handbook (7610.1 Rev-4), section 1-3(B). Half of the department's program objectives are related to reducing defaults or foreclosures.

[4] See McCarthy & Quercia.

[5] Where available, pre-refinance counseling is usually designed to help homeowners avoid predatory loans and may involve the counselor reviewing the terms of the prospective loan with the homeowner before closing to make sure they do not qualify for a better loan or to spot hidden, disadvantageous terms. Some community-based non-profits and government agencies offer this service to borrowers. However it is not very common and the homeowners who contact these agencies have often already entered into a predatory loan.

[6] For example, Urban League affiliates are less likely to provide telephone counseling and more likely to provide individual counseling, which one study documented was the most effective method of reducing 90-day delinquency rates. Telephone counseling had no statistically significant impact. See Hirad and Zorn.

[7] NUL proposes to do research in the form of a survey and report on the housing counseling and education industry. The report will be a comprehensive assessment of the industry and document the types of services currently provided; the number of homeowners who received each type of service; the

method of delivering the service; the amount of resources devoted to offering these services; an estimate of the need, if unmet; and, the problems and challenges faced in expanding the quality and quantity of these services.

[8] See Jeffrey Lubell, "Strengthening the Ladder for Sustainable Homeownership." National Housing Conference, the Annie E. Casey Foundation, 2005.

ESSAY 11

The Subprime Meltdown: Disarming the "Weapons of Mass Deception"

By Stephanie J. Jones, J.D.
National Urban League Policy Institute

I n the wake of the subprime meltdown, some politicians and commentators are perpetuating a dangerous myth: that minority and low-income borrowers and measures to expand their opportunities for homeownership, such as the Community Reinvestment Act (CRA), are responsible for the subprime crisis.[1] Although the facts prove otherwise, these persons are spreading this myth to shift blame away from where it lies to the people who were victimized by the breakdown in the system.

In fact, the crisis was triggered primarily by the actions of unregulated lenders not covered by the CRA who steered borrowers into the high-priced subprime market where even creditworthy borrowers were subjected to abusive terms that led many to financial ruin. Unregulated non-CRA financial services companies were the major originators of subprime loans in the years leading up to the subprime meltdown and it was Wall Street investors—not Fannie Mae and Freddie Mac—who were the major purchasers of subprime loans.

For years, the National Urban League and others warned that these lenders' predatory lending practices harmed borrowers, particularly in minority and low-income communities and urged that the Community Reinvestment Act and other regulations curtailing such practices be applied to these mortgage companies and other non-bank financial institutions. Unfortunately, our calls for stronger regulatory oversight and enforcement were ignored by Congress and the media. The irresponsible perpetuation of this dangerous myth—which National Urban League President Marc Morial has labeled "the Weapons of Mass Deception"[2]— threatens to undermine much neded regulatory reform and has caused division and scapegoating of minorities that this nation can ill-afford.

MYTH v. FACT

Myth: The Community Reinvestment Act was the primary cause for the foreclosure crisis because it required companies to lend to borrowers, mostly minorities, who could not afford their homes.

Fact: As shown in Figure 1, Non-CRA financial services companies were the major originators of subprime loans between 2004 and 2007, the period for which data is available. [3]

Myth: Fannie Mae and Freddie Mac were the major purchasers/ investors of subprime during this period.

Fact: Wall Street investors—not Fannie Mae and Freddie Mac— were the major purchasers/ investors of subprime loans during this period.[4] (Figure 1)

Figure 1

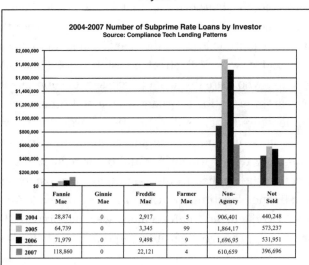

	Fannie Mae	Ginnie Mae	Freddie Mac	Farmer Mac	Non-Agency	Not Sold
2004	28,874	0	2,917	5	906,401	440,248
2005	64,739	0	3,345	99	1,864,17	573,237
2006	71,979	0	9,498	9	1,696,95	531,951
2007	118,860	0	22,121	4	610,659	396,696

2004-2007 Number of Subprime Rate Loans by Investor
Source: Compliance Tech Lending Patterns

Myth: The majority of subprime loans were taken out by minority and low-income borrowers.

Fact: While minorities and low-income borrowers received a disproportionate share of subprime loans, the vast majority of subprime loans went to white and upper income borrowers.[5] In each year between 2004-2007, non-Hispanic whites had more subprime rate loans than all minorities combined.[6] (Figure 2)

African Americans and Hispanics were given subprime loans disproportionately compared with whites, according to ComplianceTech, and black borrowers are more than twice as likely to receive subprime loans than white borrowers are.[7]

Figure 2

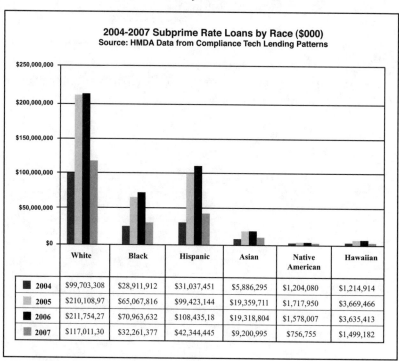

2004-2007 Subprime Rate Loans by Race ($000)
Source: HMDA Data from Compliance Tech Lending Patterns

	White	Black	Hispanic	Asian	Native American	Hawaiian
2004	$99,703,308	$28,911,912	$31,037,451	$5,886,295	$1,204,080	$1,214,914
2005	$210,108,97	$65,067,816	$99,423,144	$19,359,711	$1,717,950	$3,669,466
2006	$211,754,27	$70,963,632	$108,435,18	$19,318,804	$1,578,007	$3,635,413
2007	$117,011,30	$32,261,377	$42,344,445	$9,200,995	$756,755	$1,499,182

Figure 3

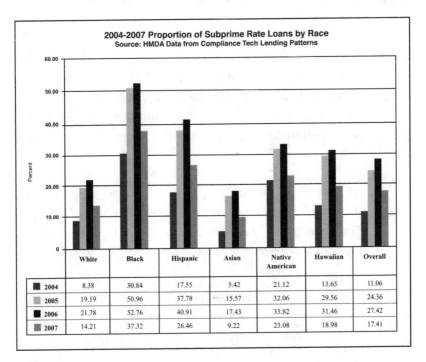

	White	Black	Hispanic	Asian	Native American	Hawaiian	Overall
2004	8.38	30.84	17.55	5.42	21.12	13.65	11.06
2005	19.19	50.96	37.78	15.57	32.06	29.56	24.36
2006	21.78	52.76	40.91	17.43	33.82	31.46	27.42
2007	14.21	37.32	26.46	9.22	23.08	18.98	17.41

For example, as Figure 3 shows, 2006, 52.76 percent of black borrowers were given subprime loans, versus 21.78 percent of whites.[8]

Myth: Most subprime loans originated in minority communities.

Fact: As shown in Figure 4, The vast majority (approximately 60 percent) of subprime rate loans were originated in largely white census tracts, i.e., census tracts less than 30 percent minority.[9]

Figure 4

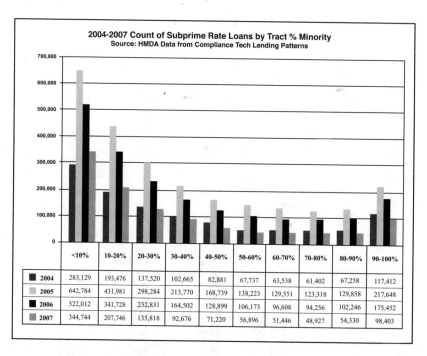

	<10%	10-20%	20-30%	30-40%	40-50%	50-60%	60-70%	70-80%	80-90%	90-100%
2004	283,129	193,476	137,520	102,665	82,881	67,737	63,538	61,402	67,258	117,412
2005	642,784	431,981	298,284	213,770	168,739	138,223	129,551	123,318	129,858	217,648
2006	522,012	341,728	232,831	164,502	128,899	106,173	96,608	94,256	102,246	175,452
2007	344,744	207,746	135,818	92,676	71,220	56,896	51,446	48,927	54,330	98,403

Myth: Most subprime loans were taken out by low-income borrowers.

Fact: Contrary to popular belief, low income borrowers had the lowest share of subprime rate loans. Upper income borrowers had the highest share of subprime rate loans during each year except 2004, where middle income borrowers had the highest share.[10] (Figure 5)

It is clear that, while certain commentators and politicians continue to insist that efforts to expand homeownership opportunities to minorities (and sometimes minorities themselves) were the root cause of the subprime crisis, the empirical data prove otherwise. These facts, if broadly disseminated, can disarm the Weapons of Mass Deception, once and for all.

Figure 5

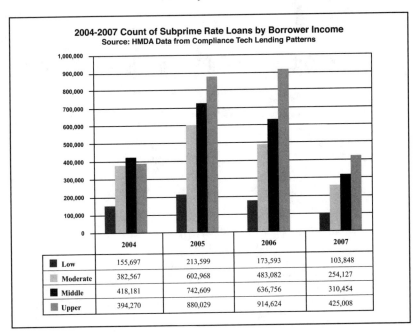

	2004	2005	2006	2007
Low	155,697	213,599	173,593	103,848
Moderate	382,567	602,968	483,082	254,127
Middle	418,181	742,609	636,756	310,454
Upper	394,270	880,029	914,624	425,008

NOTES

[1] For example, October 5, 2008 edition of "This Week with George Stephanopoulos," commentator George Will stated:

In fact, much of the crisis we're in today is because the government set out to fiddle the market. That is we had regulation, in effect, with legislation that would criminalize as racism and discrimination if you didn't lend to unproductive borrowers. Fannie Mae and Freddie Mac existed to gibber – to rig the housing market because the market would not have put people into homes they could not afford." SOURCE: Nexis

More recently, the February 20, 2009 edition of MSNBC's Morning Joe talk show, featured the following colloquy between commentator Pat Buchanan, medical analuyst Nancy Snyderman and host Joe Scarborough:

BUCHANAN: The feds, Joe, the feds leaned on banks and threatened some of these banks, "You've got to make more loans," so the banks — and pushed them out — you gotta help, frankly, in minority communities. And they pushed them out and the guys put nothing down and stuff, and then the banks sell the loans off to Fannie and Freddie.

SCARBOROUGH: And that's what happened. Banks made bad loans. They sold it to Fannie and Freddie. Fannie and Freddie sold it to Wall Street.

DR. NANCY SNYDERMAN: That's right.

SCARBOROUGH: They turned it into securities, chopped it up, sent it around the world, and here we are with the Dow Jones at its lowest rate since 1932. SOURCE: Media Matters for America, http://mediamatters.org/items/200902200006

Among other things, these examples demonstrate the need for diversity on news analyst shows called for in *Sunday Morning Apartheid (State of Black America 2007)* since it is unlikely that such comments would go unchallenged – and perhaps would not even be made – in a more racially diverse discussion.

[2] Testimony of Marc H. Morial before the Senate Committee on Banking, Housing and Urban Affairs, October 16, 2008.

[3] Home Mortgage Disclosure Act Data (HMDA) from ComplianceTech Lending Patterns.

[4] Ibid.

[5] Ibid.

[6] Ibid.

[7] Ibid.

[8] Ibid. *See also*, 2008 National Urban League Equality Index, *The State of Black America 2008* (National Urban League)

[9] HMDA Data.

[10] Ibid.

ESSAY 12

Wealth for Life

By Earl G. Graves, Jr.
Black Enterprise Magazine

Racial barriers and attitudes traditionally have complicated African Americans' path toward financial empowerment, with the ramifications reaching well beyond our earning power. However, if we are able to close the wealth gap—the stubborn imbalance in the net worth of African Americans versus that of white Americans—then we can finally begin to bridge those other persistent disparities and cure the ills that plague our community.

Make no mistake, this wealth chasm between African Americans and the majority is no mere perception; it is a stark reality. Nationally, the typical African-American family today possesses less than 10 percent of the net worth of the average white family.[1] Almost 30 percent of black families have zero or negative net worth.[2] And far fewer blacks than whites benefit from inherited wealth or assets.

Until recently, these figures represented millions of black families walking a financial tightrope. Now, with the economy in freefall—and jobs, 401Ks and available credit disappearing like vapors—our increased vulnerability has plunged many of us into a state of crisis. Some are facing bankruptcy and the possibly losing their homes, while others may never own a home because the capital and credit history necessary is so out of reach. The price to be paid for this level of economic disparity is always steep. The implications here go far beyond the welfare of the families involved, however tragic the individual circumstances. What's really at stake are the health and stability of the African-American community as a whole and the pace of our progress in America.

The new Obama administration recognizes this disparity. The president's 2010 budget, released on February 26, 2009, contains a section "Growing Imbalance: Accumulating Wealth and Closing Doors to the Middle Class," in which it is noted that the wealthiest 10 percent of households hold 70 percent of the total wealth. The combined net worth of the top one percent of families was larger than that of the bottom 90 percent and the top one percent. [3] But while it is important for the administration to advance innovative policies that close these disparities, the responsibility does not lie solely with the government.

Bottom line: If we ever hope to strengthen our families, communities and institutions, then we must adopt and apply principles to build, keep and transfer wealth.

Since its inception more than 40 years ago, *Black Enterprise* magazine has stressed economic fundamentals to our readers—saving, smart investment, the responsible leveraging of credit and home equity. At the same time, our agenda has always been informed by the social realities that inform the lives of African Americans.

In recent years, we've stepped up our efforts to help the widest possible income spectrum of African Americans gain that well-deserved slice of the American Dream with our "Black Wealth Initiative." Conceived to encourage our readers to make a firm and binding personal commitment to sound financial practices, this initiative called for participants to literally declare their financial independence, pledging to pay themselves first, make responsible home-ownership a priority, and develop a systematic program of saving and investing to secure their families for generations to come.

In framing this concept for the Black Wealth Initiative, publisher, Earl G. Graves, Sr., made the following assertion: "Our initiative must be to create wealth by building the cornerstones of economic empowerment: education, equity, enterprise and excellence. It requires that we be aggressive even to the point of zealotry."

Since we developed that program, the dynamics of wealth building have changed significantly. Wealth preservation has emerged as an even more urgent priority in the wake of the current financial crisis. In the second half of 2008, the American public has watched the financial system shaken as century-old institutions have been severely weakened or failed. The plunge in housing prices has caused some homeowners to deal with an equity deficit in which they are paying mortgages for homes that are worth less than when they first purchased the properties. The increased volatility of the stock market continues to make investors jittery and more risk averse. It's understandable considering that some market indices have tested their historic lows in recent months. For instance, in late November, the S&P 500 marked an annual decline of 48.8 percent, the worst yearly percentage drop in 80 years.[4] As for the Dow industrial average, it dipped below 8,000— its lowest level in more than a decade.[5] Along with these tumultuous times, there is a new generation of young entrants into the workforce who bring with them uncertain expectations of what the future holds.

In response to these developments, Black Enterprise has taken what we believe to be the next logical step in the evolution of our original Black Wealth Initiative. We call it Wealth for Life, and the emphasis here rests squarely on financial discipline. Through 10 newly modified principles, we offer African Americans a step-by-step guide to responsible saving, investing and spending in order to build wealth that can be passed on to future generations. Through consistent application of these principles, families will be able to establish a viable financial legacy, regardless of what the economy and financial markets look like. The 10 Wealth for Life principles are:

1. **Live within your means.** Not just African Americans, but the nation as a whole has been living precariously on credit for far too long. Well, the bill has come due, leaving millions of families drowning in sky-high interest payments. Recovery starts with making an honest assessment of income versus debts and keeping spending strictly within the bounds of what you earn.

2. **Maximize your income potential through education and training.** Whatever your profession, the need to keep pace with technology and emerging economic trends is essential to staying competitive and enhancing your value in the marketplace. Set aside space in your schedule and your budget every year for skills building – and that includes increasing your financial literacy as well.

3. **Effectively manage your budget, credit, debt and tax obligations.** It's estimated that Americans lose a significant portion of their dollars because they do not develop a budget, and the current credit crunch has made it even harder for families to access emergency capital. Only those with exemplary credit scores are able to secure home or business loans.

4. **Save at least 10 percent of your income.** If the idea of saving 10 percent seems impossible, then it's time to rethink your lifestyle and strip away nonessentials. As long as your spending exceeds your income, you will never be able to accumulate wealth. Pay yourself first.

5. **Use homeownership as a foundation for building wealth.** Even in the current downturn in the housing market, homeownership remains the key to wealth accumulation because it allows you to build equity that can be leveraged to further your financial goals. In fact, most African Americans have their assets in their home. It's essential, however, to approach homeownership responsibly. Never buy more house than you can afford and keep a sharp eye on trends that affect home value.

6. **Devise an investment plan for retirement needs and children's education.** According to a recent study on black investing conducted by Ariel Investments and Charles

Schwab, one area where African Americans are on equal footing with whites is enrollment in employer-sponsored defined contribution plans. About 90 percent of working blacks and whites participate in a 401(k) plan. Unfortunately, blacks on average contribute half as much, resulting in a far smaller nest egg than their white co-workers. At the same time, we are half as likely to identify retirement as an investment priority and lag behind when it comes to owning stocks and mutual funds. Clearly African Americans will have to adopt a more diverse, informed and disciplined approach to investing, especially if we expect to afford the ever-rising cost of higher education for our children.

7. **Ensure that your entire family adheres to sensible money management principles.** You're never too young or too old to learn the value of a dollar and how to spend responsibly. View your child's weekly allowance or that first savings account as an opportunity to impart valuable lessons in how to save, invest and build on the money they earn.

8. **Support the creation and growth of minority-owned businesses.** At a time when an African American of out-standing ability and character can be elected president, there are no more excuses when it comes to finding African-American ventures deserving of our patronage and investment. We are always stronger in partnership than when we stand alone.

9. **Guarantee that your wealth is passed on to future generations through proper insurance and estate planning.** When it comes to the creation and nurturing of wealth, the generational barrier may be the last, great hurdle for African Americans. Now's the time to sit down

with a smart estate planner to ensure that you will pass on to your children a legacy to build on instead of debts.

10. **Strengthen your community through philanthropy.** Success, ultimately, is the opportunity to give back. Remember, the civil rights movement didn't just happen; it was largely underwritten by African-American entrepreneurs. As successful as these men and women were as individuals, they saw it as their responsibility to contribute to the social advancement of African Americans as a whole. Today, we need these same types of social, economic and political partnerships if we are to overcome the many challenges we face. Economic success and financial independence give us the power and the freedom to be effective, valued partners in this shared effort.

These 10 principles are designed as a set of guidelines for creating wealth in the midst of the day's economic challenges—wealth that can be maintained and passed on for the benefit of future generations. Much like the times we find ourselves in, they demand our vigilance and sacrifice, and our commitment to success over the long haul.

Wealth building is not a sprint; it's a marathon. It's a race that is in our power to win.

NOTES

[1] *The State of Black America* 2009, Equality Index, page 27

[2] "Breaking Asset Poverty: Better Homeownership—and More," *Shelterforce*, published by the National Housing Institute

[3] "A New Era of Responsibility: Renewing America's Promise," Office of Management and Budget, www.budget.gov, p. 9.

[4] "Market's Fall Deepens as Concerns Mount on Banks," Wall Street Journal, November 21, 2008

[5] "Dow Jones Drops Below 8,000 on Bank Worries," International Herald Tribune, January 20, 2008

The Fullness of Time for a More Perfect Union: The Movement Continues...

By Gwendolyn Grant
Urban League of Kansas City, Missouri

On November 4, 2008, Americans decided whether to look toward an optimistic future or remain trapped in a worn out past. We chose hope over fear, and change over stagnation. We rejected the notion of a fractured nation and reached out for a more perfect union.

Here we are—390 years since Africans first came here in chains; 233 years after our Founding Fathers signed the Constitution, our nation's birth certificate; 145 years since Lincoln's Emancipation Proclamation and 44 years since Johnson signed the Civil Rights Act—having elected the first African-American President of the United States.

We've awakened to a world unlike anything we could have ever imagined. Dr. King said, "Occasionally in life there are those moments of unutterable fulfillment which cannot be completely explained by those symbols called words. Their meanings can only be articulated by the inaudible language of the heart." Such is our moment, and as the preacher often says, "It is the fullness of time, and the time is now."

Now! Now is the clarion call to act in the face of enormous challenges: a disintegrating global economic system, crumbling schools, collapsing roads, insane health system, whole countries going bankrupt, entire industries failing, and, meanwhile, we have overextended ourselves militarily all over the globe. In the face of mounting troubles, it is our responsibility as leaders to change the course and conscience of our country. We have done it before, as then-Senator Obama reminded us during the announcement speech of his candidacy for the U.S. presidency in Springfield, Illinois, on February 10, 2007:

> *The genius of our founders is that they designed a system of government that can be changed. And we should take heart, because we've changed this country before. In the face of tyranny, a band of patriots brought an Empire to its knees. In the face of secession, we unified a nation and set the captives free. In the face of Depression, we put people back to work and lifted millions out of poverty. We welcomed immigrants to our shores, we opened railroads to the west, we landed a man on the moon, and we heard a King's call to let justice roll down like water, and righteousness like a mighty stream.*

Avoid Complacency

I believe that with the right plan and moral vision, we will become an even greater nation as we emerge from the crucible once again. But as I look back at the great popular movements in our nation's history, I fear that with the election of the first black president, we may fall prey to a false sense of accomplishment and self-satisfaction, and that apathy and complacency may set in. However, instead of reigniting the movement, I fear that this monumental event may cause the fight to falter before the unfinished work is completed.

Consider the women's suffrage movement, which fought for the right of women to vote. Though the vote was merely the starting point, the movement lost steam after the Nineteenth Amendment granted women the right to vote in 1920. Another example is the slavery abolition movement, which struggled until the passage of the Thirteenth Amendment in 1865. Though legal liberty represented the very first step in the long struggle, the broader movement for civil rights for blacks was somehow muted.

Even when we consider the great Civil Rights Movement of the fifties and sixties, we are reminded that it too stalled with the passage of civil rights legislation, the faint promise of integration, and the murder of its most prominent leaders: Martin, Medgar and Malcolm. Since then, we have seen our communities crumble, our schools disintegrate, our children failed, our justice jailed and our economics curtailed.

So as we move past this historic moment, let us not repeat the history of our greatest popular movements and allow injustice to prevail, simply because a black family lives in the White House. We must use this moment to reinvigorate the movement and reengage the nation in a struggle to finish the job of equality, liberty and justice for all.

Toward that end, I'd like to propose a modest three-pronged approach to the challenges of leadership that lie ahead for the Urban League and all organizations committed to achieving justice in America. Fashioned after the great Obama campaign, the new movement should be built on three key elements: *idealistic pragmatism, participatory interdependence* and *personal responsibility.*

Idealistic Pragmatism

As we've marveled at Obama all these many months, one characteristic of his leadership style stands out: *idealistic pragmatism,* a blend of principled ideas with a practical, non-dogmatic approach to problem solving. Obama repeated that chorus of optimism in his speech on election night:

> *So let us summon a new spirit of patriotism; of service and responsibility where each of us resolves to pitch in and work harder; and look after not only ourselves, but each other. Let us remember. . .in this country, we rise or fall as one nation; as one people.*

He reminded us that, while we must have the audacity to hope, hollow rhetoric without work is a mockery of idealism, and that ideological rigidity will lead to paralysis. During the campaign, he often compromised to the chagrin of many progressives on a range of issues and was never bombastic. And we too, as leaders, must reject the politics of confrontation.

Let us build coalitions between corporations and social service agencies. Let's consider how we can work with churches without disrespecting their values. Let's stop fighting with politicians, and join hands together by showing how we all share common goals of fairness, opportunity and access to all, because cooperation and collaboration are the watchwords of the day. We cannot conquer these enormous tasks alone, so we must find friends and build relationships knowing that many hands working together will lighten the workload. Dare to dream but get the job done. This is the model that achieved the unimaginable election of President Obama and which should guide us on to even greater achievement.

In this spirit of pragmatism and coalition building, we need to confront the everyday issues facing the community. Specifically, we need to address the glaring gaps in equality, which continue to plague urban and disadvantaged communities. We certainly don't have to look far for a blueprint. We can build on the cornerstones and guiding principles of the National Urban League's *Opportunity Compact*. The goals are clear: opportunity for children to thrive, opportunity to have a job with a living wage, opportunity to have safe, affordable housing, and opportunity to prosper with businesses of our own. These fundamental issues must remain our focus as we seek to close the gaps in education, income, wealth and health. If we forsake these fundamentals, the election of Obama will only have symbolic meaning.

Certainly, we can deploy some of the same tactics used by the Obama campaign, considered one of the best-organized campaigns ever. We too have to get back to that word which has always been central to the movement: *organize*. We need to get back to the basics of organizing with a contemporary twist: Internet-based organization—which brings people together, allows for shared information and resources, and provides the backbone joining forces efficiently. Consequently, we must upgrade our movement to reflect new technology and shifting demographics.

Idealism, pragmatism, organization and coalition building, and problem solving at the local level—such are the elements for the new empowerment agenda today.

Participatory Interdependence

Another major theme of this historic election is *participatory interdependence.* The Obama coalition was broad and deep—a multi-racial, multi-ethnic, multi-generational, cross-gender and cross-regional coalition. It reflected the rich diversity of America, one of our most important and unique attributes. He inspired more people to vote and expanded the electorate by millions. He earned unprecedented support from whites, women, Hispanics, young people, new voters and lapsed voters from all income levels and socio-economic levels, who joined together, got involved and dared to change the world.

Though not a new concept, participatory interdependence has given way to cynicism and apathy. Therefore, it is our task as leaders to rekindle a spirit of involvement and higher purpose, recognizing, as Dr. King reminded us, "I can never be what I ought to be until you are what you ought to be. This is the way our world is made. No individual or nation can stand out boasting of being independent. We are interdependent."

This is the core challenge of leadership for the New Movement, and Obama has shown us how. Activate young people with realness and motivate working people for a common cause. Rally everyday people to care, to act and to change the world, one heart at a time. Dare them to dream, because we must communicate common cause and not emphasize parochial and partisan differences. Excellent schools, fair courts, working roads and bridges, universal health care and a thriving economy are important to all Americans.

"Our destinies are tied together," as Dr. King once said. "There is not a separate black path to power and fulfillment that does not have to intersect with white roots. Somewhere along the way, the two must join together, black and white together, we shall overcome."

175

Personal Responsibility

The third pillar of the new movement is personal responsibility, which has always played a central role in our struggle. After all, who else can we rely on but ourselves? Obama addressed this issue at the National Urban League's Annual Conference last year:

> *That's why your opportunity agenda is a 'Compact' —not a guarantee, not a promise—but a call to responsibility. Because we know that government can't solve all our problems, and government can't and shouldn't do for us what we should be doing for ourselves: raising our kids the right way, being good neighbors and good citizens, becoming leaders in our industries and communities. We know that the American dream isn't something that happens to you—it's something you strive for and work for and seize with your own two hands. And we've got a responsibility as a nation to keep that dream alive for all of our people.*

But I'm also reminded of what Dr. King said about self-reliance at a Passion Sunday sermon at the National Cathedral in Washington in 1968: "It's all right to tell a man to lift himself by his own bootstraps, but it is a cruel jest to say to a bootless man that he ought to lift himself by his own bootstraps."

So while we fight for better schools, fair wages, universal health care and equal opportunity, we must reemphasize self-reliance, especially to our youth by modeling self-reliance in our communities and personal lives. That has been the heartbeat of the civil rights movement; it is the spirit of all great movements, and it is the path to change.

Race and the Constitution

One hundred years ago, W. E. B. DuBois said, "the problem of the 20th century is the problem of the color line." Unfortunately, as the data show, it still is! In his trailblazing book, *A More Perfect Union*

— *Advancing New American Rights*, Rep. Jesse L. Jackson, Jr. argues for a permanent solution: through a set of Constitutional amendments guaranteeing that all Americans have equal opportunity, full employment, living wages, universal health care, affordable housing and a quality education from preschool to college. Until then, the dream of a more perfect union will be postponed.

We've arrived at an amazing moment in America, and we are on the brink of enormous change, spurred on by catastrophic challenges. It is the fullness of time, ripe and ready to explode into a new universe. And from this vantage point, we can finally see a more perfect union here in America with liberty and justice for all, the promise of our forefathers, and our birthright as Americans. Obama is evidence of the audacity of hope for a greater America to come, but we must be the heroes and initiate the change we want to see. We don't have to wait for destiny, because the future started yesterday, and we're already late. The movement continues...

REPORT FROM
THE NATIONAL URBAN LEAGUE POLICY INSTITUTE

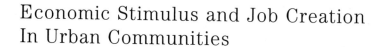

Economic Stimulus and Job Creation In Urban Communities

By Valerie Rawlston Wilson, Ph.D.
and Bernard E. Anderson, Ph.D.

I n July 2007, the National Urban League released its *Opportunity Compact,* a comprehensive set of recommendations designed to empower all Americans to be full participants in the economic and social mainstream of this nation. *The Opportunity Compact* identified four cornerstones that reflect the values represented by the American dream: 1) *The Opportunity to Thrive* (Children and Families); 2) *The Opportunity to Earn* (Jobs); 3) *The Opportunity to Own* (Housing and Asset Development); and 4) *The Opportunity to Prosper* (Entrepreneurship) and set forth 10 specific recommendations for advancing them.[1] Among other things, *The Opportunity Compact* offered a vigorous plan for creating sustainable jobs in urban communities through such mechanisms as an Urban Infrastructure Bank to fund reinvestments in our cities and an increased investment in job training and "second chance" programs.

The *Compact* and its recommendations were endorsed by several presidential candidates, including then-Senator Barack Obama, whose campaign platform included all ten of the *Compact's* recommendations.[2]

When the economy declined drastically in the fall of 2008, the National Urban League renewed its call for a concerted effort to create jobs in urban America. In December 2008, the League offered the President-Elect and Congress its Economic Recovery Plan to help stabilize the economy. Broadly speaking, this plan recommended that at least three things be done to spur the economy:

1) focus on *immediate* relief;
2) create jobs that are sustainable; and
3) train people for industries that are producing jobs.

At a time when 11.6 million people are unemployed, and that number continues to rise everyday, the passage and President Obama's signing of the American Recovery and Reinvestment Act in February 2009 is a significant step toward getting people back to work and getting our country back on its feet. At the heart of the President's stimulus plan is $575 billion in new spending for aid programs, such as extended unemployment benefits and food stamps, and for projects intended to save or create 3.5 to 4 million jobs, largely related to infrastructure and energy. This spending includes $100 billion in education funding, of which $53.6 billion is designated for a state fiscal stabilization fund. The plan will also provide almost $212 billion in tax cuts for individuals and businesses.

Overall, the National Urban League is pleased with this legislation which goes a long way toward meeting some of our recommendations for addressing the foreclosure crisis, rebuilding our urban infrastructure, and increasing the investment in workforce development programs. While this is an important first step, the current trends in urban employment demonstrate that much more needs to be done to create and sustain jobs in America's urban communities.

Trends in Urban Employment

The economic recovery that took place between November 2001 and December 2007 significantly lagged behind previous recoveries in terms of job creation.[3] Not only was monthly job creation lower than it was during previous recoveries, but job growth has also trailed monthly labor force and population growth since November 2001. The consequences of this slower job creation have been particularly grave for urban youth and other economically disadvantaged groups.

As reported in the November 9, 2008 edition of the *New York Times*, "...the hardships of the gathering recession are sweeping down to hurt the working poor and younger job seekers most of all...especially black males in their late teens or early 20s without more than a high-school education." By contrast, the economic expansion of the 1990s, the longest peacetime boom on record, brought unemployment rates below 4 percent in more than four out of ten metropolitan areas[4] and created 22 million new jobs between 1993 and 2000.[5] During this time, young men—especially young African-American men—in labor markets with continuously low unemployment rates—experienced a boost in employment and earnings.[6] Whereas there was marked improvement in the employment-population ratio (increased) and unemployment rate (decreased) of black teens from 1993-2000, the opposite has been true since 2001.[7]

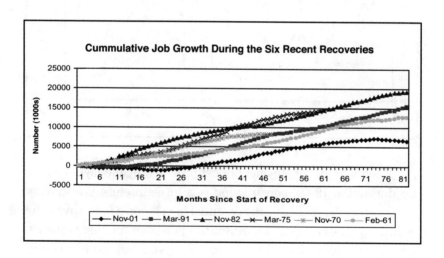

181

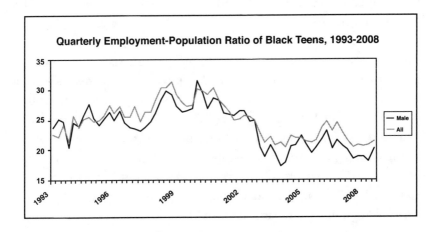

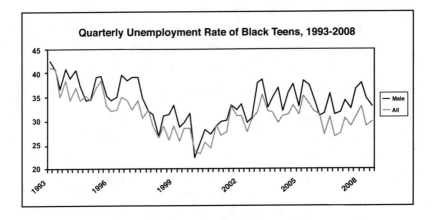

Much like the employment boost provided by the high-tech sector during the 1990s, construction (via infrastructure investments) and green-collar jobs have the potential to usher in a new wave of job growth in this country. However, the potential for this growth to have an immediate impact on the unemployed in urban communities will be limited by the fact that jobs created through infrastructure investments take time to materialize. Also, it will take time for disadvantaged workers, many of whom lack a high school diploma or have a limited skill set, to acquire the skill and education necessary to compete for many of the new energy and green-collar jobs. Even in the long-run, unless the needs of this group are specifically addressed, many will not have the opportunity to contribute or benefit from economic growth.

Proposals for Fiscal Stimulus Job Creation

The American Recovery and Reinvestment Act is an important first step on the road to revitalizing our urban communities and addressing the needs of disadvantaged workers. However, it only went part of the way and more must be done to ensure that this population is an essential part of the nation's recovery efforts. History has taught us that, unless this population is specifically targeted in legislation, these individuals are unlikely to be hired and helped.

Therefore, the National Urban League calls upon President Obama and the United States Congress to move forward with economic recovery and jobs legislation and policies that accomplish the following:

1. Increase funding for proven and successful models of workforce training and job placement for under-skilled workers between the ages of 16 and 30 such as the Department of Labor's "Responsible Reintegration of Youthful Offenders."

- Non-profit national intermediaries, including national minority non-profit intermediaries, with a demonstrated track record of effectiveness in serving this targeted population should be explicitly utilized to ensure a timely and effective use of training funds. The country cannot afford to fund only state and local governments as a means of job training and job creation. Often it takes months, and even years, for these dollars to hit the streets after federal and local RFPs are issued.

2. Direct a percentage of all infrastructure monies to job training, job placement and job preparation for disadvantaged workers.

3. Target workforce investment dollars to the construction industry jobs that an infrastructure program will create and, where reigniting the construction industry is a goal, pre-apprenticeship programs must be funded in that sector.

4. Fund infrastructure development for public building construction and renovations of schools, community centers, libraries, recreation centers, parks, etc., that will rebuild and revitalize urban communities.

- Funding infrastructure of this type can be accomplished by increasing funding for the Community Development Block Grant (CBDG) public facilities program that is authorized under existing law that allows for construction of public facilities and improvements for eligible purposes.

5. Re-establish a temporary Public Service Employment (PSE) program aimed at creating 150,000 – 200,000 jobs in urban areas to forestall a reduction in public services and an increase in job losses;

- The precedent for such a program is The Emergency Jobs and Unemployment Assistance Act of 1974 which established title VI of the Comprehensive Employment and Training Act (CETA) as a temporary countercyclical program of public service employment. By June of 1975, this program was responsible for providing jobs for 155,000 people. Two years later, President Carter's 1977 economic stimulus package added $4 billion for PSE to the fiscal year 1978 budget, resulting in jobs for 10 percent of all unemployed persons in the labor force. A field evaluation of PSE programs revealed that roughly 85 percent of PSE jobs represented new job creation as opposed to job displacement and for every 100 PSE dollars 86 went to directly stimulating the economy through paying salaries.

Though the program was initially intended to combat cyclical employment, research indicates that in many jurisdictions, the program showed potential for alleviating structural employment. PSE workers were also found to provide important primary services to local communities.[8] The majority of jobs created were lower-skilled, making them accessible to urban youth and others with less of education.

Conclusion

As we rebuild our economy with more and better paying jobs, we also must consider a large segment of the population that is often forgotten—those who are out of school and out of work who are not prepared to compete in a strong global economy. Because these conditions result in lost economic input, higher dependency on government programs and an increase in crime, among other things, failure to address their needs is detrimental, not only to these individuals, but to the entire country. Therefore, it is imperative that when we go to work rebuilding America, those who live in urban America are not left behind.

NOTES

[1] 1) Commit to mandatory early childhood education beginning at age three as well as guarantee access to college for all; 2) Close the gaps in the health insurance system to ensure universal healthcare for all children; 3) Establish policies that provide tools for working families to become economically self-sufficient; 4) Create an urban infrastructure bank to fund reinvestment in urban communities (e;g; parks, schools, roads); 5) Increase economic self-sufficiency by indexing the minimum wage to the rate of inflation and expanding the Earned Income Tax Credit to benefit more working families; 6) Expand "second chance" programs for high school drop outs, ex-offenders and at-risk youth to secure GEDs, job training and employment; 7) Adopt the "Homebuyer's Bill of Rights" as recommended by the National Urban League;

8) Reform public housing to assure continuing national commitment to low-income families; 9) Strongly enforce federal minority business opportunity goals to ensure greater minority participation in government contracting; 10) Build capacity of minority business through expansion of micro-financing, equity financing and the development of strategic alliances with major corporations. *The Opportunity Compact*, available at www.nul.org. *See, also, The State of Black America 2008* (National Urban League, 2008).

[2] "Renewing America's Promise," 2008 Democratic National Platform, http://www.democrats.org/a/party/platform.html

[3] Source: Nonfarm Payroll Establishment data. U.S. Department of Labor, Bureau of Labor Statistics (www.bls.gov). Each series is benchmarked to the start of its recovery as defined by the NBER Business Cycle Dating Committee.

[4] Rodgers, William M. III. "A Critical Assessment of Skills Explanations of Black-White Employment and Wage Gaps." *The State of Black America 1999* (National Urban League, 1999).

[5] Anderson, Bernard E. "The Black Worker: Continuing Quest for Economic Parity." *The State of Black America 2002* (National Urban League, 2002).

[6] Freeman, Richard B. and William M. Rodgers, III. "Area Economic Conditions and the Labor Market Outcomes of Young Men in the 1990s Expansion." NBER Working Paper #7073 (NBER, Inc., 1999).

[7] Source: Bureau of Labor Statistics (www.bls.gov)

[8] Nathan, Richard P., et al. *Public Service Employment: A Field Evaluation* (Brookings Institution, 1981).

NATIONAL URBAN LEAGUE RECOMMENDATIONS

OPPORTUNITY TO THRIVE

Education

1. Fully fund No Child Left Behind (NCLB), ensure that all monies authorized are appropriated to reach all eligible children and close the equality gap by ending resource inequities in our schools.

2. Require states to compare and publicly report resources available to achieve a sound and basic education for every child in every school.

3. Replace Annual Yearly Progress (AYP) with a Comprehensive Accountability Framework that can more accurately capture student performance using multiple measures of achievement;

4. Enact a federal teacher and principal supply policy to identify and support highly qualified and effective teachers and leaders for all students;

5. Establish a private right of action that gives parents and other concerned parties the ability to hold districts, states, and the U.S. Department of Education accountable for implementing the requirements of NCLB;

6. Guarantee that all three- and four-year olds have access to full day, developmentally appropriate, high quality early childhood education;

7. Change Supplemental Education Services (SES) eligibility requirements to offer immediate academic support to all students not "proficient;"

8. Provide increased funding to states for SES and require districts to provide academic support to ALL eligible students;

9. Create a new federal secondary school improvement fund to support low-performing middle and high schools;

10 Increase funds to provide for more meaningful, understandable and timely information regarding key school and student performance data.

Health

1. Implement a comprehensive and universal health insurance system for all Americans;

2. Develop a comprehensive health infrastructure for the delivery of health education, prevention and intervention initiatives for African Americans;

3. Conduct a thorough examination of the criminal justice system as it relates to treatment and rehabilitation of African-American males;

4. Examine chronic health conditions in a context of economic, sociologic and environmental contributors;

5. Increase the Career Pipeline and Access for Minorities in the Health Professions.

OPPORTUNITY TO EARN

1. Increase funding for proven and successful models of workforce training and job placement for under-skilled workers between the ages of 16 and 30 such as the Department of Labor's "Responsible Reintegration of Youthful Offenders."

2. Direct a percentage of all infrastructure monies to job training, job placement and job preparation for disadvantaged workers.

3. Target workforce investment dollars to the construction industry jobs that an infrastructure program will create and, where reigniting the construction industry is a goal, pre-apprenticeship programs must be funded in that sector.

4. Fund infrastructure development for public building construction and renovations of schools, community centers, libraries, recreation centers, parks, etc., that will rebuild and revitalize urban communities.

5. Re-establish a temporary Public Service Employment (PSE) program aimed at creating 150,000 – 200,000 jobs in urban areas to forestall a reduction in public services and an increase in job losses;

OPPORTUNITY TO OWN

Pass a "Homebuyers' Bill of Rights" that:

1. Funds homeownership education and counseling, financial literacy workshops, credit counseling, fair housing

advocacy and foreclosure prevention assistance that uses national minority housing intermediaries with a track record of providing effective counseling assistance in underserved minority urban communities;

2. Provides for Individual Development Accounts for home-ownership administered by employers as matched savings plans for the future purchase of a home and offer housing tax credits for people below a certain income level.

3. Strengthens the Community Reinvestment Act (CRA) as it is applied to banks and expands its reach to non-bank financial institutions in to encourage banks to respond to a variety of needs in low- and moderate-income communities and enforce stricter standards that eliminate incentives for predatory loans and provides greater transparency.

4. Creates a HUD Task Force to vigorously investigate and prosecute violations of fair-housing laws and authorize congressional oversight hearings to hold HUD accountable.

5. Demystifies the credit reporting system through creation of a public education and awareness campaign about credit scoring and its impact on wealth creation, and establishment of a penalty structure for credit reporting bureaus that maintain inaccurate client files.

6. Reauthorizes and improves HOPE VI.

OPPORTUNITY TO PROSPER

1. Restore and Make Permanent the Small Business Administration's Community Express Loan Program.

2. Continue Funding for the New Market Tax Credit Program Beyond 2009.

3. Strengthen and Enforce Federal Minority Business Opportunity Goals in Government Contracting.

4. Expand the Number of Small Minority Businesses Involved in STEM (Science, Technology, Engineering and Math).

5. Develop an Affordable National Health Insurance Option.

The Congressional Black Caucus and President Barack Obama: Speaking With One Voice to Fill the Moral Gaps in Our World

By Congresswoman Barbara Lee

To understand the mission of the Congressional Black Caucus (CBC) is to understand what government is supposed to be in America. Government has two moral missions: protection and empowerment. Protection includes military and police protection, but also worker, consumer and environmental protection. Empowerment includes building and maintaining infrastructure, education, the economy and the court system. No one can make a living in America without protection and empowerment by the government.

Since America is a democracy, the government has a further moral mission to ensure that government protection and empowerment extends equally to everyone—that is *moral equality*. Where there is a major disparity between rich and poor or between one race or gender and another, there is a moral gap. Consequently, the job of government in America is to help fill in the moral gaps.

The African-American community knows those moral gaps intimately. The CBC has documented those disparities, and in every case, they are greatest for African Americans—education, healthcare, jobs, housing and homeownership, civil rights, the environment, and much more. To fill in these gaps for African Americans would be to fill them in for *all* Americans.

For 40 years, the Congressional Black Caucus has sought moral equality for African Americans and ultimately all Americans. The CBC has led the Congress on issues, with intelligence, commitment and power. It has been, and continues to be, the conscience of the Congress and the voice for the voiceless.

Though we face the dawning of a new day, the moral gaps left behind by the Bush Administration are huge. Yet with the ascension of a former member of the Congressional Black Caucus, Barack Obama, to the Presidency at a time of crisis for America, we have both new challenges and new opportunities.

President Barack Obama and the CBC share a common agenda that at its root seeks to fill the moral gaps in this country, and President Obama has sent out a clarion call for unity. The CBC must heed that call for unity while acknowledging that race is still a factor in America that must be addressed. We are confident that President Obama and the CBC will speak with one voice, and unify our country around this common agenda.

We recognize that there are three branches of government—legislative, executive and judicial—that are central to our democracy. In order for us to achieve our goals, everyone must play their part and work in concert for the greater good of all people. Once we have achieved that harmony, only then can we begin to fill the moral gaps.

Together, we must turn around the economy and build a workforce for the 21st century, provide healthcare and quality education for all, tackle poverty head on and provide meaningful opportunity for all, end the war in Iraq, restore our nation's standing in the world, and above all treat all people with human dignity.

Treating people with human dignity requires us to prioritize the establishment of healthy communities. Healthy communities are created by the presence of jobs, education, healthcare and a clean environment. As members of Congress, we recognize the role of government to empower communities and create opportunities. As individuals, we affirm the responsibility of each person to our families and our neighbors. To measure success or failure in America is to measure it in our communities.

Our first priority is to work toward economic empowerment within African-American communities. Jobs along with sound businesses, housing and agriculture are the bedrock of economic empowerment. To achieve this empowerment, government must be committed like never before to strengthening our economy. From there, we will work to ensure that people of color are able to benefit from newly implemented public infrastructure and economic development projects through workforce training, green jobs for future industries, and funds to help formally incarcerated individuals transition back into our communities and workforce. Additionally, there must also be increased support for small, minority- and women-owned businesses which generate a number of jobs in this country.

Housing will also be a key to the economic empowerment of African Americans. Everyone should be able to live in a safe and affordable home and neighborhood, but the foreclosure crisis and the lack of affordable housing has crippled the only means which has consistently afforded African Americans the opportunity to create wealth. The CBC has long called on our government to address this issue, and now that it has reached a catastrophic level, we must have a continued effort to stem this problem and put in place programs that will help keep people in their homes and create opportunities for new homeowners to realize the American dream.

Health and wellness must be paramount in our communities. We must eliminate healthcare disparities and make high quality, affordable healthcare accessible for all. African Americans are disproportionately affected by some of the most fatal diseases including cancer, diabetes, cardiovascular disease and HIV/AIDS. We will work to address these tremendous and deadly disparities by supporting the establishment of the Disparity and Minority Health Research Center at the National Institutes of Health, work to create a comprehensive national HIV/AIDS strategy and support programs, like the Minority AIDS Initiative, that directly address the problem. Additionally, we will commit to supporting minority health professional schools, HBCUs, and other minority serving institutions and organizations to help strengthen their infrastructure and ensure their viability. This coupled with increased emphasis on prevention and increased care for our seniors and the disabled will help to bridge the health disparities gap in communities of color.

There must also be a renewed interest in parenting and creating strong, stable families. President Obama has shown the way in his Father's Day speech in 2008. Parenting, he pointed out, requires what our country requires: responsibility for ourselves and our children and a commitment to excellence so that as we work to better ourselves we become shining examples for our children to emulate.

There is no greater way to foster healthy communities than by empowering young men and women to be responsible, self-reliant participants in their families and communities. We must focus attention and resources on young black men and women that have become disconnected and marginalized from society. Government and communities must be there to support them through job training, early childhood education programs, and day care programs, all of which are necessary for strong, stable families.

There must be a total reinvestment in our communities including increased funding to provide access to a quality education for all, infrastructure development and redevelopment, investment in science and technology and a commitment to service. The "No Child Left Behind" law must be reformed so students are not focused solely on testing but are given a comprehensive curriculum that includes financial literacy, creative arts and the appropriate preparation for higher education. Our roads, bridges and sewer systems are crumbling. There is an urgent need to fortify our infrastructure so we will not have to witness another tragedy like that of the collapse of the Mississippi River Bridge in Minnesota or the devastation of Hurricanes Katrina and Rita. Greater investment in new technologies will help to restore our communities and allow us to live cleaner, greener and more environmentally sound lives. And we must recommit ourselves to the service of others. Our communities will not prosper without a large investment of human kindness.

We will continue to push for civil rights by focusing on a full count of African Americans in the census, funding for community reentry programs, voting rights and voting reform as well as the establishment of voting rights for the District of Columbia and a presidential vote for American citizens living in the territories. Additionally, our caucus will advocate for the consideration of more African Americans for judicial appointments and nominations and administration positions.

Lastly, we will work to strengthen our relationships with other countries so that the United States can again be respected in the world. To do so, we must help bring about a responsible and swift end to the war in Iraq along with providing additional support for our troops and veterans. We must also bring a renewed focus to Africa and the Caribbean, including the genocide in Darfur, the humanitarian crisis in Haiti and Zimbabwe, and the overall needs of these regions to address global poverty and deadly diseases like HIV/AIDS, Tuberculosis and Malaria.

The Congressional Black Caucus is without question ready and willing to work with President Obama. The road ahead will not be easy, but the 42 members of the Congressional Black Caucus recognize the magnitude of this moment. We will work with President Obama, his administration and Congress to turn these obstacles into opportunities as we seek to fill these moral gaps.

COMMENTARY

If Not For Me...Then For My Children

By David J. Johns

Brother President,

I am proud of you and celebrate your accomplishment of becoming our first African-American president. In addition to your other notable achievements, your shattering of this particular ceiling will have an indelible impact upon generations who toiled for the privileges entrusted to a chosen few and a generation of young people who will never know that the thought of a black president was once inconceivable.

I recall the stories of Frederick Douglass, Malcolm X and so many African-American men and women who were told that their aspirations to become "successful" were unrealistic. But today, I smile at the thought of the student I met at a Boys and Girls Club of America gala, whose stomach swelled when he screamed at the top of his 9-year-old lungs, "I want to be president when I grow up!"

Thank you for making the image of an intelligent and successful black man "cool" and thereby validating young people who participate in student government and find joy in searching for library books. I cannot wait to see how many more children will think it is "cool" to excel in school, simply because they want to be like Barack Obama.

Thank you for underscoring the importance of learning both through your personal commitment to higher education and through efforts such as your campaign pledge of $10 billion dollars for early childhood education and your congressional work to improve summer learning opportunities and support predominantly black institutions. With your accomplishments in mind, as you formally begin to shape your administrative legacy, I urge you make early childhood education a key priority. The commitment you have made to your family and your role as a father make this request especially relevant and critical.

Thank you for shattering the myth that black men are not fathers and do not participate in the institution of marriage. Thank you for caring for your wife, Michelle, and your daughters, Sasha and Malia, as if providing for them is the most important thing you will ever do in your lifetime. Images of you and your loving family are particularly powerful when stories of absent fathers and the damage resulting from broken black homes are frequently recycled in the news and in popular culture. It does not help that these stories are often reinforced by personal experience. While celebrating you and your family, it is especially important that we remember and acknowledge unnamed men who gracefully carry out the duties associated with responsible manhood every day. We must also acknowledge that, according to the Children's Defense Fund, every minute a baby is born to a teen mother and every 21 seconds a baby is born to an unmarried mother. Each day in America, 292 black babies are born to teen mothers and 1,202 are born to unmarried mothers. Too many of these children and countless others experience life without the comfort of a father's embrace or the stability that often accompanies a father's unbounded love. This is why as a father and as our president, you must call upon this country to recommit to investing in our children.

It is imperative that your thought leadership and attention remain focused on establishing and supporting agencies, individuals and entities charged with ensuring that every child is provided with early opportunities to learn and prepare for success in school and in life. Children are our most precious resource. It is our responsibility to ensure that they can realize the dreams we dare them to dream, as well as the ones we hold on to ourselves. To do this, we must ensure that all children are supported in early learning and development. While parents and communities play a pivotal role in the development and success of children, government also has a responsibility to create environments and provide opportunities that are stimulating and supportive. As we make critical investments in our economic infrastructure, it would be unwise and narrow-minded not to recognize and appropriately fund early childhood education. Quality early learning programs have been shown to produce greater academic success, decrease referrals to special education programs, as well as provide greater economic success and positive social relationships in adulthood. These investments are necessary to maintain our national economy and to bolster our workforce.

Brother President, we stand at a precipice. Your administration and this critical juncture in our history provide us with an opportunity to re-envision the system through which we educate our children. Responding to the changes in our economy and social practices as well as to the demands of a technology-rich, global society requires that we do the work to truly identify how parents and community members are empowered to provide stimulating and nurturing opportunities for all children, regardless of race, class or any other distinguishing characteristic. These opportunities must begin during a child's formative years and extend throughout a student's time in school. Your leadership and commitment to ensuring that public education reform begins with an early commitment to children is an essential component of rebuilding and strengthening our social fabric, our economy and our country.

Beyond the moral responsibility we have to end the cyclical quest to determine just which group of children are being left behind, we owe it to ourselves and to the promise of achieving the American Dream to devise a system in which all children are fully prepared to succeed in school and in life. This process begins with ensuring that every child is supported in his or her earliest years. I can think of nothing more important than conveying my desire for my future children, for your children, and for *all* children to have the opportunities that we have had; the opportunity to develop a love for learning and to truly realize our dreams.

November 4, 2008: An Ode to Black America

By Michelle D. Bernard, J.D.

Lynchings, beatings, rape, water hoses and epithets such as "boy," "nigger," "bitch" and "whore." These are but a few of the many indignities that African Americans suffered on the path to freedom and equality in the United States.

The 2008 election forever changed America and wiped away these sins. In many respects, it was an emotional cleansing of all of the injustices we faced as a people since the first slave ships landed on the shores of this great nation of ours. Whatever one's partisan preference, the symbolic result is one that all Americans should celebrate. But the election was an especially powerful affirmation of the moral worth and human dignity of black Americans, and especially black men.

The United States was imperfectly born. As British author Samuel Johnson caustically asked of the American revolutionaries: "How is it that we hear the loudest *yelps* for liberty among the drivers of Negroes?" Thus, the U.S. has always presented two faces to black Americans: The enormous promise of prosperity and freedom and the bitter limits on enjoying that prosperity and freedom. Black men fought in America's wars but were not eligible to be full citizens in America. The United States styled itself a city on a hill setting an example to the world, even as it denied its black citizens the liberties that the country claimed to represent.

African Americans have long recognized this national hypocrisy. Frederick Douglass gave voice to these sentiments in a celebrated address on July 4, 1852. America's founders were "great" and "brave" men, he explained; "statesmen, patriots and heroes, and for the good they did, and the principles they contended for, I will unite with you to honor their memory." But the promise of the nation they helped create had not been fulfilled. "What, to the American slave, is your 4th of July," he asked? Douglass answered with sadness: "To him, your celebration is a sham; your boasted liberty, an unholy license; your national greatness, swelling vanity; your sounds of rejoicing are empty and heartless; your denunciation of tyrants, brass-fronted impudence; your shouts of liberty and equality, hollow mockery."

What Frederick Douglass said was true in 1852. And, far more shockingly, it was still true 100 years later. But today is a new day. After November 4, Frederick Douglass would have to say something much different about America.

Racism has not disappeared, and discrimination still occurs. America's promise remains only imperfectly fulfilled. That will always be the case with imperfect human beings and the imperfect nations which they create. However, America finally has proved that any citizen can do anything in this great republic of ours.

While black Americans fought hardest for this change and are the most obvious beneficiaries of it, white Americans became our partners to ensure that the United States lived up to its great ideals. African Americans long could win elections in largely black districts. Over time, the Edward Brookes, Tom Bradleys, Doug Wilders and Carol Moseley Brauns proved that race was no bar to winning in majority white jurisdictions. Now, Barack Obama has demonstrated that to be true across the nation.

Americans have come together, white and black, Christian and Jew, and people of all colors, faiths, and backgrounds, to right the great wrong of America's past. The United States always has been a great and good country, despite its flaws. Today, America has dramatically demonstrated to the entire world its greatness and goodness.

While November 4 is a victory for all Americans, it remains of particular importance for the African-American community and especially for black men.

In America, one did not have to look far to see artificial limits to black achievement. They were clear. No matter that many intelligent and skilled African Americans followed in the footsteps of Frederick Douglass by living lives of great distinction obvious even to the white majority. There were untold positions, jobs, neighborhoods, schools, clubs, marriages and even friendships that were off-limits to blacks. The color of our skin, rather than the content of our character, was all that mattered.

This process represented a particular emasculation of African-American men. Today we take for granted the role of women in the workplace, higher education and politics. But for much of our nation's history most women stayed closer to home. Even in a hostile world, many black women could raise families and gain satisfaction as wives and mothers.

Men, in contrast, typically found more of their self-respect through their work, schools, and political associations. Yet these avenues of achievement were most often closed off by racial discrimination and Jim Crow laws. Long before the black family collapsed and black men seemed to flee from their roles as fathers and community leaders, white America did its best to prevent black men from being real men.

Frustration with the lack of respect according them as workers, citizens and human beings was reflected in the 1968 sanitation workers' strike—which tragically drew Martin Luther King, Jr. to Memphis where he was murdered. The striking employees wore signs proclaiming: "I am a man." But years of struggle and frustration remained before our nation was ready to affirm their manhood.

On November 4, America emphatically and publicly did so.

Barack Obama's victory has not just restored respect long lacking for African Americans. It also has recognized a new form of black political leadership of women and men alike.

Black Americans today owe much to the Civil Rights generation. For instance, Rep. John Lewis (D-Ga.) was a leader in the Student Nonviolent Coordinating Committee and organized countless demonstrations on behalf of equal rights. Thurgood Marshall fought for racial equality before and on the U.S. Supreme Court. Many, many more blacks risked their livelihoods and even their lives to give full meaning to the Declaration of Independence's proclamation that "all men are created equal."

Today, we now are witnessing the rise of a new type of black leadership and black politics. We are seeing African-American leaders who represent the changes that permeate America. There is Adrian Fenty, the young and energetic mayor of Washington, D.C. There is Cory Booker, who, though not yet forty, already has been mayor of Newark, N.J. for two years. There are United Nations Ambassador Susan Rice and former Secretary of State Condoleezza Rice. There are former congressmen J.C. Watts and Harold Ford, Jr.

And then there is Barack Obama, a black man who grew up without his father. A black man who hungrily grabbed every opportunity that opened before him. And a black man who just won the highest political office in the land—and most important government position in the world.

This newer generation provides a powerful antidote to the hopelessness felt by many young African Americans, and especially African-American males. The point is not that the many obstacles facing young blacks have magically disappeared. Or that success is now automatically guaranteed.

But no young African American can ever again believe that he or she cannot overcome hardship and discrimination. No young African American can ever again believe that any position lies beyond his or her reach. No young African American can ever again believe that the future has been set, that his or her destiny has been pre-determined.

Today, the promise of America truly is the promise for all Americans, black as well as white. Today the United States has demonstrated that it is committed to upholding the true meaning of the Declaration of Independence.

Imagine the frustration that must have ravaged Frederick Douglass throughout his life. He was the living refutation of the myth of black inferiority upon which slavery was based. He was intelligent, educated and passionate, yet he had to run for his freedom and pay off his master to assure his liberty. Americans prided themselves on their commitment to both liberty and equality, yet he had no assurance of either. We should not be surprised that he declared on that 4th of July long ago: "for revolting barbarity and shameless hypocrisy, America reigns without a rival."

Yet he concluded his oration with a message of hope. "Notwithstanding the dark picture I have this day presented of the state of the nation, I do not despair," he said. More than a decade before the promulgation of the Emancipation Proclamation, he perceived "forces in operation which must inevitably work the downfall of slavery," and predicted that "No nation can now shut itself up from the surrounding world and trot round in the same old path of its fathers without interference."

He was proved right.

The process was long and hard. Millions of African Americans struggled and suffered. All Americans paid a price for their nation's hypocrisy. But the United States finally has left "the same old path of its fathers." Today, the American government truly belongs to every American.

COMMENTARY

The Game Changer: Are We Beyond What is Next to What is Now?

By Cassye D. Cook, J.D.

I remember the day when the then junior United States Senator Barack Obama announced his candidacy for president of the United States of America, my general thought was "Interesting timing" and "Is he really serious?" I thought it was maybe a little touch of hubris and a case of listening to too many eager advisors and supporters. There were some that were in his camp early, but there were far more like me that thought that this would be another *symbolic exercise* in democracy. A moment that would be reduced to a footnote in history, a time that could possibly expand the national dialogue and rally a different type of electorate support, but not quite reach the threshold needed to actually prove viable or more so electable.

I was very familiar with then Senator Obama, his race for Illinois U.S. Senate, his popularity in Chicago and his impressive speech at the 2004 Democratic National Convention that introduced him to millions. But "President Obama?" The jury was still out on that one. As the 2008 election primary season unfolded, it was clear that this time things were going to be different—he won the Iowa caucus. In that moment, more people started paying attention, especially those in the post- baby boomer generation, which I'll affectionately call the e-Generation. They saw something rare, uncommon and longed for: a politician who communicated on a new level and in a 21st century way that was inclusive and technologically inviting.

The journey that ensued for nearly two years was a tremendously exciting period in history that produced countless firsts in American politics. But most importantly, it revealed a leader who was calm, thoughtful, competent and smart. But now that the elections are over, Barack Obama has prevailed as the 44th president of the United States of America and people are settling into the reality of this historic moment. But what now? Will "44" really become the game changer that will induce lasting results and change our history?

Before I point out the hopes and dreams that can be born out of this time, let me be translucent. Obama's historic victory will not rescind all of our problems; it has not created a post-racial society. His presidency does not close the innumerable barriers that people of color and lower socio-economic status across our country face, and it does not stop the inequities of justice that are so pervasive in our society. The President will not fill that void, and we do him, ourselves and American society as a whole a great disservice when we create unrealistic goals and expectations. We should neither confuse nor replace the necessary, truthful assessments of the challenges ahead with complacency. However, we can acknowledge that President Obama has influenced an expanded, new and constructive vision in so many people, and we cannot deny that we live in a different optimism as a country today because of the 2008 U.S. presidential election.

Obama's presidency signals the elicitation of meaningful input from citizens about important issues, and its return to participatory democracy having universal appeal. Historically, few leaders have executed such a style of national decision-making process and made it effective on a large scale. But the resurgence of accessible, participatory democracy appears to ring true to the masses again, especially with the e-Generation.

This is evidenced by the over 400,000 people who have sent resumes to the administration looking for a way into President Obama's administration, because they are interested in government and public service. Compare this to when George W. Bush became president eight years ago, and only 90,000 people applied for jobs in his administration. Asking the electorate to step up is not a new ideal, but it is a profound time when people heed the call. President John F. Kennedy in fact sounded the call in his 1961 inauguration speech to take part in service to the country. When American citizens of all colors and varying creeds from different parts of the country are eager to become part of this new movement for change, it epitomizes the democratic ideals by which this nation was founded.

Often, I think about what role I would have played during the Civil Rights Movement. Would I have been bold enough, vocal enough or marched enough? The generation after Kennedy and King are beneficiaries to the struggle, yet had no "common voice" that delivered a message that resonated with the clear, unwavering expectation that it's our responsibility to get up and serve. For many of the e-Generation, President Obama has been the inspiration to embrace their own mountain top experience, and it has truly connected a generation to the ideological battles born in the streets in the 1960s.

The 2008 election proved that it has never been about apathy with the youth vote, but that it has always been about the absence of something they could believe in and commonalities they could identify with. For people who speak to our highest ambitions, there will always be a response and so many responded because people desire leadership. It was about each individual and their hopes and desires. It was also about all the factors historically serving as barriers—such as age, race, gender, and religion—that did not hinder a broader, universal message that the ownership of America's destiny is for all of us to embrace and for all of us to contribute in.

Often, many in the e-Generation are referred to as the next generation of leaders. And for some time, I took no issue with that classification or description. But after some reflection on national leadership and lessons from President Obama's historic race to the White House, I truly believe it should be acknowledged that this prophetic designation is flawed. We are *now*, our time is *now* and the future is *now*.

We are all now, and often being labeled "next" implies that we must not be serious or ready. The "next" moniker somehow authenticates our inaction, because it is not our time; because we somehow need a king maker to grant us access. While I don't discount serious preparation and experience to be ready for that moment, waiting on permission can stifle the ability to offer our best. To step up in service and leadership, we need to get our head around the idea of *now* or any given moment and realize that we have to be *now*, because the need for leadership in the country is so urgent.

President Barack Obama and this election season brought forth a revived appetite for making a difference, pushing a universal cause, and bringing issues to the forefront. His success has challenged my own thinking about questioning readiness, and he validated the right of the underdog—the less likely candidate to be able to have a seat— to be a player in the game. It is readiness, ambition, thick skin, confidence and belief in a higher purpose that can bring *change.*

Our narrative will have to change, because a new chapter is unfolding. It is time for new dreams, new visions and *now* dreamers to understand that they stand on broad shoulders poised to glance over one's own mountain top and stand ready to build on the civil rights' victories. With great thanks to our President, who inspired us to engage in the heavy lifting ourselves, that inspiration will allow us not only to offer support, but it will also require us to examine his policies, his approach and decisions that will impact our country.

That is the only way our "next" will transform us to our "now." It's time for the e-Generation to change the game and make that "e" signify execution, excitement and higher expectations for ourselves, our government and our country as a whole.

It's game time. What *now?*

Did I Ever?

By The Honorable Nathaniel R. Jones, LL.D.

"Did you ever think you would live to see a black President?"

Whenever I am asked this question—and I have been frequently asked it in the days since Barack Obama's election as America's 44th President—my mind flips back to an early point in time which, for me, was the beginning of my awareness of race.

As a child, my mother took me to lectures at the segregated YMCA in my hometown of Youngstown, Ohio. It was there that I heard speeches by nationally-renowned persons who were on the front line of the battle against racial discrimination. The forums I attended as a youngster were typical of meetings held in black communities all across America, North and South, in which speakers implored audiences to not give in to racial stereotypes or accept the limitations on their potential even though the toxicity of racism and discrimination were present in all of the institutions that affected their lives.

This was during a period when "separate-but-equal" was still the law of the land and the toxicity of racism had infected all of the institutions that governed the destiny of black and white people. Stereotypical attitudes about white superiority and black inferiority were reinforced by law and custom. The Supreme Court in its 1857 *Dred Scott* decision held that blacks were not persons within the meaning of the Constitution. Chief Justice Roger Taney made twenty-one references to blacks as sub-human species.

Following the Emancipation Proclamation and the Civil War, Reconstruction offered hope to the newly-freed slaves of real opportunity to fully participate in the American mainstream. However, the infamous Hayes-Tilden Deal of 1876 that led to President Hayes' withdrawal of the federal troops from the South opened the legal doors to the restoration of States Rights and stripping voting rights from blacks, since the disenfranchisement and marginalization of blacks was crucial to a restoration of whites to their former position of political dominance. Such groups as the Ku Klux Klan and the Knights of the White Camellia, along with others, were able to accomplish this by intimidation and violence. Lynchings soared during the 1880s and 1890s with the result that former slaves were disfranchised once again. In addition to outright violence, the grandfather clause, literacy tests, poll tax laws, all-white primaries and property requirements were proxies for outright racial exclusion of blacks from the voting booths.

These tactics were cemented and sanctioned at the highest levels of government with the 1896 Supreme Court decision in *Plessy v. Ferguson,* which flipped the 14th Amendment on its head and injected the "separate but equal" poison into America's institutional arteries. By any measure, the ringing dissent by Justice John Marshall Harlan dwarfed the much-acclaimed academic achievements of Henry Billings Brown who authored the majority opinion.

Roy Wilkins, the preeminent civil rights leader, often said blacks were exposed to a "smothering pattern of a thousand different personal humiliations." These humiliations, in many instances, were the concrete legacy of *Plessy, Dred Scott,* and other government actions that did such serious damage to hopes and aspirations of black Americans for generations thereafter. One instance that has stayed with me was what my black friends and I experienced as children during summer months. The summer playground program was racially tailored. On Tuesday mornings when white children were taken to the city-owned swimming pools, the black youngsters were sent on nature hikes. Such was the impact of these unforgettable "personal humiliations" that they remain fresh in my mind more than 70 years later.

Despite these events that threatened to challenge my faith in the system, thanks to the early messages of hope I had received, and the refusal to allow the racial stereotypes to define my goals, I pushed ahead to acquire the tools needed to fight for equality—education and the vote. Much of the inspiration for my actions was derived from the work of civil rights lawyers and other activists who tirelessly fought to break racism's hold on the institutions that run our lives.

The legal strategy for overcoming this legacy was devised by the NAACP's Charles Hamilton Houston. At the core of the justification for institutional racism was the notion that blacks were stained with a badge of inferiority, so powerfully and shamefully argued by Chief Justice Taney in the *Dred Scott* decision. Thus, Houston's two early targets for undoing the Taney thesis were to knock out barriers to equal education and voting. They were the pathways to undercutting the rationale for denying Constitutional rights to blacks.

The litigation strategy led eventually to the unanimous 1954 decision of *Brown v. Board of Education*, which held that separate-but-equal was inherently unfair and violative of the 14th Amendment to the United States Constitution. In *Brown*, the Supreme Court finally recognized that segregation itself, in and of itself, deprived minority children of equal educational opportunities. *Brown*, like *Plessy*, ushered in a new era in American history. Although it was a case about schools and educational opportunities, *Brown* laid the framework for desegregating all aspects of American life.

It was clear to blacks from the beginning of the struggle against segregation that they were a numerical minority. Since, in a democratic society, numbers are important, African Americans at that time knew that while they had to become politically active, it was essential to enlist support of whites and to form interracial coalitions. One of the most reliable allies was the Jewish community. While some Protestant denominations adhered to segregationist positions, there were others who spoke out boldly on behalf of rights of Negroes. In addition, though craft unions had exclusionary policies, the industrial unions were much more liberal on racial issues. A. Philip Randolph, the Sleeping Car Porters Union, and the NAACP led the fight within the trade union movement. The policy of the YMCA okayed segregation within its units. On the other hand, the YWCA took a more forward looking position on integration. These and other groups combined with the NAACP, the black church and other liberal organizations to fight against segregation and discrimination. Thus, the foundation for the coalition that came together for Barack Obama began to form decades ago.

President Dwight Eisenhower set off much discussion among the black leadership when he appointed Frederick Morrow, a black, as his assistant. He made history by appointing J. Ernest Wilkins of Chicago as Assistant Secretary of Labor. President Kennedy named a black, Andrew Hatcher, as his assistant press secretary. That appointment was noteworthy for the visibility attached to the position.

President Nixon made appointments of blacks to sub-Cabinet positions, such as Sam Jackson and Arthur Fletcher at the Labor Department, but the White House power center remained lily-white. His senior staff sometimes conferred with the Urban League's Whitney Young and Vernon Jordan and the NAACP's Clarence Mitchell on legislation.

Unfortunately, during the 70s, the slow pace in implementing *Brown v. Board of Education*, the 1964 Civil Rights Act and the 1965 Voting Rights Act was a point of significant frustration. A number of blacks began to respond to the siren song of black power and black racial separatism. Adherents drove from the coalition white allies who had been toiling in the vineyard for decades. Particular targets were some Jewish organizations. Slowly, healing began to take place. The campaign of Barack Obama brought together and solidified, once again, the fractured coalitions and old allies. It was this reunification, which I had observed emerging over the years, coming together during the period of the 2008 political campaign that led me to believe that Senator Obama's election as President was a distinct possibility.

In recent years, particularly since the attacks on civil rights mounted by Richard Nixon and Ronald Reagan, civil rights adherents were dismissed as merely being "special interest" groups seeking "preferential" treatment. History belies that.

Rather than being selfish, blacks were in fact, acting in the national interest. Should there be any doubt, one need only look at the strength and diversity of America's workforce today by virtue of the laws enacted outlawing discrimination in the workplace; and the distance we have come in providing quality education for diverse Americans even though unacceptable gaps still exist; the vitality of the military since its integration; and the strength of the American political system by virtue of the expansion of voting rights. These changes did not just benefit African Americans; they enhanced our entire nation.

In reflecting on this history, I find myself reviewing my own rocky pathway to the present. I recalled the feeling I had when, many years later as an adult and a lawyer, I stepped into the shoes once worn by Thurgood Marshall as the chief legal officer of the NAACP, the oldest and largest civil rights organization. I was positioned to lead the fight against school segregation by bringing lawsuits to implement the 1954 *Brown v. Board of Education* decision in the North. I took Mr. Marshall's baton and continued to run the race.

Did I ever? My answer is informed, in part, by my DNA that includes decades of observation and involvement in the struggle to change attitudes, participate in the building of coalitions and working to effect change in relations and attitudes. That spans the period of my attending those YMCA forums as a youth, sitting in on the informal discussions of national and local civil rights strategists, challenging the racial policies and efforts to redefine me, recruiting the participation of white colleagues to join in those change efforts, and the numerous activities that followed. It was a combination of those life experiences that made me a believer when I heard Senator Obama explain to delegates to the National Urban League at its 2007 annual meeting in St. Louis his strategy for capturing the White House.

As his strategy unfolded, in particular with his victories in the Iowa and South Carolina primaries, I recalled what he laid out to the delegates, and later to me in a personal chat; how he proposed to activate more young people, dispirited, and long disenfranchised blacks, particularly in the so-called "Red States." Combining that game plan with the changes I observed in human and political relationships, it seemed to me that Senator Obama had properly measured the extent of change that had occurred by virtue of altered relationships, at the workplace, in neighborhoods, on campuses, in schools and in recreational activities. He was the messenger poised to seize upon these profound and historic realignments.

Hovering around me in the glow of the election of this remarkable African American as President, is an unease that it will be misread as signaling an end to historic racism and a reason for terminating programs aimed at ending economic and educational disparities. Only if there is an understanding of how the road of remedies was paved with an assortment of legal and political strategies, will there be permanence to this election's significance. There must be no relaxation in the struggle for economic and social justice.

But that does not detract from sense of forward movement we feel as President Barack Obama takes on the enormous task of governing this nation. As I watch our young president, I see not only his person, but the America described by Langston Hughes in his moving poem, "I, Too Sing America."

I am the darker brother.
They send me to eat in the kitchen
When company comes,
But I laugh,
And eat well,
And grow strong.

Tomorrow,
I'll sit at the table
When company comes,
Nobody'll dare
Say to me,
"Eat in the kitchen,"

Then.

Besides,
They'll see how beautiful I am
And be ashamed—

I, too, am America.

So, when I am asked "Did you ever think you would live to see a black President?" I answer a resounding "YES, I DID."

The Journey Continues

By Stephanie J. Jones

Dear Mr. President:

Two years ago, you concluded your Foreword to *The State of Black America 2007* with the following charge to us all:

> *[I]t is in our shared interests and in the interest of every American to stop ignoring these challenges and start finding the solutions that will work. For in the end, we want the story for Black America to be one universal story where success is the norm and struggles are overcome.*
>
> *This is the journey we are on together.*[1]

You completed this Foreword just a few weeks before you launched the campaign that led to your election as the first African-American President of the United States. But that historic campaign did not mark the beginning of your journey. In fact, as you told us during the National Urban League's Annual Conference last summer, your journey began many years before when you became "a foot soldier in the movement the Urban League built—the movement to bring opportunity to every corner of our cities."

While you may be the most prominent of Urban League Movement "foot soldiers," you are certainly not alone. For 99 years, the Urban League has empowered millions of African Americans and others in urban communities across the country to achieve their full economic and social potential. Like you, we were community organizers long before it was cool!

Given our shared goals and history, we—like most Americans of all races, ages, political persuasions—feel the excitement and pride in your enormous achievement. But that excitement and pride are dwarfed by an even stronger sense of obligation and mission: to share with you our experience, knowledge and perspectives we have developed during our nearly century-long journey.

The State of Black America 2009: Message to the President does more than report on the conditions of our urban communities. It offers you, your administration, Congress and others a clear roadmap of specific steps that you can and should take to revitalize our cities, empower our people and grow our economy. In addition to a rich blend of National Urban League's empirical data, unparalleled "hands-on" experience gained through our work in urban communities, analysis and commentary by America's most insightful thinkers and doers, we present the quiet yet powerful voices of ordinary people who simply want their government to respond to their concerns.

This 33rd edition of *The State of Black America* is directed to you, but it also speaks to America. Your successful campaign reminded us that movements begin one person at a time and that individuals speaking and working together can be as powerful as the most daunting special interests. Your presidency, at this critical juncture in our nation's history and in the African-American narrative, presents an opportunity for each of us to step up and take responsibility for helping to shape the policies that will impact us, our families and our communities. We must define our own issues, concerns and potential solutions rather than allow them to be defined for us by others in a vacuum. After all, if we don't speak for ourselves, stand up for our families, advocate for our communities, who will? And as we speak, stand and advocate, our public officials can learn an important truth—that our ideas and voices bring enormous depth and value to the public policy conversation.

We hope that the information and ideas in *The State of Black America 2009: Message to the President* will provide you a roadmap for the strong, bold and decisive action needed to set our nation on the road to full economic and social equality for all of its citizens and to create that "one universal story where success is the norm and struggles are overcome." It is in this spirit that we offer our hands and our help to you and your administration in hopes that we will achieve the goals we have shared and strived for all these many years.

Yes, Mr. President, this IS the journey we—all of us—are on together.

NOTES

[1] *State of Black America 2007: Portrait of the Black Male* (National Urban League 2007)

APPENDIX I

In Memoriam

Bo Diddley

Bo Diddley was a singer, songwriter and guitarist and a major pioneer of rock 'n' roll. The uniqueness and innovation of his music, stage presence — and even the specifications of the guitar he played — made him one of the most identifiable performers in the history of popular music. Also, the original musical rhythms he cultivated influenced some of rock music's most prominent artists.

Bo Diddley was born Otha Ellas Bates in McComb, Miss., on December 30, 1928. His mother's cousin, Gussie McDaniel, adopted him after birth and moved the family — Otha and her other children — to Chicago when he was six. Shortly after settling on Chicago's South Side, he began studying the violin at the age of seven and took up the guitar when he was 12.

He quit school as a teenager and began performing with several other musician friends who called themselves "The Jivecats." In 1954, the group presented a demo recording to Phil and Leonard Chess of Chess Records in Chicago. The brothers were extremely impressed with Diddley's guitar work and subsequently offered him and his group a recording contract.

It was in and around this time that he changed his name to Bo Diddley, but the origins of the name have always been unclear. Thinking it would make a catchy and commercial stage name for the new, up-and-coming musician, some contend that Leonard Chess took the name from a popular, local Chicago comedian. And some others say the name was derived from a one-stringed instrument from the Mississippi Delta called the "diddley bow."

His new name became the title of his first record, *"Bo Diddley,"* released by Checker Records, a subsidiary of Chess, in 1955. Fittingly enough, the self-titled tune, a number one hit on the R&B charts in 1955, became his signature song and illustrated his original, trademark musical beat — three strokes/rest/two strokes. Also, similar to the beat of his music, even the guitar Diddley played, which he made himself, was unique. The rectangular body of his instrument starkly contrasted conventional guitar models and was integral in establishing Diddley's legendary identity.

During the late 1950s and early 1960s, Diddley recorded more hit songs — *"You Can't Judge A Book By Its Cover," "Road Runner"* and *"Mona."* He became one of the premier stars of rock 'n' roll, and the syncopated beat of his music heavily influenced other rock stars. Buddy Holly was regarded by many as a rock 'n' roll legend, and Diddley's beat influenced one of the late guitarist's hit songs — *"Not Fade Away."* In addition, legendary English rock groups, such as the Rolling Stones and the Yardbirds, covered some of Diddley's original compositions. And some music authorities contend that other rock guitar icons —such as Chuck Berry and Jimi Hendrix — incorporated certain aspects of Diddley's guitar showmanship into their stage acts.

However, the rock 'n' roll craze began to subside by the mid-sixties, and as Diddley's musical career went downward, his recordings and performances became infrequent. However, the popular punk rock band The Clash invited him to be their opening act during their tour in 1979. And in later years, Diddley also appeared at numerous nostalgic rock 'n' roll revues, and in 1987, he was inducted into the Rock 'N' Roll Hall of Fame.

Bo Diddley died of heart failure on June 2, 2008, at his home in Archer, Fla., at the age of 79.

David McCoy Franklin

David McCoy Franklin was an entrepreneur and one of the entertainment industry's most successful attorneys. The Atlanta native was also a savvy political campaign organizer who played an integral role in the 1973 election of Atlanta's first black mayor, Maynard Jackson.

Franklin was born in Atlanta, where he was raised by his mother and grandmother. He graduated from Atlanta's Turner High School and attended Morehouse College. After graduating from Morehouse, he relocated to Washington, D.C., where he worked for the Department of Labor and attended the American University Washington College of Law at night. It was also during his years in the District that he met his future wife — and a future mayor of Atlanta — Shirley Franklin, then a student at Howard University.

After passing the D.C. Bar, Franklin began his career managing entertainers. While still in the District, he met Donny Hathaway, then an up-and-coming musician, and agreed to handle his business matters. He displayed strong negotiating skills while managing Hathaway's career and soon gained a reputation in the entertainment industry of attaining lucrative deals for performers. High-profile stars began to seek his services, and his clientele included Roberta Flack, Gladys Knight, Lou Gossett, Luther Vandross, Peabo Bryson and Richard Pryor. It was said that Franklin was the first black attorney to negotiate six-figure deals for his clients.

He returned back to his hometown of Atlanta during the early 1970s, where he began another successful career as a political campaigner. He became a chief campaign strategist for Maynard Jackson, then vice mayor of Atlanta and candidate for mayor in the 1973 election, while partnering with Jackson in a law firm. Franklin orchestrated a successful fund-raising campaign for Jackson's candidacy by having some of his star clients in the entertainment industry — such as Roberta Flack, Donny Hathaway and Gladys Knight—perform at a fund-raising event at the Omni in Atlanta. Also, he devised a "get out and vote" campaign that transported thousands of black voters to city voting polls on election day. Consequently, Maynard Jackson was elected the first African-American mayor of Atlanta, and many contend that Franklin played a key role in the victory.

In later years, Franklin served as a political strategist for national-level politicians, such as Senator Edward Kennedy (D-MA) and 1984 Democratic presidential nominee and former Vice President Walter Mondale (D-MN).

Franklin also experienced success as an entrepreneur having went on to found Franklin & Wilson Airport Concessions, which at one time housed 15 retail stores at Atlanta's Hartsfield-Jackson International Airport. He also co-founded the Black Entertainment and Sports Lawyers Association and served as the organization's first chairman.

Franklin died at the age of 65 on September 7, 2008, of natural causes.

Isaac Hayes

Isaac Hayes was an instrumentalist, songwriter, singer and actor regarded as one of the most creative recording artists in the history of R&B music. He was one of the recording industry's most successful solo artists during the 1970s, and during his musical career with Stax Records, he was said to have played a significant role in popularizing the legendary "Sound of Memphis."

Hayes was born in Covington, Tenn., on August 20, 1942. After his father abandoned the family shortly after his birth, and his mother dying a year later, Hayes' maternal grandparents, who were sharecroppers, raised him and his sister in severely impoverished conditions of a Southern rural area.

After the family relocated to Memphis when Hayes was six, he became drawn to music as a high school student and performed with numerous R&B and gospel groups as a teen. The musical ability he displayed during his performances was so exceptional that upon graduation from Manassas High School in North Memphis, he was offered over a dozen music scholarships from various colleges and universities. However, because he had recently married and was soon to become a father, he opted instead to work in a Memphis meat-packing plant.

Nevertheless, he still performed music in nightclubs and small juke joints throughout Memphis and various towns of Mississippi. In 1963, Stax Records in Memphis hired him as a session musician, where he played keyboards on recordings by the late soul vocalist Otis Redding. He also began a songwriting partnership with David

Porter, and the prolific songwriting team wrote several hits for Stax's popular 1960s vocal duo Sam & Dave — *"Hold On, I'm Coming," "I Thank You"* and, a song that became a number one hit in 1967 and an R&B classic, *"Soul Man."*

During that year, Hayes also released his first solo album, fittingly entitled *"Presenting Isaac Hayes."* But it was his second album, *"Hot, Buttered, Soul"* released two years later, where he made his breakthrough as a recording artist, with the album selling over a million copies. He also achieved further success with subsequent solo albums—*"To Be Continued," "Black Moses"* and *"The Isaac Hayes Movement."* His rich baritone singing voice, coupled with his brilliant orchestral musical arrangements, made him one of the most innovative and influential musical artists of the 1970s. Many in fact credit Hayes as being a major pioneer of the decade's most popular musical genre—disco.

However, it was the highly acclaimed musical soundtrack that he composed for the 1971 Gordon Parks-directed film *"Shaft"* in which Hayes achieved his greatest recognition. He won two Grammys for the film's musical score and the film's theme song won an Academy Award for "Best Original Song." In doing so, he became the first African American to win an Oscar in a musical category.

The fame he garnered as a musical performer also opened the door for acting opportunities in Hollywood. He made numerous guest appearances in movies and television shows during the seventies and eighties.

In recent years, he found a new generation of fans in an unlikely fashion as the voice of the cartoon character "Chef" in the popular but controversial animated cable-TV series, *"South Park."* However, he left the show in 2006, after he was offended by a particular episode he felt blasphemed the Scientology religion, a faith he had practiced for years. Also in 2006, Hayes was inducted into the Songwriter's Hall of Fame.

Two years later on August 10, 2008, he died after his wife found him lying unconscious next to a running treadmill in their home. He was 65.

Freddie Hubbard

Freddie Hubbard was a Grammy-award winning musician and considered one of the greatest trumpet players of jazz music. The virtuosity and melodic creativity he displayed as a trumpeter made him one of the genre's most influential artists.

Frederick Dewayne Hubbard was born on April 7, 1938, in Indianapolis, IN. The youngest of seven children, he was born into a musical family. His mother played piano and his other siblings played various musical instruments. The first instrument Hubbard learned to play was mellophone, and by junior high school, he was studying other horn instruments, such as the trumpet, flugelhorn and tuba.

During his mid-teens, he took musical lessons from Max Woodbury, a trumpeter with the Indianapolis Symphony Orchestra at the Arthur Jordan Conservatory of Music. He also performed locally with other Indianapolis musicians, including the Montgomery Brothers who featured another future jazz great—guitarist Wes Montgomery.

In 1958, when he was 20, he moved to New York where he played with some of jazz music's greatest artists, including Philly Joe Jones, Sonny Rollins, Quincy Jones and John Coltrane and also performed for several years with Art Blakely's Jazz Messengers. During the early 1960s, he joined the legendary Blue Note label, where he recorded jazz albums with noted jazz artists, such as Herbie Hancock, Oliver Nelson and John Coltrane. Though still in his early 20s, he received the prestigious Down Beat Critics' Poll Award for his remarkable trumpet work.

Hubbard also collaborated with avant-garde jazz greats during this period, appearing on Ornette Coleman's album *"Free Jazz"* (1960) and Eric Dolphy's *"Out to Lunch"* (1964). Hubbard estimated that he played on more than 300 jazz albums during the 1960s.

However, by 1970, he relocated to the West Coast, and similar to most jazz artists during the 1970s and 80s, he began mixing—or "fusing"—jazz music with elements of pop and rock. He toured with other jazz-rock fusion artists, Wayne Shorter, Tony Williams and Miles Davis, and recorded several well-received albums on the CTI label, including *"Red Clay"* and *"Straight Life."* In 1972, his album *"First Light"* won a Grammy for "best jazz performance."

Throughout his musical career, he displayed a unique technical mastery of the trumpet, enabling him to play intricate melodies and phrases with tremendous fluidity and ease. However, his intense style of playing caused him to split his lip while performing on a 1992 European tour. The injury caused a serious infection to his lip and permanently and adversely affected his trumpet playing.

Despite having to struggle with the physical impediment, Hubbard continued performing in nightclubs and recorded on a sporadic basis. At one point, he switched to playing the less demanding fluegelhorn, in an attempt to recapture the musical virtuosity he was renowned for. In 2006, he received a jazz master's award from the National Endowment for the Arts.

Hubbard died on December 29, 2008, from complications stemming from a heart attack that he previously suffered. He was 70.

Stephanie Tubbs Jones

Stephanie Tubbs Jones was former prosecutor and judge and the first African American woman to represent Ohio in Congress. As a groundbreaking African-American legal practitioner and politician, she was a tireless and outspoken champion for equal opportunity and justice for all Americans.

She was born Stephanie Tubbs on September 10, 1949, in Cleveland, OH., and her father was an airport skycap and her mother worked as a cook. Tubbs Jones attended Cleveland public schools and received both her undergraduate and law degrees from Case Western Reserve University in Cleveland in 1971 and 1974, respectively.

Tubbs Jones began her career as legal counsel to Cleveland sewer district, and in 1976, she became an assistant prosecutor for Cuyahoga County in Ohio. At the age of 31, she was elected as a Cleveland municipal court judge, and later became the first African-American woman to serve on Ohio's Court of Common Pleas. She was appointed chief prosecutor of Cuyahoga County in 1990, and became the first woman and the first African American in state history to be appointed to the position.

In 1998, she became the first black woman to represent Ohio in Congress. She represented the predominately Democratic 11th Congressional District on the east side of Cleveland, succeeding Rep. Louis Stokes who had retired from the seat after holding it for over 30 years. During her career in Congress, Tubbs Jones chaired the House Ethics Committee and became the first black woman to serve on the Ways and Means Committee.

Considered a liberal Democrat, she co-sponsored legislation to expand health care coverage for low- and middle-income citizens and programs to assist the re-entry of ex-offenders in the societal mainstream during her tenure in Congress. She was also a staunch proponent of gun control, protection of small businesses and credit unions, and restrictions on predatory lending. Tubbs Jones also opposed the Iraq War, voting against the use of U.S. military force against Iraq in 2002, and in 2003, once the war was underway, was one of 11 House members who opposed a resolution to support the U.S. war effort.

An ardent supporter of voting rights, she lead a congressional fight in January 2005 to oppose certification of the 2004 U.S. presidential election, alleging improper conduct in the tallying of electoral votes in her home state, Ohio. Later in 2005 and on the 42nd anniversary of "Bloody Sunday"—a historic but violent voting rights protest during the 1960s' American Civil Rights Movement—Tubbs Jones, along with Sen. Hillary Rodham Clinton (D-NY), reintroduced electoral voter reform legislation, in an effort to ensure legitimate elections and ample voting opportunities for all.

She died on August 20, 2008, after suffering a brain hemorrhage that was caused by an aneurysm as she was driving her car in Cleveland. She was 58 years old.

In honor of her strong public service commitment on health issues, such as on organ donation, while serving on the House Ways and Means Subcommittee on Health, President George W. Bush signed the Stephanie Tubbs Jones Congressional Gift of Life Medal

Act (HR 7198) into law on October 14, 2008. The medal is awarded to organ donors, such as Mrs. Tubbs Jones, and their families in recognition of the donor's act of courage.

Eartha Kitt

For over six decades, Eartha Kitt entertained worldwide audiences as a multi-talented singer, dancer and actress. Her sensual and sultry style of performing and singing captivated millions across the world, and she was regarded as one of the entertainment industry's most renowned and resilient sex symbols.

Kitt was born on January 17, 1927, on a cotton plantation in North, S.C., but at the age of eight, she was sent to live with an aunt in New York City. During her teenage years, she studied piano and attended the city's high school for the performing arts. She dropped out of school at 15, but in 1946, she landed a job as a dancer with the famed Katherine Dunham Dance Troupe and performed throughout Europe. While performing in Paris, she caught the eye of the legendary Orson Wells—who he once dubbed as "the most exciting woman in the world"—who cast her as Helen of Troy in a European production of *Faust*. While performing internationally as a singer and dancer, she learned over a dozen different languages and performed songs in French, Spanish and Turkish.

During the early 1950s, she returned back to the United States and performed in clubs, cabarets, and on stage and also began a musical recording career. She appeared in a Broadway musical, *"New Faces of 1952"* and in the 1954 production of *"Mrs. Patterson,"* in which she earned a Tony nomination. Also, in 1954, her first solo album was released, *"RCA Presents Eartha Kitt."* The debut album included some of her classic songs — *"I Want To Be Evil," "C'est Si Bon"* and *"Santa Baby."* She also had leading lady roles in Hollywood films, starring with Nat King Cole in *St. Louis Blues* (1958) and Sammy Davis Jr. in *"Anna Lucasta"* (1959).

During the 1960s, she played roles on television and received an Emmy nomination in 1966 for an appearance on the T.V. drama *"I, Spy."* And in 1967, she reached her peak of stardom appearing as the seductive and sultry villainess "Catwoman" on the campy hit TV series "Batman."

However, she became the center of controversy during the following year. In 1968, Lady Bird Johnson, wife of the late U.S. President Lyndon B. Johnson, invited Kitt to a White House ladies' luncheon. While speaking at the function, she criticized the U.S. presidential administration's escalation of the Vietnam War and cited it as the reason for the turbulence among American youth at that time. Her outspokenness alienated many attending the luncheon—including Lady Bird. As a result, it was alleged that President Johnson had her blacklisted throughout the U.S. entertainment industry, and that the FBI and CIA placed her under surveillance.

Unable to find work in the United States, she returned overseas and for the next several years performed on stage and theater in Europe and South Africa. However, she returned back to the United States to perform at Carnegie Hall in 1974, and in 1978, she resurrected her stature in the U.S. entertainment industry with a starring role in the hit musical *"Timbuktu!"* Triumphantly, President Jimmy Carter invited her back to the White House for a visit while the musical was being performed in Washington, D.C., during that year.

In later years, Kitt remained an active entertainer, performing at the famed Café Carlyle in New York and appearing with Eddie Murphy in the 1992 box-office hit *"Boomerang."* In 1996, and nearing the age of 70, she received a Grammy nomination for her album *"Back in Business."* In recent years, she won several awards for her voice-over work on the animated Disney-TV series *"The Emperor's New School."*

She died of colon cancer on Christmas Day in 2008 at the age 81.

Bernie Mac

Bernie Mac was a comedian and actor who appeared in numerous Hollywood films and TV sitcoms. As with many prominent comics of the modern entertainment era, his uncompromising and profane comedic style drew criticism and controversy; yet he became one of the entertainment industry's most successful and popular comedians.

He was born Bernard Jeffrey McCullough in Chicago, IL. on October 5, 1957. Born into poverty on Chicago's South Side, Mac displayed comedic talent as a child and often performed comedy routines for family and neighborhood friends. After graduating from high school in 1976, he worked a string of different jobs during his young adult life, as a janitor, bus driver and a worker at a General Motors auto plant. However, still in pursuit of his dream to become a successful comedian, Mac performed in comedy clubs at night and even told jokes for tips on the Chicago subway.

His big break came in 1990, after he received national recognition by winning the *Miller Lite Comedy Search* contest and appearing as a comic on the HBO-produced *"Def Comedy Jam,"* which showcased up-and-coming, young black standup comedians. The notoriety he gained by performing stand-up comedy opened the door for movie roles, and Mac appeared in numerous comedy films during the early nineties, *"Mo' Money"* (1992), *"Who's The Man?"* (1993) and *"House Party 3"* (1994). In later years, he also had starring roles in films such as *"Ocean's Eleven"* (2001), *"Bad Santa"* (2003) and *"Mr. 3000"* (2004). In 1996, he started performing on television with a recurring role as "Uncle Bernie" on the TV family sitcom *"Moesha,"* which ran for five seasons.

In 2000, Mac appeared with three other star black comics—Steve Harvey, Cedric the Entertainer and D.L Hugley—in the 2000 box-office smash *"The Original Kings of Comedy."* The Spike Lee-produced documentary was nominated for a 2001 Chicago Film Critics Association Award for "best documentary," and the soundtrack from the film received a 2001Grammy award nomination for "best comedy album."

However, Mac will probably be best remembered for his self-titled TV-family sitcom, *"The Bernie Mac Show,"* in which he played a married comedian caring for his sister's three young children. His role as a tough-loving and at times abrasive guardian of his two nieces and nephew was somewhat unconventional by comedy sitcom standards. In fact, a *New York Times Magazine* writer characterized Mac's fatherly role on the show as "more Ike Turner than Dr.

Spock." Nevertheless, the series effectively captured Mac's hard-nosed humor and became one the most popular comedy shows on television. During its five-year run, the series won a Peabody Award in 2002, and Mac was twice nominated for an Emmy for "best lead actor in a comedy series."

Bernie Mac died on August 9, 2008 at the age of 50 from complications stemming from pneumonia. He had suffered from sarcoidosis, an inflammatory lung disease for most of his adult life. However, he had stated that the disease went into remission in 2005.

Odetta

Odetta Holmes, more commonly known solely by her first name, Odetta, was a singer and human rights activist. Often referred to as the "voice of the civil rights movement," she often sang protest anthems at civil rights rallies during the 1960s. She was also regarded as one of the most influential musical artists of the folk music revival during the 1960s.

Odetta was born in Birmingham, Ala. on New Year's Eve in 1930. At the age of six, she relocated with her mother to Los Angeles, where she received her first formal training in music. Although schooled in classical music and opera during her youth, she became interested in folk music when she was 19 while touring with a musical troupe in San Francisco. She began performing in small clubs and coffeehouses throughout the city, and in 1954, she recorded her first album, *"The Tin Angel."*

Over the late fifties and early sixties, she became a popular folk singer and toured extensively throughout the country, appearing at folk festivals and clubs. She also released several more albums, *"Odetta Sings Ballads and Blues "*(1956), *At the Gate of Horn* (1957) and *Odetta Sings Folk Songs"* (1963), which became one of the best-selling folk albums of 1963. She also made several appearances at the annual Newport Folk Festival between 1959 and 1965.

She became a popular fixture at civil rights rallies during the sixties, where she performed and marched with other protestors. Perhaps her most notable appearance was when she appeared at the historic March on Washington in 1963, singing a soul-stirring rendition of "*O Freedom*." Dr. Martin Luther King, Jr. once coined Odetta as the "queen of folk music."

Her powerful voice moved audiences and her riveting musical style influenced major performers, including Harry Belafonte, Janis Joplin, Joan Baez and Bob Dylan. In fact, Dylan, arguably folk-rock music's most prolific songwriter, once stated in an interview that on hearing her album "*Odetta Sings Ballads and Blues,*" it inspired him to switch from playing electric guitar to an acoustic in an effort to adapt a more folk music-oriented sound.

However, as the popularity of folk music and protest songs began to wane by the end of the 1960s, her performances and recordings became sporadic. Although she did receive a few acting roles on television and appeared in a few Hollywood movies in later years. In 1974, she appeared as a slave woman in the made-for-television movie, "*The Autobiography of Miss Jane Pittman.*"

In 1999, President Clinton awarded her with the National Medal of Arts, in recognition of her musical contributions. In 2004, she received the Living Legend Award from the Library of Congress and during the same year, she became a Kennedy Center nominee.

But over the last ten years of her life, she struggled with health ailments, such as chronic heart disease and pulmonary fibrosis. In 2008, her illnesses required hospitalization, but she vigorously tried to recuperate as she wanted desperately to perform at Barack Obama's presidential inauguration. Unfortunately, she succumbed to heart disease on December 2, 2008. She was 77.

R. Eugene Pincham

R. Eugene Pincham was a Chicago civil rights attorney, a former circuit court judge and justice of the Appellate Court of Illinois. Throughout his career as a legal practitioner, he gained a reputation as being a crusader of equal rights for those who had been treated unfairly by the justice system, particularly for the poor and disadvantaged.

Pincham was born in Chicago on June 28, 1925. But after his parents divorced when he was seven months, his mother relocated him and his brother to Athens, Ala., where he was reared. In 1941, after graduating from Athens' Trinity High School, a school founded by missionaries to educate children of former slaves, he enrolled in LeMonye College in Memphis, Tenn. However, he later transferred to Tennessee State University, where he received a bachelor's degree in political science in 1947.

Aspiring to be a lawyer, he returned to Chicago a year later and enrolled at the Northwestern University School of Law. While in law school, Pincham, the lone black student out of a class of 80 at Northwestern, supported himself by waiting tables and shining shoes. However, in 1951, he earned a Juris Doctor degree and began his legal career working as a state and federal government attorney. In 1954, he served in private practice as a partner in the law firm of Evins, Pincham, Fowlkes and Cooper.

In 1976, he became a circuit county judge of Cook County in Illinois and was assigned to the criminal division. And eight years later, he became a justice of the Illinois Appellate Court.

He resigned from the bench in 1989 and embarked on a political career. In 1990, he ran for president of the Cook County Board of Commissioners. In 1991, he unsuccessfully challenged Richard M. Daley Chicago mayoral campaign after Daley had become mayor upon the death of Harold Washington, Pincham's close friend and the first African American to serve as mayor of Chicago.

An outspoken critic of unfair treatment and racism within the criminal justice system, he defended many African-American suspects believed to have had been wrongly accused of committing severe criminal acts. His most high-profile case involved two young boys from Chicago's South side, aged seven and eight, who were indicted for allegedly murdering an 11-year-old girl in 1998. Pincham represented one of the boys who, along with the youth, had been accused of bludgeoning the young girl to death. After DNA samples taken from the girl's body were linked to an adult sex offender, who later confessed to killing the young girl, the charges against the two boys were subsequently dropped. A lawsuit was filed for wrongful arrest and both youths were awarded multi-million dollar settlements from the city. Pincham also represented Anthony Porter, a death row inmate wrongly convicted and imprisoned for a double homicide.

R. Eugene Pincham died on April 3, 2008, after suffering from a longtime illness. He was of 82.

Pat Tobin

Pat Tobin was a highly successful public relations consultant and event organizer. In a field historically dominated by non-white male professionals, she became known as "the queen of public relations" and headed one of the most successful woman/minority-owned public relations firms in the world.

Patricia Tobin was born in White Plains, N.Y., on February 28, 1943. Her family later relocated to Philadelphia, where she graduated from Overbrook High School and earned an associate degree from the Charles Morris Price School of Journalism.

In 1977, she moved to Los Angeles and found a job as an event organizer for a CBS television affiliate. She was particularly successful in arranging networking functions, in which various professionals from the communications/journalism field could interact and establish business relationships and contacts.

It was during this time that Tobin began to realize that opportunities for minorities to work in the public relations were limited, and that few advertisers realized the potential buying power of black American consumers. Seeking to take advantage of this untapped market, she formed her own public relations and advertising firm in 1983—Tobin & Associates.

Several years later in 1987, when the then prime minister of Japan publicly made derogatory comments about African Americans, it prompted various black leaders in America to protest his racist comments, and for a time, many black Americans had negative perceptions of the nation's government and businesses. Tobin shrewdly used the controversy to her advantage by offering her marketing and public relations services to various Japanese businesses in an effort to improve their image and relations with the African-Americans consumers. Toyota Motor Sales, USA, Inc. awarded her firm a contract to provide consulting services on community and public relations with minorities, which she provided for more than twenty years.

The success and notoriety she garnered from her work with Toyota spawned other opportunities in providing public relations services. She soon built a high profile clientele, providing consultation on black community public relations to large entities such as Shell and AT&T, as well as enhancing public relations campaigns for African-American celebrities such as Johnnie Cochran, Spike Lee and Tavis Smiley. Tobin was also a key figure in promoting Fitzgerald's Casino and Hotel in Las Vegas, owned by Don H. Baren, the first African American to wholly own a casino establishment in Las Vegas.

In addition to providing consulting services to various businesses, Tobin also consulted many burgeoning black-owned public relations firms across the country. She was also the co-founder of the Black Public Relations Association, where she served as a past president and board member.

She died on June 10, 2008, after a long-standing battle with cancer. She was 65 years old.

Gene Upshaw

Gene Upshaw was an NFL Hall of Fame football player and the former executive director of the NFL Players' Association. In addition to being one of the greatest offensive linemen ever to play in professional football, he was highly instrumental in substantially increasing players' salaries in his role as head of the NFL players' union.

Eugene Thurman Upshaw was born in Robstown, Tex., in 1945 and worked in cotton fields as a youth. Although he did not begin playing organized football until he was a senior in high school, he enrolled at Texas A&I University (now Texas A&M University-Kingsville) where he became a standout lineman on the school's football team and received N.A.I.A. All-American honors for outstanding play.

During the first NFL-AFL combined draft in 1967, he was the first-round pick of the Oakland Raiders. The rare combination of his massive size, at 6-5, 255 pounds, coupled with his exceptional speed made him one the league's best offensive linemen and the prototype for an NFL "pulling" guard. During his 15-year tenure with the Oakland Raiders, he was an 11-time all-pro selection and was the only player to play in three Super Bowls in three different decades with the same team. In addition to his outstanding athletic ability, he displayed effective leadership qualities and intelligence, prompting his Raiders teammates to nickname him, "The Governor." He was inducted into the NFL Hall of Fame in 1987 and was the first player enshrined who had played the guard position exclusively throughout an entire NFL career.

After his retirement from the NFL, Upshaw was named as executive director of the NFL Players Association in 1983 and became the first African American to head a major sports union. During his 25-year tenure as executive director, he persistently challenged team owners to increase salaries and retirement benefits for NFL players.

When Upshaw first became the head of the players' union, it was estimated that the average salary for an NFL player was $90,000, which was by far the lowest of all professional team sports. However, in 1993, the players' union, led by Upshaw, filed a landmark anti-trust suit against the NFL, and a compromise was reached that granted free agency to the players in exchange for a salary cap for NFL teams. This unprecedented free agency enabled players to negotiate for higher salaries with other teams when their current contracts expired, which, in turn, resulted in dramatic increases in player salary. It is currently estimated that the average salary for an NFL player is $1.75 million, and many credit Upshaw's relentless work as the reason for the considerable salary boost.

Gene Upshaw died of pancreatic cancer at his vacation home in Lake Tahoe, Cali., on August 20, 2008. Ironically, he died at the age of 63; the number he wore during his entire NFL career as an Oakland Raider. In honor of his remarkable accomplishments as both an NFL player and union chieftain, the league emblazoned a "GU" emblem on the helmets of all NFL players during the 2008 football season.

APPENDIX II

About the Authors

Bernard E. Anderson, Ph.D.
Bernard E. Anderson is the Whitney M. Young Professor of Management in the Wharton School of the University of Pennsylvania. An expert on labor economics and human resource management, Dr. Anderson is a former Assistant Secretary of the U.S. Department of Labor for the Employment Standards Administration. He chairs the National Urban League President's Council of Economic Advisers.

Michelle D. Bernard, J.D.
Michelle D. Bernard is an MSNBC political analyst and president and CEO of the Independent Women's Forum and Independent Women's Voice. Bernard is author of *Women's Progress: How Women Are Wealthier* and *Healthier and More Independent Than Ever Before.*

Cassye D. Cook, J.D.
Cassye D. Cook is vendor manager at Sysco Corporation and serves as the national president of the National Urban League Young Professionals. She is a *cum laude* graduate of Clark Atlanta University and earned her J.D. degree from the Thurgood Marshall School of Law at Texas Southern University.

Christopher J. Dodd
Senator Christopher J. Dodd is the senior U.S. senator from Connecticut and serves as chairman of the United States Senate Committee on Banking, Housing and Urban Affairs. He is also is a senior member of the Health, Education, Labor and Pensions Committee and is the Chairman of its Children and Families Subcommittee.

Chaka Fattah

Congressman Chaka Fattah serves in the U.S. House of Representatives, representing the Second Congressional District of Pennsylvania. He chairs the Congressional Urban Caucus, which addresses critical urban issues, such as employment, education, housing and health.

Darrell J. Gaskin, Ph.D.

Darrell J. Gaskin is associate professor of Health and Economics at the University of Maryland at College Park African-American Studies Department. He was awarded the Academy Health 2002 Article-of-the-Year Award for his health services research article entitled, "*Are Urban Safety-Net Hospitals Losing Low-Risk Medicaid Maternity Patients?*"

Gwendolyn Grant

Gwendolyn Grant is president and CEO of the Urban League of Greater Kansas City. She also authors an op-ed column for *The Kansas City Call* and is also a member of the Kansas City Missouri School District Buildings Corporation Board of Directors and the Institute for Urban Education Advisory Board.

Earl G. Graves, Jr.

Earl "Butch" Graves, Jr. is president and CEO of *Black Enterprise* magazine, where he is responsible for the strategic positioning and overall profitability of the corporation. He previously held marketing executive positions in the corporation and also played briefly as a professional basketball player in the NBA.

John H. Jackson, Ph.D.

John H. Jackson is president and CEO of the Schott Foundation for Public Education, where he oversees the foundation's operations and philanthropic strategy to promote advocacy and public policy reforms in education. He previously served as Chief Policy Officer and National Director of Education for the NAACP.

David J. Johns

David J. Johns is an educator and consultant who has researched and written extensively on black male issues. He currently serves as a senior federal policy advisor.

Nathaniel R. Jones, LL.D.

Nathaniel R. Jones is senior counsel and chief diversity officer of the Blank Rome LLP law firm in Cincinnati, Ohio. He previously served as a judge on the U.S. Court of Appeals for the Sixth Circuit for 23 years and was general counsel of the NAACP from 1969 to 1979.

Stephanie J. Jones, J.D.

Stephanie Jones is the executive director of the National Urban League Policy Institute and is also editor-in-chief of the organization's two flagship publications: *The State of Black America* and *Opportunity Journal*. She previously served as chief counsel to former North Carolina Sen. John Edwards and chief of staff to Rep. Stephanie Tubbs Jones.

Barbara Lee

Congresswoman Barbara Lee serves in the U.S. House of Representatives, representing California's 9th Congressional District. She is also chairwoman of the Congressional Black Caucus and a member of the House Appropriations Committee and the Labor, Health and Human Services, Education and the Financial Services Subcommittees.

Lisa Bland Malone

Lisa Bland Malone is vice president and chief of staff at the National Urban League Policy Institute and also serves as editorial director of the organization's two flagship publications: *The State of Black America* and *Opportunity Journal*.

Eboni Morris

Eboni Morris is a health policy fellow at the National Urban League Policy Institute, where she monitors legislative and administrative activity on health issues impacting African-Americans and conducting health policy analysis and research.

Cy Richardson

Cy Richardson is vice president for housing and community development at the National Urban League, where he is responsible for designing and implementing policies and programs that promote asset building and wealth creation for people of color in urban America.

William M. Rodgers III, Ph.D.

William M. Rodgers is a professor at the Edward J. Bloustein School of Planning and Public Policy at Rutgers University and chief economist at the John J. Heldrich Center for Workforce Development. Professor Rodgers previously served as chief economist at the U.S. Department of Labor from 2000 to 2001. He is a member of the National Urban League President's Council of Economic Advisers.

Hal Smith, Ph.D.

Hal Smith is vice president of education and youth development at the National Urban League. He previously served as a director of quality assurance with the city of New York and as a senior associate at the Annenberg Institute for School Reform.

William E. Spriggs, Ph.D.

William E. Spriggs is a professor and chair of the department of economics at Howard University in Washington, D.C. and previously served at the Economic Policy Institute as senior fellow. He also previously served as executive director of the National Urban League's Institute for Opportunity and Equality from 1988 to 2004.

J. Phillip Thompson, Ph.D.

J. Phillip Thompson is associate professor of Urban Politics in the Department of Urban Studies and Planning of the Massachusetts Institute of Technology. The urban planner and political scientist also has worked as deputy general manager of the New York Housing Authority and as director of the Mayor's Office of Housing Coordination.

Valerie Rawlston Wilson, Ph.D.

Valerie Rawlston Wilson is senior resident scholar at the National Urban League Policy Institute, where she is responsible for directing the institute's research agenda. Her research focuses on labor economics, economics of higher education, poverty and discrimination. She also serves on the National Urban League President's Council of Economic Advisers.

APPENDIX III

Index of Authors and Articles

In 1987, the National Urban League began publishing *The State of Black America* in a smaller, typeset format. By so doing, it became easier to catalog and archive the various essays by author and article.

The 2009 edition of *The State of Black America* is the fifteenth to contain an index of the authors and articles that have appeared since 1987. The articles have been divided by topic and are listed in the alphabetical order of their authors' names.

Reprints of the articles catalogued herein are available through the National Urban League, 120 Wall Street, New York, New York 10005; 212/558-5300.

Affirmative Action

Arnwine, Barbara R., "The Battle Over Affirmative Action: Legal Challenges and Outlook," 2007, pp. 159-172.

Special Section. "Affirmative Action/National Urban League Columns and Amici Brief on the Michigan Case," 2003, pp. 225–268.

Afterword

Daniels, Lee A., "Praising the Mutilated World," 2002, pp. 181–188.

Jones, Stephanie J., "Women's Voices, Women's Power," 2008, pp. 203-204.

Jones, Stephanie J., " The Journey Continues," 2009, pp. 221–223.

AIDS

Rockeymoore, Maya, "AIDS in Black America and the World," 2002, pp. 123–146.

An Appreciation

National Urban League, "Ossie Davis: Still Caught in the Dream," 2005, pp. 137-138.

Jones, Stephanie J., "Rosa Parks: An Ordinary Woman, An Extraordinary Life," 2006, pp. 245-246.

Black Males

Bell, William C., "How are the Children? Foster Care and African-American Boys," 2007, pp. 151-157.

Carnethon, Mercedes R., "Black Male Life Expectancy in the United States: A Multi-level Exploration of Causes," 2007, pp. 137-150.

Dyson, Eric Michael, "Sexual Fault Lines: Robbing the Love Between Us," 2007, pp. 229-237.

Hanson, Renee, Mark McArdle, and Valerie Rawlston Wilson, "Invisible Men: The Urgent Problems of Low-Income African-American Males," 2007, pp. 209-216.

Holzer, Harry J., "Reconnecting Young Black Men: What Policies Would Help," 2007, pp. 75-87.

Johns, David J., "Re-imagining Black Masculine Identity: An Investigation of the 'Problem' Surrounding the Construction of Black Masculinity in America," 2007, pp. 59-73.

Lanier, James R., "The Empowerment Movement and the Black Male," 2004, pp. 143–148.

———, "The National Urban League's Commission on the Black Male: Renewal, Revival and Resurrection Feasibility and Strategic Planning Study," 2005, pp. 107–109.

Morial, Marc H., "Empowering Black Males to Reach Their Full Potential," 2007, pp. 13-15.

Reed, James, and Aaron Thomas, The National Urban League: The National Urban League: Empowering Black Males to Reach Their Full Potential, 2007, pp. 217–218.

Rodgers III, William, M., "Why Should African Americans Care About Macroeconomic Policy," 2007, pp. 89-103.

Rodgers III, William M., "Why Reduce African-American Male Unemployment?," 2009, pp. 109–121.

Wilson, Valerie Rawlston, "On Equal Ground: Causes and Solutions for Lower College Completion Rates Among Black Males," 2007, pp. 123-135.

Business

Emerson, Melinda F., "Five Things You Must Have to Run a Successful Business," 2004, pp. 153–156.

Glasgow, Douglas G., "The Black Underclass in Perspective," 1987, pp. 129–144.

Henderson, Lenneal J., "Empowerment through Enterprise: African-American Business Development," 1993, pp. 91–108.

Price, Hugh B., "Beacons in a New Millennium: Reflections on 21st-Century Leaders and Leadership," 2000, pp. 13–39.

Tidwell, Billy J., "Black Wealth: Facts and Fiction," 1988, pp. 193–210.

Turner, Mark D., "Escaping the 'Ghetto' of Subcontracting," 2006, pp. 117–131.

Walker, Juliet E.K., "The Future of Black Business in America: Can It Get Out of the Box?," 2000, pp. 199–226.

Children and Youth

Bell, William C., "How are the Children? Foster Care and African-American Boys," 2007, pp. 151-157.

Comer, James P., "Leave No Child Behind: Preparing Today's Youth for Tomorrow's World," 2005, pp.75–84.

Cox, Kenya L. Covington, "The Childcare Imbalance: Impact on Working Opportunities for Poor Mothers," 2003, pp. 197–224d.

Edelman, Marian Wright, "The State of Our Children," 2006, pp. 133–141.

———, "Losing Our Children in America's Cradle to Prison Pipeline," 2007, pp. 219-227.

Fulbright-Anderson, Karen, "Developing Our Youth: What Works," 1996, pp. 127–143.

Hare, Bruce R., "Black Youth at Risk," 1988, pp. 81–93.

Howard, Jeff P., "The Third Movement: Developing Black Children for the 21st Century," 1993, pp. 11–34.

Knaus, Christopher B., "Still Segregated, Still Unequal: Analyzing the Impact of No Child Left Behind on African-American Students," 2007, pp. 105-121.

McMurray, Georgia L. "Those of Broader Vision: An African-American

Perspective on Teenage Pregnancy and Parenting," 1990, pp. 195–211.

Moore, Evelyn K., "The Call: Universal Child Care," 1996, pp. 219–244.

Scott, Kimberly A., "A Case Study: African-American Girls and Their Families," 2003, pp. 181–195.

Williams, Terry M., and William Kornblum, "A Portrait of Youth: Coming of Age in Harlem Public Housing," 1991, pp. 187–207.

Civic Engagement

Alton, Kimberley, "The State of Civil Rights 2008," 2008, pp. 157–161.

Campbell, Melanie L., "Election Reform: Protecting Our Vote from the Enemy That Never Sleeps," 2008, pp. 149-156.

Grant, Gwendolyn, Lessons from the President, "The Fullness of Time for a More Perfect Union: The Movement Continues...," 2009, pp. 171–177.

Lindsay, Tiffany, "Weaving the Fabric: The Political Activism of Young African-American Women," 2008, pp. 187–192.

Civil Rights

Alton, Kimberley, "The State of Civil Rights 2008," 2008, pp. 157–161.

Archer, Dennis W., "Security Must Never Trump Liberty," 2004, pp. 139–142.

Burnham, David, "The Fog of War," 2005, pp. 123-127.

Campbell, Melanie L., "Election Reform: Protecting Our Vote from the Enemy That Never Sleeps," 2008, pp. 149-156.

Grant, Gwendolyn, Lessons from the President, "The Fullness of Time for a More Perfect Union: The Movement Continues...," 2009, pp. 171–177.

Jones, Nathaniel R., "The State of Civil Rights," 2006, pp. 165–170.

Ogletree, Jr., Charles J., "Brown at 50: Considering the Continuing Legal Struggle for
Racial Justice," 2004, pp. 81–96.

Shaw, Theodore M., "The State of Civil Rights," 2007, pp. 173-183.

Criminal Justice

Curry, George E., "Racial Disparities Drive Prison Boom," 2006, pp. 171–187.

Drucker, Ernest M., "The Impact of Mass Incarceration on Public Health in Black Communities," 2003, pp. 151–168.

Edelman, Marian Wright, "Losing Our Children in America's *Cradle to Prison*

Pipeline," 2007, pp. 219-227.

Lanier, James R., "The Harmful Impact of the Criminal Justice System and War on Drugs on the African-American Family," 2003, pp. 169–179.

Diversity

Bell, Derrick, "The Elusive Quest for Racial Justice: The Chronicle of the Constitutional Contradiction," 1991, pp. 9–23.

Cobbs, Price M., "Critical Perspectives on the Psychology of Race," 1988, pp. 61–70.

————, "Valuing Diversity: The Myth and the Challenge," 1989, pp. 151–159.

Darity, William Jr., "History, Discrimination and Racial Inequality," 1999, pp. 153–166.

Jones, Stephanie J., "Sunday Morning Apartheid: A Diversity Study of the Sunday Morning Talk Shows," 2006, pp. 189-228.

Watson, Bernard C., "The Demographic Revolution: Diversity in 21st-Century America," 1992, pp. 31–59.

Wiley, Maya, "Hurricane Katrina Exposed the Face of Diversity," 2006, pp. 143–153.

Drug Trade

Lanier, James R., "The Harmful Impact of the Criminal Justice System and War on Drugs on the African-American Family," 2003, pp. 169–179.

Economics

Alexis, Marcus and Geraldine R. Henderson, "The Economic Base of African-American Communities: A Study of Consumption Patterns," 1994, pp. 51–82.

Bradford, William, "Black Family Wealth in the United States," 2000, pp. 103-145.

————, "Money Matters: Lending Discrimination in African-American Communities," 1993, pp. 109–134.

Burbridge, Lynn C., "Toward Economic Self-Sufficiency: Independence Without Poverty," 1993, pp. 71–90.

Edwards, Harry, "Playoffs and Payoffs: The African-American Athlete as an Institutional Resource," 1994, pp. 85–111.

Gordon, III, Sam, Letter to the President, 2009, p. 99.

Graves Jr., Earl, "Wealth for Life," 2009, pp. 165–170.

Hamilton, Darrick, "The Racial Composition of American Jobs," 2006, pp. 77-115.

Harris, Andrea, "The Subprime Wipeout: Unsustainable Loans Erase Gains Made by African-American Women," 2008, pp. 125-133.

Henderson, Lenneal J., "Blacks, Budgets, and Taxes: Assessing the Impact of Budget Deficit Reduction and Tax Reform on Blacks," 1987, pp. 75–95.

———,"Budget and Tax Strategy: Implications for Blacks," 1990, pp. 53–71.

———, "Public Investment for Public Good: Needs, Benefits, and Financing Options," 1992, pp. 213–229.

Herman, Alexis, "African-American Women and Work: Still a Tale of Two Cities," 2008, pp. 109-113.

Holzer, Harry J., "Reconnecting Young Black Men: What Policies Would Help," 2007, pp. 75-87.

Jeffries, John M., and Richard L. Schaffer, "Changes in Economy and Labor Market Status of Black Americans," 1996, pp. 12-77.

Malveaux, Julianne, "Shouldering the Third Burden: The Status of African-American Women," 2008, pp. 75-81.

———, "The Parity Imperative: Civil Rights, Economic Justice, and the New American Dilemma," 1992, pp. 281–303.

Mensah, Lisa, "Putting Homeownership Back Within Our Reach," 2008, pp. 135-142.

Morial, Marc H. and Marvin Owens, "The National Urban League Economic Empowerment Initiative," 2005, pp. 111-113.

Myers, Jr., Samuel L., "African-American Economic Well-Being During the Boom and Bust," 2004, pp. 53–80.

National Urban League, "Recommendations: Opportunity to Thrive, Opportunity to Earn, Opportunity to Own, Opportunity to Prosper," 2009, pp. 187-191.

National Urban League, The National Urban League's Homebuyer's Bill of Rights, 2008, pp. 143-147.

National Urban League Research Staff, "African Americans in Profile: Selected Demographic, Social and Economic Data," 1992, pp. 309–325.

———, "The Economic Status of African Americans During the Reagan-Bush Era

Withered Opportunities, Limited Outcomes, and Uncertain Outlook," 1993, pp. 135–200.

———, "The Economic Status of African Americans: Limited Ownership and Persistent Inequality," 1992, pp. 61–117.

———, "The Economic Status of African Americans: 'Permanent' Poverty and Inequality," 1991, pp. 25–75.

———, "Economic Status of Black Americans During the 1980s: A Decade of Limited Progress," 1990, pp. 25–52.

———, "Economic Status of Black Americans," 1989, pp. 9–39.

———, "Economic Status of Black 1987," 1988, pp. 129–152.

———, "Economic Status of Blacks 1986," 1987, pp. 49–73.

National Urban League, Recommendations: Opportunity to Thrive; Opportunity to Earn; Opportunity to Own; Opportunity to Prosper, 2009, pp. 187–191

Reuben, Lucy J., "Make Room for the New 'She'EOs: An Analysis of Businesses Owned by Black Females," 2008, pp. 115-124.

Richardson, Cy, "What Must Be Done: The Case for More Homeownership and Financial Education Counseling," 2009, pp. 145–155.

Rodgers III, William, M., "Why Should African Americans Care About Macroeconomic Policy," 2007, pp. 89-103.

Shapiro, Thomas M., "The Racial Wealth Gap," 2005, pp. 41–48.

Spriggs, William E., "Nothing Trickles Down: How Reaganomics Failed America," 2009, pp. 123-133.

Taylor, Robert D., "Wealth Creation: The Next Leadership Challenge," 2005, pp. 119–122.

Thompson, J. Phillip, "The Coming Green Economy," 2009, pp. 135–142.

Tidwell, Billy J., "Economic Costs of American Racism," 1991, pp. 219–232.

Turner, Mark D., "Escaping the 'Ghetto' of Subcontracting," 2006, pp. 117-131.

Watkins, Celeste, "The Socio-Economic Divide Among Black Americans Under 35," 2001, pp. 67-85.

Webb, Michael B., "Programs for Progress and Empowerment: The Urban League's National Education Initiative," 1993, pp. 203-216.

Education

Allen, Walter R., "The Struggle Continues: Race, Equity and Affirmative Action in U.S. Higher Education," 2001, pp. 87-100.

Bailey, Deirdre, "School Choice: The Option of Success," 2001, pp. 101-114.

Bradford, William D., "Dollars for Deeds: Prospects and Prescriptions for African-American Financial Institutions," 1994, pp. 31–50.

Cole, Johnnetta Betsch, "The Triumphs and Challenges of Historically Black Colleges and Universities," 2008, pp. 99-107.

Comer, James P., Norris Haynes, and Muriel Hamilton-Leel, "School Power: A Model for Improving Black Student Achievement," 1990, pp. 225–238.

——"Leave No Child Behind: Preparing Today's Youth for Tomorrow's World," 2005, pp. 75–84.

Dilworth, Mary E. "Historically Black Colleges and Universities: Taking Care of Home," 1994, pp. 127–151.

Edelman, Marian Wright, "Black Children In America," 1989, pp. 63–76.

Fattah, Chaka, "Needed: Equality in Education," 2009, pp. 57–60.

Freeman, Dr. Kimberly Edelin, "African-American Men and Women in Higher Education: 'Filling the Glass' in the New Millennium," 2000, pp. 61–90.

Gordon, Edmund W., "The State of Education in Black America," 2004, pp. 97–113.

Guinier, Prof. Lani, "Confirmative Action in a Multiracial Democracy," 2000, pp. 333–364.

Hall, Isiah R., Letter to the President, 2009, p. 43

Hanson, Renee R., "A Pathway to School Readiness: The Impact of Family on Early Childhood Education," 2008, pp. 89-98.

Jackson, John H., "From Miracle to Movement: Mandating a National Opportunity to Learn, 2009, pp. 61–70.

Journal of Blacks in Higher Education (reprint), "The 'Acting White' Myth," 2005, pp.115–117.

Knaus, Christopher B., "Still Segregated, Still Unequal: Analyzing the Impact of No Child Left Behind on African American Students," 2007, pp. 105-121.

McBay, Shirley M. "The Condition of African American Education: Changes and Challenges," 1992, pp. 141–156.

McKenzie, Floretta Dukes with Patricia Evans, "Education Strategies for the 90s," 1991, pp. 95–109.

Robinson, Sharon P., "Taking Charge: An Approach to Making the Educational Problems of Blacks Comprehensible and Manageable," 1987, pp. 31–47.

Rose, Dr. Stephanie Bell, "African-American High Achievers: Developing

Talented Leaders," 2000, pp. 41–60.

Ross, Ronald O., "Gaps, Traps and Lies: African-American Students and Test Scores," 2004, pp. 157–161.

Smith, Hal F., "The Questions Before Us: Opportunity, Education and Equity," 2009, pp. 45–55.

Sudarkasa, Niara, "Black Enrollment in Higher Education: The Unfulfilled Promise of Equality," 1988, pp. 7–22.

Watson, Bernard C., with Fasaha M. Traylor, "Tomorrow's Teachers: Who Will They Be, What Will They Know?" 1988, pp. 23–37.

Willie, Charles V., "The Future of School Desegregation," 1987, pp. 37–47.

Wilson, Reginald, "Black Higher Education: Crisis and Promise," 1989, pp. 121–135.

Wilson, Valerie Rawlston, "On Equal Ground: Causes and Solutions for Lower College Completion Rates Among Black Males," 2007, pp. 123-135.

Wirschem, David, "Community Mobilization for Education in Rochester, New York: A Case Study," 1991, pp. 243-248.

Emerging Ideas

Huggins, Sheryl, "The Rules of the Game," 2001, pp. 65-66.

Employment

Anderson, Bernard E., "The Black Worker: Continuing Quest for Economic Parity, 2002, pp. 51-67

Darity, William M., Jr., and Samuel L.Myers, Jr., "Racial Earnings Inequality into the 21st Century," 1992, pp. 119–139.

Dodd, Christopher J., "Infrastructure and Job Creation—A Priority for Urban America," 2009, pp. 101-108.

Hamilton, Darrick, "The Racial Composition of American Jobs," 2006, pp. 77–115.

Hammond, Theresa A., "African Americans in White-Collar Professions," 2002, pp. 109–121.

Herman, Alexis, "African-American Women and Work: Still a Tale of Two Cities," 2008, pp. 109-113.

Reuben, Lucy J., "Make Room for the New 'She'EOs: An Analysis of Businesses Owned by Black Females," 2008, pp. 115-124.

Rodgers III, William M., "Why Reduce African-American Male Unemployment?," 2009, pp. 109–121.

Thomas, R. Roosevelt, Jr., "Managing Employee Diversity: An Assessment," 1991, pp. 145–154.

Tidwell, Billy, J., "Parity Progress and Prospects: Racial Inequalities in Economic Well-being," 2000, pp. 287–316.

——, "African Americans and the 21st- Century Labor Market: Improving the Fit," 1993, pp. 35–57.

——, "The Unemployment Experience of African Americans: Some Important Correlates and Consequences," 1990, pp. 213–223.

——, "A Profile of the Black Unemployed," 1987, pp. 223–237.

Equality

Fattah, Chaka, "Needed: Equality in Education," 2009, pp. 57–60.

Jackson, John H., "From Miracle to Movement: Mandating a National Opportunity to Learn," 2009, pp. 61–79.

Raines, Franklin D., "What Equality Would Look Like: Reflections on the Past, Present and Future, 2002, pp. 13-27.

Smith, Hal F., "The Questions Before Us: Opportunity, Education and Equity," 2009, pp. 45-55

Equality Index

Global Insight, Inc., The National Urban League Equality Index, 2004, pp. 15-34.

——, The National Urban League Equality Index, 2005, pp. 15-40.

Orozco, Ana and Robert Tomarelli of Global Insight, Inc., The National Urban League 2009 *Equality Index*, 2009, pp. 25-41.

Thompson, Rondel and Sophia Parker of Global Insight, Inc.,The National Urban League Equality Index, 2006, pp. 13-60.

Thompson, Rondel and Sophia Parker of Global Insight, Inc., The National Urban League Equality Index, 2007 pp. 17-58.

Wilson, Valerie Rawlston, The National Urban League 2008 Equality Index: Analysis, 2008, pp. 15-24.

Wilson, Valerie Rawlston, Introduction to the 2009 Equality Index, 2009, pp. 15–24.

Families

Battle, Juan, Cathy J. Cohen, Angelique Harris, and Beth E. Richie, "We Are Family: Embracing Our Lesbian, Gay, Bisexual, and Transgender (LGBT) Family Members," 2003, pp. 93-106.

Billingsley, Andrew, "Black Families in a Changing Society," 1987, pp. 97–111.

———, "Understanding African-American Family Diversity," 1990, pp. 85–108.

Cox, Kenya L. Covington, "The Childcare Imbalance: Impact on Working Opportunities for Poor Mothers," 2003, pp. 197-224d.

Drucker, Ernest M., "The Impact of Mass Incarceration on Public Health in Black Communities," 2003, pp. 151-168.

Dyson, Eric Michael, "Sexual Fault Lines: Robbing the Love Between Us," 2007, pp. 229-237.

Hanson, Renee R., "A Pathway to School Readiness: The Impact of Family on Early Childhood Education," 2008, pp. 89-98.

Hill, Robert B., "Critical Issues for Black Families by the Year 2000," 1989, pp. 41–61.

———, "The Strengths of Black Families' Revisited," 2003, pp. 107-149.

Ivory, Steven, "Universal Fatherhood: Black Men Sharing the Load," 2007, pp. 243-247.

Rawlston, Valerie A., "The Impact of Social Security on Child Poverty," 2000, pp. 317–331.

Scott, Kimberly A., "A Case Study: African-American Girls and Their Families," 2003, pp. 181-195.

Shapiro, Thomas M., "The Racial Wealth Gap," 2005, pp. 41-48

Stafford, Walter, Angela Dews, Melissa Mendez, and Diana Salas, "Race, Gender and Welfare Reform: The Need for Targeted Support," 2003, pp. 41-92.

Stockard (Jr.), Russell L. and M. Belinda Tucker, "Young African-American Men and Women: Separate Paths?," 2001, pp. 143-159.

Teele, James E., "E. Franklin Frazier: The Man and His Intellectual Legacy," 2003, pp. 29-40

Thompson, Dr. Linda S. and Georgene Butler, "The Role of the Black Family in Promoting Healthy Child Development," 2000, pp. 227–241.

West, Carolyn M., "Feminism is a Black Thing"?: Feminist Contribution to Black Family Life, 2003, pp. 13-27.

Willie, Charles V. "The Black Family: Striving Toward Freedom," 1988, pp. 71–80.

Foreword
Height, Dorothy I., "Awakenings," 2008, pp. 9-10.
Obama, Barack, Foreword, 2007, pp. 9-12.
King III, Martin, Luther, "The American Narrative," pp. 9-10.

From the President's Desk
Morial, Marc H., "The State of Black America: The Complexity of Black Progress," 2004, pp. 11-14.
———, "The State of Black America: Prescriptions for Change," 2005, pp. 11–14
———, "The National Urban League Opportunity Compact," 2006, pp. 9–11.
———, "Empowering Black Males to Reach Their Full Potential," 2007,pp. 13-15.
———, From the President's Desk, 2008, pp. 11-14.
———, From the President's Desk, 2009, pp. 11–13.

Health
Browne, Doris, "The Impact of Health Disparities in African-American Women," 2008, pp. 163-171.
Carnethon, Mercedes R., "Black Male Life Expectancy in the United States: A Multi-level Exploration of Causes," 2007, pp. 137-150.
Cooper, Maudine R., "The Invisibility Blues' of Black Women in America," 2008, pp. 83-87.
Christmas, June Jackson, "The Health of African Americans: Progress Toward Healthy People 2000," 1996, pp. 95–126.
Gaskin, Darrell J., "Improving African Americans Access to Quality Healthcare," 2009, pp. 73–86
Leffall, LaSalle D., Jr., "Health Status of Black Americans," 1990, pp. 121–142.
McAlpine, Robert, "Toward Development of a National Drug Control Strategy," 1991, pp. 233–241.
Morris, Eboni D., "By the Numbers: Uninsured African-American Women," 2008, pp. 173-177.
Morris, Eboni and Lisa Bland Malone, "Health Is Where the Home Is: The

Relationship Between Housing, Neighborhoods and Health Status," 2009, pp. 87–98.

Nobles, Wade W., and Lawford L. Goddard, "Drugs in the African-American Community: A Clear and Present Danger," 1989, pp. 161–181.

Primm, Annelle and Marisela B. Gomez, "The Impact of Mental Health on Chronic Disease," 2005, pp. 63–73.

Primm, Beny J., "AIDS: A Special Report," 1987, pp. 159–166.

———, "Drug Use: Special Implications for Black America," 1987, pp. 145–158.

Smedley, Brian D., "Race, Poverty, and Healthcare Disparities," 2006, pp. 155–164.

Williams, David R., "Health and the Quality of Life Among African Americans," 2004, pp. 115-138.

Williams, Erica Marie, Letter to the President, 2009, p. 71.

Housing

Calmore, John O., "To Make Wrong Right: The Necessary and Proper Aspirations of Fair Housing," 1989, pp. 77–109.

Clay, Phillip, "Housing Opportunity: A Dream Deferred," 1990, pp. 73–84.

Cooper, Maudine R., "The Invisibility Blues' of Black Women in America," 2008, pp. 83-87.

Dokes, Malinda, Letter to the President, 2009, p. 143.

Freeman, Lance, "Black Homeownership: A Dream No Longer Deferred?," 2006, pp. 63–75.

Graves, Jr., Earl G., "Wealth for Life," 2009, pp. 165–170.

Harris, Andrea, "The Subprime Wipeout: Unsustainable Loans Erase Gains Made by African-American Women," 2008, pp. 125–133.

James, Angela, "Black Homeownership: Housing and Black Americans Under 35," 2001, pp. 115-129.

Jones, Stephanie J., "The Subprime Meltdown: Disarming the 'Weapons of Mass Deception'," 2009, pp. 157–164.

Leigh, Wilhelmina A., "U.S. Housing Policy in 1996: The Outlook for Black Americans," 1996, pp. 188–218.

Morris, Eboni and Lisa Bland Malone, "Health Is Where the Home Is: The Relationship Between Housing, Neighborhoods and Health Status," 2009, pp. 87-98.

Richardson, Cy, "What Must Be Done? The Case for More Homeownership and Financial Education Counseling," 2009, pp. 145–155

Spriggs, William E., "Nothing Trickles Down: How Reaganomics Failed America," 2009, pp. 123–133

In Memoriam

National Urban League, "William A. Bootle, Ray Charles, Margo T. Clarke, Ossie Davis, Herman C. Ewing, James Forman, Joanne Grant, Ann Kheel, Memphis Norman, Max Schmeling," 2005, pp. 139–152.

————, "Renaldo Benson, Shirley Chisholm, Johnnie Cochran, Jr., Shirley Horn, John H. Johnson, Vivian Malone Jones, Brock Peters, Richard Pryor, Bobby Short, C. Delores Tucker, August Wilson, Luther Vandross, and NUL members Clarence Lyle Barney, Jr., Manuel Augustus Romero;" 2006, pp. 279–287.

————, "Ossie Davis: Still Caught in the Dream," 2005, pp. 137–138.

————, "Ed Bradley, James Brown, Bebe Moore Campbell, Katherine Dunham, Mike Evans, Coretta Scott King, Gerald Levert, Gordon Parks, June Pointer, Lou Rawls, and Helen E. Harden," 2007, pp. 249-257.

————, "Effi Barry, Jane Bolin, Daniel A. Collins (NUL Member), Oliver Hill, Yolanda King, Calvin Lockhart, Mahlon Puryear (NUL Member), Max Roach, Eddie Robinson, William Simms (NUL Member), Darryl Stingley, and Ike Turner," 2008, pp. 205-217.

————, In Memoriam, 2009, pp. 225–241

Jones, Stephanie J., "Rosa Parks: An Ordinary Woman, An Extraordinary Life," 2006, pp. 245–246.

Military Affairs

Butler, John Sibley, "African Americans and the American Military," 2002, pp. 93-107.

Music

Boles, Mark A., "Breaking the 'Hip Hop' Hold: Looking Beyond the Media Hype," 2007, pp. 239-241.

Brown, David W., "Their Characteristic Music: Thoughts on Rap Music and Hip-Hop Culture," 2001, pp. 189–201.

Bynoe, Yvonne, "The Roots of Rap Music and Hip-Hop Culture: One Perspective," 2001, pp. 175–187.

Op-Ed/Commentary

Archer, Dennis W., "Security Must Never Trump Liberty," 2004, pp. 139–142.

Bailey, Moya, "Going in Circles: The Struggle to Diversify Popular Images of Black Women," 2008, pp. 193-196.

Bernard, Michelle D., "November 4, 2008: An Ode to Black America," pp. 203–207.

Boles, Mark A., "Breaking the 'Hip Hop' Hold: Looking Beyond the Media Hype," 2007, pp. 239-241.

Burnham, David, "The Fog of War," 2005, pp. 123–127.

Cook, Cassye D., "The Game Changer: Are We Beyond What is Next to What is Now?," 2009, pp. 209–212.

Covington, Kenya L., "The Transformation of the Welfare Caseload," 2004, pp. 149–152.

Dyson, Eric Michael, "Sexual Fault Lines: Robbing the Love Between Us," 2007, pp. 229-237.

Edelman, Marian Wright, "Losing Our Children in America's *Cradle to Prison Pipeline*," 2007, pp. 219-227.

Emerson, Melinda F., "Five Things You Must Have to Run a Successful Business," 2004, pp. 153–156.

Ivory, Steven, "Universal Fatherhood: Black Men Sharing the Load," 2007, pp. 243-247.

Johns, David J., "If Not for Me … Then for My Children," 2009, pp. 199-202.

Jones, Nathaniel R., "Did I Ever?," 2009, pp. 213–219.

Journal of Blacks in Higher Education (reprint), "The 'Acting White' Myth," 2005, pp. 115–117.

Lanier, James R., "The Empowerment Movement and the Black Male," 2004, pp. 143–148.

Lee, Barbara, "The Congressional Black Caucus and President Barack Obama: Speaking with One Voice to Fill the Moral Gaps in Our World," 2009, pp. 193–197.

Lindsay, Tiffany, "Weaving the Fabric: the Political Activism of Young African-American Women," 2008, pp. 187-192.

Malveaux, Julianne, "Black Women's Hands Can Rock the World: Global Involvement and Understanding," 2008, pp. 197-202.

Ross, Ronald O., "Gaps, Traps and Lies: African-American Students and Test Scores," 2004, pp. 157–161.

Taylor, Susan L., "Black Love Under Siege," 2008 pp. 179-186.

Taylor, Robert D., "Wealth Creation: The Next Leadership Challenge," 2005, pp. 119–122.

West, Cornel, "Democracy Matters," 2005, pp. 129–132.

Overview

Morial, Marc H., "Black America's Family Matters," 2003, pp. 9-12.

Price, Hugh B., "Still Worth Fighting For: America After 9/11," 2002, pp. 9-11

Politics

Alton, Kimberley, "The State of Civil Rights 2008," 2008, pp. 157-161.

Campbell, Melanie L., "Election Reform: Protecting Our Vote from the Enemy Who Never Sleeps," 2008, pp. 149-156.

Coleman, Henry A., "Interagency and Intergovernmental Coordination: New Demands for Domestic Policy Initiatives," 1992, pp. 249–263.

Hamilton, Charles V., "On Parity and Political Empowerment," 1989, pp. 111–120.

———, "Promoting Priorities: African-American Political Influence in the 1990s," 1993, pp. 59–69.

Henderson, Lenneal J., "Budgets, Taxes, and Politics: Options for the African-American Community," 1991, pp. 77–93.

Holden, Matthew, Jr., "The Rewards of Daring and the Ambiguity of Power: Perspectives on the Wilder Election of 1989," 1990, pp. 109–120.

Kilson, Martin L., "African Americans and American Politics 2002: The Maturation Phase," 2002, pp. 147–180.

———, "Thinking About the Black Elite's Role: Yesterday and Today," 2005, pp. 85-106.

Lee, Silas, "Who's Going to Take the Weight? African Americans and Civic Engagement in the 21st Century," 2007, pp. 185-192.

Lindsay, Tiffany, "Weaving the Fabric: The Political Activism of Young African-American Women," 2008, pp. 187-192.

McHenry, Donald F., "A Changing World Order: Implications for Black America," 1991, pp. 155–163.

Persons, Georgia A., "Blacks in State and Local Government: Progress and Constraints," 1987, pp. 167–192.

Pinderhughes, Dianne M., "Power and Progress: African-American Politics in the New Era of Diversity," 1992, pp. 265–280.

———, "The Renewal of the Voting Rights Act," 2005, pp. 49–61.

———, "Civil Rights and the Future of the American Presidency," 1988, pp. 39–60. Price, Hugh B., "Black America's Challenge: The Re-construction of Black Civil Society," 2001, pp. 13-18.

Tidwell, Billy J., "Serving the National Interest: A Marshall Plan for America," 1992, pp. 11–30.

West, Cornel, "Democracy Matters," 2005, pp. 129–132.

Williams, Eddie N., "The Evolution of Black Political Power", 2000, pp. 91–102.

Poverty

Cooper, Maudine R., "The Invisibility Blues' of Black Women in America," 2008, pp. 83-87.

Edelman, Marian Wright, "The State of Our Children," 2006, pp. 133–141.

Prescriptions for Change

National Urban League, "Prescriptions for Change," 2005, pp. 133-135.

Relationships

Taylor, Susan L., "Black Love Under Siege," 2008, pp. 179-186.

Religion

Lincoln, C. Eric, "Knowing the Black Church: What It Is and Why," 1989, pp. 137–149.

Richardson, W. Franklyn, "Mission to Mandate: Self-Development through the Black Church," 1994, pp. 113–126.

Smith, Dr. Drew, "The Evolving Political Priorities of African-American Churches: An Empirical View," 2000, pp. 171–197.

Taylor, Mark V.C., "Young Adults and Religion," 2001, pp. 161–174.

Reports from the National Urban League

Hanson, Renee, Mark McArdle, and Valerie Rawlston Wilson, "Invisible Men: The Urgent Problems of Low-Income African-American Males," 2007, pp. 209-216.

Lanier, James, "The National Urban League's Commission on the Black Male: Renewal, Revival and Resurrection Feasibility and Strategic Planning Study," 2005, pp. 107–109.

Jones, Stephanie J., "Sunday Morning Apartheid: A Diversity Study of the Sunday Morning Talk Shows" 2006, pp. 189–228.

National Urban League Policy Institute, The Opportunity Compact: A Blueprint for Economic Equality, 2008, pp. 43-74.

Wilson, Valerie Rawlston and Bernard E. Anderson, "Economic Stimulus and Job Creation in Urban Communities," 2009, pp. 179–186

Reports

Joint Center for Political and Economic Studies, A Way Out: Creating Partners for Our Nation's Prosperity by Expanding Life Paths for Young Men of Color – Final Report of the Dellums Commission, 2007, pp. 193-207.

Reed, James and Aaron Thomas, The National Urban League: Empowering Black Males to Meet Their Full Potential, 2007, pp. 217-218.

Sexual Identity

Bailey, Moya, "Going in Circles: The Struggle to Diversify Popular Images of Black Women," 2008 pp. 193-196.

Battle, Juan, Cathy J. Cohen, Angelique Harris, and Beth E. Richie, "We Are Family: Embracing Our Lesbian, Gay, Bisexual, and Transgender (LGBT) Family Members," 2003, pp. 93-106.

Taylor, Susan L., "Black Love Under Siege," 2008, pp. 179-186.

Sociology

Cooper, Maudine R., "The Invisibility Blues' of Black Women in America," 2008, pp. 83-87.

Taylor, Susan L., "Black Love Under Siege," 2008, pp. 179-186.

Teele, James E., "E. Franklin Frazier: The Man and His Intellectual Legacy," 2003, pp. 29-40.

Special Section: Black Women's Health

Browne, Doris, "The Impact of Health Disparities in African-American Women," 2008, pp. 163-171.

Morris, Eboni D., "By the Numbers: Uninsured African-American Women," 2008, pp. 173-177.

Special Section: Katrina and Beyond

Brazile, Donna L., "New Orleans: Next Steps on the Road to Recovery," 2006, pp. 233–237.

Morial, Marc H., "New Orleans Revisited," 2006, pp. 229–232.

National Urban League, "The National Urban League Katrina Bill of Rights," 2006, pp. 239–243.

Surveys

The National Urban League Survey, 2004, pp. 35-51.

Stafford, Walter S., "The National Urban League Survey: Black America's Under-35 Generation," 2001, pp. 19-63.

——, "The New York Urban League Survey: Black New York—On Edge, But Optimistic," 2001, pp. 203-219.

Technology

Dreyfuss, Joel, "Black Americans and the Internet: The Technological Imperative," 2001, pp. 131-141.

Wilson Ernest J., III, "Technological Convergence, Media Ownership and Content Diversity," 2000, pp. 147–170.

Urban Affairs

Allen, Antoine, and Leland Ware, "The Geography of Discrimination: Hypersegregation, Isolation and Fragmentation Within the African-American Community," 2002, pp. 69–92.

Bates, Timothy, "The Paradox of Urban Poverty," 1996, pp. 144–163.

Bell, Carl C., with Esther J. Jenkins,"Preventing Black Homicide," 1990,pp. 143–155.

Bryant Solomon, Barbara, "Social Welfare Reform," 1987, pp. 113–127.

Brown, Lee P., "Crime in the Black Community," 1988, pp. 95–113.

Bullard, Robert D. "Urban Infrastructure: Social, Environmental, and Health Risks to African Americans," 1992, pp.183–196.

Chambers, Julius L., "The Law and Black Americans: Retreat from Civil Rights," 1987, pp. 15–30.

———, "Black Americans and the Courts: Has the Clock Been Turned Back Permanently?" 1990, pp. 9–24.

Edelin, Ramona H., "Toward an African-American Agenda: An Inward Look," 1990, pp. 173–183.

Fair, T. Willard, "Coordinated Community Empowerment: Experiences of the Urban League of Greater Miami," 1993, pp. 217–233.

Gray, Sandra T., "Public-Private Partnerships: Prospects for America. . . Promise for African Americans," 1992, pp. 231–247.

Harris, David, " 'Driving While Black' and Other African-American Crimes: The Continuing Relevance of Race to American Criminal Justice," 2000, pp. 259–285.

Henderson, Lenneal J., "African Americans in the Urban Milieu: Conditions, Trends, and Development Needs," 1994, pp. 11–29.

Hill, Robert B., "Urban Redevelopment: Developing Effective Targeting Strategies," 1992, pp. 197–211.

Jones, Dionne J., with Greg Harrison of the National Urban League Research Department, "Fast Facts: Comparative Views of African-American Status and Progress," 1994, pp. 213–236.

Jones, Shirley J., "Silent Suffering: The Plight of Rural Black America," 1994, pp.171–188.

Massey, Walter E. "Science, Technology, and Human Resources: Preparing for the 21st Century," 1992, pp. 157–169.

Mendez, Jr. Garry A., "Crime Is Not a Part of Our Black Heritage: A Theoretical Essay," 1988, pp. 211–216.

Miller, Warren F., Jr., "Developing Untapped Talent: A National Call for African-American Technologists," 1991, pp. 111–127.

Murray, Sylvester, "Clear and Present Danger: The Decay of America's Physical Infrastructure," 1992, pp. 171–182.

Pemberton, Gayle, "It's the Thing That Counts, Or Reflections on the Legacy of W.E.B. Du Bois," 1991, pp. 129–143.

Pinderhughes, Dianne M., "The Case of African-Americans in the Persian Gulf:

The Intersection of American Foreign and Military Policy with Domestic Employment Policy in the United States," 1991, pp. 165–186.

Robinson, Gene S. "Television Advertising and Its Impact on Black America," 1990, pp. 157–171.

Sawyers, Dr. Andrew and Dr. Lenneal Henderson, "Race, Space and Justice: Cities and Growth in the 21st Century," 2000, pp. 243–258.

Schneider, Alvin J., "Blacks in the Military: The Victory and the Challenge," 1988, pp. 115–128.

Smedley, Brian, "Race, Poverty, and Healthcare Disparities," 2006, pp. 155–164.

Stafford, Walter, Angela Dews, Melissa Mendez, and Diana Salas, "Race, Gender and Welfare Reform: The Need for Targeted Support," 2003, pp. 41–92.

Stewart, James B., "Developing Black and Latino Survival Strategies: The Future of Urban Areas," 1996, pp. 164–187.

Stone, Christopher E., "Crime and Justice in Black America," 1996, pp. 78–94.

Tidwell, Billy J., with Monica B. Kuumba, Dionne J. Jones, and Betty C. Watson, "Fast Facts: African Americans in the 1990s," 1993, pp. 243–265.

Wallace-Benjamin, Joan, "Organizing African-American Self-Development: The Role of Community-Based Organizations," 1994, pp. 189–205.

Walters, Ronald, "Serving the People: African-American Leadership and the Challenge of Empowerment," 1994, pp. 153–170.

Allen, Antoine, and Leland Ware, "The Geography of Discrimination: Hypersegregation, Isolation and Fragmentation Within the African-American Community," 2002, pp. 69–92.

Wiley, Maya, "Hurricane Katrina Exposed the Face of Poverty," 2006, pp. 143–153.

Welfare

Bergeron, Suzanne, and William E. Spriggs, "Welfare Reform and Black America," 2002, pp. 29–50.

Cooper, Maudine R., "The Invisibility Blues' of Black Women in America," 2008, pp. 83-87.

Covington, Kenya L., "The Transformation of the Welfare Caseload," 2004, pp. 149–152.

Spriggs, William E., and Suzanne Bergeron, "Welfare Reform and Black

America," 2002, pp. 29–50.

Stafford, Walter, Angela Dews, Melissa Mendez, and Diana Salas, "Race, Gender and Welfare Reform: The Need for Targeted Support," 2003, pp. 41-92.

Women's Issues

Bailey, Moya, "Going in Circles: The Struggle to Diversify Popular Images of Black Women," 2008, pp. 193-196.

Browne, Doris, "The Impact of Health Disparities in African-American Women," 2008, pp. 163-171.

Cooper, Maudine R., "The Invisibility Blues' of Black Women in America," 2008, pp. 83-87.

Harris, Andrea, "The Subprime Wipeout: Unsustainable Loans Erase Gains Made by African-American Women," 2008, pp. 125-133.

Herman, Alexis, "African-American Women and Work: Still a Tale of Two Cities," 2008, pp. 109-113.

Lindsay, Tiffany, "Weaving the Fabric: The Political Activism of Young African-American Women," 2008, pp. 187–192.

Malveaux, Julianne, "Black Women's Hands Can Rock the World: Global Involvement and Understanding," 2008, pp. 197-202.

——, "Shouldering the Third Burden: The Status of African-American Women," 2008, pp. 75-81.

Mensah, Lisa, "Putting Homeownership Back Within Our Reach," 2008, pp. 135-142.

Morris, Eboni D., "By the Numbers: Uninsured African-American Women," 2008, pp. 173-177.

Reuben, Lucy J., "Make Room for the New 'She'EOs: An Analysis of Businesses Owned by Black Females," 2008, pp. 115-124.

Stafford, Walter, Angela Dews, Melissa Mendez, and Diana Salas, "Race, Gender and Welfare Reform: The Need for Targeted Support," 2003, pp. 41–92.

Taylor, Susan L., "Black Love Under Siege," 2008, pp. 179-186.

West, Carolyn M., "Feminism is a Black Thing"?: Feminist Contribution to Black Family Life, 2003, pp. 13–27.

World Affairs

Malveaux, Julianne, "Black Women's Hands Can Rock the World: Global Involvement and Understanding," 2008, pp. 197-202.

APPENDIX IV

History of the National Urban League

The National Urban League, which has played so pivotal a role in the 20th-Century Freedom Movement, grew out of that spontaneous grassroots movement for freedom and opportunity that came to be called the Black Migrations. When the U.S. Supreme Court declared its approval of segregation in the 1896 *Plessy v. Ferguson* decision, the brutal system of economic, social and political oppression, the South quickly adopted rapidly transformed what had been a trickle of African Americans northward into a flood.

Those newcomers to the North soon discovered that while they had escaped the South, they had by no means escaped racial discrimination. Excluded from all but menial jobs in the larger society, victimized by poor housing and education, and inexperienced in the ways of urban living, many lived in terrible social and economic conditions.

Still, in the North and West blacks could vote; and in that and other differences in the degree of difference between living in the South and not living in the South and North lay opportunity—and, that African Americans clearly understood.

But to capitalize on that opportunity, to successfully adapt to urban life and to reduce the pervasive discrimination they faced, they would need help. That was the reason the Committee on Urban Conditions Among Negroes was established on September 29, 1910 in New York City. Central to the organization's founding were two extraordinary, remarkable people: Mrs. Ruth Standish Baldwin and Dr. George Edmund Haynes, who would become the Committee's first executive secretary. Mrs. Baldwin, the widow of a railroad magnate and a member of one of America's oldest families, had a remarkable social conscience and was a stalwart champion of the poor and disadvantaged. Dr. Haynes, a graduate of Fisk University, Yale University, and Columbia University (he was the first African American to receive a doctorate from Columbia University), felt a compelling need to use his training as a social worker to serve his people.

A year later, the Committee merged with the Committee for the Improvement of Industrial Conditions Among Negroes in New York (founded in New York in 1906), and the National League for the Protection of Colored Women (founded in 1905) to form the National League on Urban Conditions Among Negroes. In 1920, the name was later shortened to the National Urban League.

The interracial character of the League's board was set from its first days. Professor Edwin R. A. Seligman of Columbia University, one of the leaders in progressive social service activities in New York City, served as chairman from 1911 to 1913. Mrs. Baldwin took the post until 1915.

The fledgling organization counseled black migrants from the South, helped train black social workers, and worked in various other ways to bring educational and employment opportunities to blacks. Its research into the problems blacks faced in employment opportunities, recreation, housing, health and sanitation, and education spurred the League's quick growth. By the end of World War I, the organization had 81 staff members working in 30 cities.

In 1918, Dr. Haynes was succeeded by Eugene Kinckle Jones who would direct the agency until his retirement in 1941. Under his direction, the League significantly expanded its multifaceted campaign to crack the barriers to black employment, spurred first by the boom years of the 1920s, and then, by the desperate years of the Great Depression. Efforts at reasoned persuasion were buttressed by boycotts against firms that refused to employ blacks, pressures on schools to expand vocational opportunities for young people, constant prodding of Washington officials to include blacks in New Deal recovery programs and a drive to get blacks into previously segregated labor unions.

As World War II loomed, Lester Granger, a seasoned League veteran and crusading newspaper columnist, was appointed Jones' successor.

Outspoken in his commitment to advancing opportunity for African Americans, Granger pushed tirelessly to integrate recalcitrant racist trade unions, and led the League's effort to support A. Philip Randolph's March on Washington Movement to fight discrimination in defense work and in the armed services. Under Granger, the League, through its own Industrial Relations Laboratory, had notable success in cracking the color bar in numerous defense plants. The nation's demand for civilian labor during the war also helped the organization press ahead with greater urgency its programs to train black youths for meaningful blue-collar employment. After the war, those efforts expanded to persuading Fortune 500 companies to hold career conferences on the campuses of Negro Colleges and place blacks in upper-echelon jobs.

Of equal importance to the League's own future sources of support, Granger avidly supported the organization of its volunteer auxiliary, the National Urban League Guild, which, under the leadership of Mollie Moon, became an important national force in its own right.

The explosion of the civil rights movement provoked a change for the League, one personified by its new leader, Whitney M. Young, Jr., who became executive director in 1961. A social worker like his predecessors, he substantially expanded the League's fund-raising ability—and, most critically, made the League a full partner in the civil rights movement. Indeed, although the League's tax-exempt status barred it from protest activities, it hosted at its New York headquarters the planning meetings of A. Philip Randolph, Martin Luther King, Jr., and other civil rights and labor leaders for the 1963 March on Washington. Young was also a forceful advocate for greater government and private-sector involvement in efforts to eradicate poverty. His call for a domestic Marshall Plan, a ten-point program designed to close the huge social and economic gap between black and white Americans, significantly influenced the discussion of the Johnson Administration's War on Poverty legislation.

Young's tragic death in 1971 in a drowning incident off the coast of Lagos, Nigeria brought another change in leadership. Vernon E. Jordan, Jr., formerly Executive Director of the United Negro College Fund, took over as the League's fifth Executive Director in 1972 (the title of the office was changed to President in 1977).

For the next decade, until his resignation in December 1981, Jordan skillfully guided the League to new heights of achievement. He oversaw a major expansion of its social-service efforts, as the League became a significant conduit for the federal government to establish programs and deliver services to aid urban communities, and brokered fresh initiatives in such League programs as housing, health, education and minority business development. Jordan also instituted a citizenship education program that helped increase the black vote and brought new programs to such areas as energy, the environment, and non-traditional jobs for women of color—and he developed *The State of Black America* report.

In 1982, John E. Jacob, a former chief executive officer of the Washington, D.C. and San Diego affiliates who had served as Executive Vice President under Jordan, took the reins of leadership, solidifying the League's internal structure and expanding its outreach even further.

Jacob established the Permanent Development Fund in order to increase the organization's financial stamina. In honor of Whitney Young, he established several programs to aid the development of those who work for and with the League: The Whitney M. Young, Jr. Training Center, to provide training and leadership development opportunities for both staff and volunteers; the Whitney M. Young, Jr. Race Relations Program, which recognizes affiliates doing exemplary work in race relations; and the Whitney M. Young, Jr. Commemoration Ceremony, which honors and pays tribute to long-term staff and volunteers who have made extraordinary contributions to the Urban League Movement.

Jacob established the League's NULITES youth-development program and spurred the League to put new emphasis on programs to reduce teenage pregnancy, help single female heads of households, combat crime in black communities, and increase voter registration.

Hugh B. Price, appointed to the League's top office in July 1994, had taken its reins at a critical moment for the League, for Black America, and for the nation as a whole. The fierce market-driven dynamic known as, described by the rubric of "globalization," swept the world, fundamentally altering economic relations among and within countries, including the United States.

Price, a lawyer by training, with extensive experience in community development and other public policy issues, has intensified the organization's work in three broad areas: in education and youth development, in individual and community-wide economic empowerment, and in the forceful advocacy of affirmative action and the promotion of inclusion as a critical foundation for securing America's future as a multi-ethnic democracy.

In the spring of 2003, Price stepped down after a productive nine-year tenure, and Marc H. Morial, who served two terms as Mayor of New Orleans, Louisiana, was appointed president and chief executive officer. Since taking the helm, Morial has helped thrust the League into the forefront of major public policy issues, research and effective community-based solutions. From Hurricane Katrina and extension of the Voting Rights Act to creating jobs and housing through effective economic strategies, he is considered one of the nation's foremost experts on a wide range of issues related to cities and their residents. He has also been recognized by the *Non-Profit Times* as one of America's top 50 non-profit executives and has been named by *Ebony Magazine* as one of the 100 "Most Influential Blacks in America."

Upon his appointment to the League, Morial established an ambitious five-point empowerment agenda encompassing Education & Youth, Economic Empowerment, Health and Quality of Life, Civic Engagement and Civil Rights & Racial Justice that informs the League's programs, research and advocacy efforts. He created the new quantitative "Equality Index" to measure effectively the disparities in urban communities across these five areas. The index is now a permanent part of the League's annual and much heralded signature publication—*The State of Black America.*

In 2004, Mr. Morial Launched the League's first Annual Legislative Policy Conference (LPC) in Washington, D.C. Armed with a common agenda of jobs, education and civil rights, the Urban League leadership (staff, board and volunteers) from across the country served as frontline advocates in discussions with congressional lawmakers.

During the 2007 National Urban League Annual Conference, Morial unveiled the National Urban League's *Opportunity Compact.* The *Opportunity Compact* is our blueprint for economic equality. It is a comprehensive set of principles and policy recommendations designed to empower all Americans to be full participants in the economic and social mainstream of this nation. There are four cornerstones of the *Opportunity Compact* that reflect the values represented by the American dream:

The Opportunity to Thrive (Children)
The Opportunity to Earn (Jobs)
The Opportunity to Own (Housing)
The Opportunity to Prosper (Entrepreneurship)

BOARD OF TRUSTEES
2008 – 2009
(As of March 2009)

OFFICERS

CHAIR
John D. Hofmeister

SENIOR VICE CHAIR
Robert D. Taylor

VICE CHAIR
Alma Arrington Brown

SECRETARY
Alexis M. Herman

TREASURER
Willard "Woody" W. Brittain

PRESIDENT AND CHIEF EXECUTIVE OFFICER
Marc H. Morial

NATIONAL URBAN LEAGUE

Chair
John D. Hofmeister

President and Chief Executive Officer
Marc H. Morial

Senior Vice President
Marketing & Communications
Rhonda Spears Bell

Senior Vice President
Programs
Donald E. Bowen

Senior Vice President
Human Resources and Chief Talent Officer
Wanda H. Jackson

Executive Director
Policy Institute
Stephanie J. Jones

Senior Vice President
Affiliate Services
Herman L. Lessard, Jr.

Executive Director
Centennial Commission
S. Annelle Lewis

Senior Vice President
Development
Dennis G. Serrette

Senior Vice President
Finance and Operations
Paul Wycisk

NATIONAL URBAN LEAGUE
POLICY INSTITUTE

Executive Director
Stephanie J. Jones

Vice President & Chief of Staff
Lisa Bland Malone

Senior Resident Scholar
Valerie Rawlston Wilson

Senior Legislative Director
Suzanne Bergeron

Resident Scholar
Renee R. Hanson

Research Analyst
Mark McArdle

Health Policy Analyst
Eboni Morris

Publications Director
Larry Williamson

Publications Manager
Rose Jefferson-Frazier

Office Manager
Gail Thomas

Receptionist
Richard E. Lawrence

Roster of National Urban League Affiliates

AKRON, OHIO
Akron Community Service Center and Urban League

ALEXANDRIA, VIRGINIA
Northern Virginia Urban League

ANCHORAGE, ALASKA
Urban League of Anchorage-Alaska

ALTON, ILLINOIS
Madison County Urban League

ANDERSON, INDIANA
Urban League of Madison County, Inc.

ATLANTA, GEORGIA
Atlanta Urban League

AURORA, ILLINOIS
Quad County Urban League

AUSTIN, TEXAS
Austin Area Urban League

BALTIMORE, MARYLAND
Greater Baltimore Urban League

BATTLE CREEK, MICHIGAN
Southwestern Michigan Urban League

BINGHAMTON, NEW YORK
Broome County Urban League

BIRMINGHAM, ALABAMA
Birmingham Urban League

BOSTON, MASSACHUSETTS
Urban League of Eastern Massachusetts

BUFFALO, NEW YORK
Buffalo Urban League

CANTON, OHIO
Greater Stark County Urban League, Inc.

CHAMPAIGN, ILLINOIS
Urban League of Champaign County

CHARLESTON, SOUTH CAROLINA
Charleston Trident Urban League

CHARLOTTE, NORTH CAROLINA
Urban League of Central Carolinas, Inc.

CHATTANOOGA, TENNESSEE
Urban League Greater Chattanooga, Inc.

CHICAGO, ILLINOIS
Chicago Urban League

CINCINNATI, OHIO
Urban League of Greater Cincinnati

CLEVELAND, OHIO
Urban League of Greater Cleveland

COLORADO SPRINGS, COLORADO
Urban League of Pikes Peak Region

COLUMBIA, SOUTH CAROLINA
Columbia Urban League

COLUMBUS, GEORGIA
Urban League of Greater Columbus, Inc.

COLUMBUS, OHIO
Columbus Urban League

DALLAS, TEXAS
Urban League of Greater Dallas and North Central Texas

DAYTON, OHIO
Dayton Urban League

DENVER, COLORADO
Urban League of Metropolitan Denver

DETROIT, MICHIGAN
Detroit Urban League

ELIZABETH, NEW JERSEY
Urban League of Union County

ELYRIA, OHIO
Lorain County Urban League

ENGLEWOOD, NEW JERSEY
Urban League for Bergen County

FARRELL, PENNSYLVANIA
Urban League of Shenango Valley

FLINT, MICHIGAN
Urban League of Flint

FORT LAUDERDALE, FLORIDA
Urban League of Broward County

FORT WAYNE, INDIANA
Fort Wayne Urban League

GARY, INDIANA
Urban League of Northwest Indiana, Inc.

GRAND RAPIDS, MICHIGAN
Grand Rapids Urban League

GREENVILLE, SOUTH CAROLINA
The Urban League of the Upstate

HARTFORD, CONNECTICUT
Urban League of Greater Hartford

HOUSTON, TEXAS
Houston Area Urban League

INDIANAPOLIS, INDIANA
Indianapolis Urban League

JACKSON, MISSISSIPPI
Urban League of Greater Jackson

JACKSONVILLE, FLORIDA
Jacksonville Urban League

JERSEY CITY, NEW JERSEY
Urban League of Hudson County

KANSAS CITY, MISSOURI
Urban League of Kansas City

KNOXVILLE, TENNESSEE
Knoxville Area Urban League

LANCASTER, PENNSYLVANIA
Urban League of Lancaster County

LAS VEGAS, NEVADA
Las Vegas-Clark County Urban
League

LEXINGTON, KENTUCKY
Urban League of Lexington-Fayette
County

LONG ISLAND, NEW YORK
Urban League of Long Island

LOS ANGELES, CALIFORNIA
Los Angeles Urban League

LOUISVILLE, KENTUCKY
Louisville Urban League

MADISON, WISCONSIN
Urban League of Greater Madison

MEMPHIS, TENNESSEE
Memphis Urban League

MIAMI, FLORIDA
Urban League of Greater Miami

MILWAUKEE, WISCONSIN
Milwaukee Urban League

MINNEAPOLIS, MINNESOTA
Minneapolis Urban League

MORRISTOWN, NEW JERSEY
Morris County Urban League

MUSKEGON, MICHIGAN
Urban League of Greater Muskegon

NASHVILLE, TENNESSEE
Urban League of Middle Tennessee

NEW ORLEANS, LOUISIANA
Urban League of Greater New
Orleans

NEW YORK, NEW YORK
New York Urban League

NEWARK, NEW JERSEY
Urban League of Essex County

NORFOLK, VIRGINIA
Urban League of Hampton Roads

OKLAHOMA CITY, OKLAHOMA
Urban League of Oklahoma City

OMAHA, NEBRASKA
Urban League of Nebraska

ORLANDO, FLORIDA
Metropolitan Orlando Urban League

PEORIA, ILLINOIS
Tri-County Urban League

PHILADELPHIA, PENNSYLVANIA
Urban League of Philadelphia

PHOENIX, ARIZONA
Greater Phoenix Urban League

PITTSBURGH, PENNSYLVANIA
Urban League of Pittsburgh

PORTLAND, OREGON
Urban League of Portland

PROVIDENCE, RHODE ISLAND
Urban League of Rhode Island

RACINE, WISCONSIN
Urban League of Racine &
Kenosha, Inc.

RALEIGH, NORTH CAROLINA
Triangle Urban League

RICHMOND, VIRGINIA
Urban League of Greater Richmond,
Inc.

ROCHESTER, NEW YORK
Urban League of Rochester

SACRAMENTO, CALIFORNIA
Greater Sacramento Urban League

SAINT LOUIS, MISSOURI
Urban League Metropolitan St.
Louis

SAINT PAUL, MINNESOTA
St. Paul Urban League

SAINT PETERSBURG, FLORIDA
Pinellas County Urban League

SAN DIEGO, CALIFORNIA
Urban League of San Diego County

SEATTLE, WASHINGTON
Urban League of Metropolitan
Seattle

SOUTH BEND, INDIANA
Urban League of South Bend
and St. Joseph County

SPRINGFIELD, ILLINOIS
Springfield Urban League, Inc.

**SPRINGFIELD,
MASSACHUSETTS**
Urban League of Springfield

STAMFORD, CONNECTICUT
Urban League of Southern
Connecticut

TACOMA, WASHINGTON
Tacoma Urban League

TALLAHASSEE, FLORIDA
Tallahassee Urban League

TOLEDO, OHIO
Greater Toledo Urban League

TUCSON, ARIZONA
Tucson Urban League

TULSA, OKLAHOMA
Metropolitan Tulsa Urban League

WARREN, OHIO
Greater Warren-Youngstown Urban
League

WASHINGTON, D.C.
Greater Washington Urban League

WEST PALM BEACH, FLORIDA
Urban League of Palm Beach
County, Inc.

WHITE PLAINS, NEW YORK
Urban League of Westchester
County

WICHITA, KANSAS
Urban League of Kansas, Inc.

WILMINGTON, DELAWARE
Metropolitan Wilmington Urban
League

**WINSTON-SALEM,
NORTH CAROLINA**
Winston-Salem Urban League